The
FOUR
CULTURES
of the
ACADEMY

William H. Bergquist

The FOUR CULTURES *of the* ACADEMY

Insights and Strategies for Improving Leadership in Collegiate Organizations

Jossey-Bass Publishers · San Francisco

For sales outside the United States contact Maxwell Macmillan International Publishing Group, 866 Third Avenue, New York, New York 10022

 The paper used in this book is acid-free and meets the State of California requirements for recycled paper (50 percent recycled waste, including 10 percent postconsumer waste), which are the strictest guidelines for recycled paper currently in use in the United States.

Library of Congress Cataloging-in-Publication Data

Bergquist, William H.
    The four cultures of the academy : insights and strategies for
improving leadership in collegiate organizations / William H. Bergquist.
       p.   cm.—(The Jossey-Bass higher and adult education series)
    Includes bibliographical references (p.   ) and index.
    ISBN 1-55542-431-7
    1. Universities and colleges—United States—Administration.
2. Organizational behavior—United States.   3. Educational
anthropology—United States.   I. Title.   II. Title: 4 cultures of
the academy.   III. Series.
LB2341.B476   1992
378.73—dc 20   91-37578
                                                CIP

FIRST EDITION
HB Printing   10 9 8 7 6 5 4 3 2 1   *Code 9229*

The Jossey-Bass
Higher and Adult Education Series

Contents

❖❖❖

Preface

In recent years, it has become increasingly fashionable to describe organizations as cultures. Anthropologists, management consultants, organizational psychologists, and other social scientists have become enamored of this concept and have helped to popularize the notion that cultural analyses yield important insights about the life and dynamics of an organization. The definitions of organizational culture and the methods used to study organizational cultures are as diverse as the disciplines involved (see, for example, Pettigrew, 1979; Deal and Kennedy, 1982; Peters and Waterman, 1982; Schein, 1985).

Purpose for the Book

There is a need for cultural analyses of collegiate institutions from the perspective of both those who lead and work in the institutions and those who live in a society that is significantly influenced by the institutions' efforts. Those inside the institutions may welcome understanding of organizational culture, because collegiate institutions seem to be particularly resistant to influence and change. A favorite adage of a man who recently led one of our major universities is, "A university president is like a man sitting on the edge of a dock trying to control the flight of the seagulls above." The dynamics of collegiate organizations are often difficult to understand, and any framework that can help bring order to the seeming chaos and complexity of these institutions will be greatly appreciated.

The purpose of *The Four Cultures of the Academy* is to provide an initial analysis of collegiate cultures and to offer a preliminary framework that can guide and inspire new courses of action within those complicated and often closed organizations. Four assumptions guide the design of the book.

First, we need a clearer sense of what culture means. The concept of organizational culture has, like the word *paradigm* (Kuhn, 1962), taken on a life of its own and has often been distorted for idiosyncratic purposes.

Second, the nature of and differences between various organizational cultures in academic organizations must be detailed. We must advance our theory building and knowledge in this area.

Third, we need a fuller exposition of the ways in which to use (or not to use) the concepts of organizational culture in our daily lives as leaders and members of academic organizations. American pragmatism often seems to dictate that we find a use for every concept; furthermore, contemporary organizational leaders frequently appear to need a strategy for change when confronted with the notion of culture. What we require most is not a set of recommendations about how we should change or mold a culture to meet our own needs; rather, we must determine how to work with and use the strengths and resources of the existing organizational culture to accomplish our goals.

Finally, we can clarify our definition of culture as we examine the similarities and differences among collegiate cultures. Some of our most informative anthropology, after all, is comparative in nature. Furthermore, our categorizations and our use of concepts about organizational culture are likely to become clearer when we examine several specific collegiate institutions and members of those institutions in some detail. The concepts of organizational culture can easily become highly abstruse if they are not grounded in and illustrated by the analysis of specific settings at particular times.

Four different, yet interrelated, cultures are now to be found in American higher education. They have a profound impact on the ways in which campus leaders view their current work in the academy, as well as on the ways in which faculty members, administrators, and students perceive the potential for personal career advancement and institutional change. These four cultures also influence how those outside the academy perceive the purposes and appropriate operations of collegiate institutions and how they believe they themselves should interact with the institutions.

Two of the four cultures can be traced back to the origins of American higher education. We have labeled them the *collegial* and *managerial* cultures. The other two have emerged more recently, partially in response to the seeming failure of the two original cultures to adapt effectively to changes in contemporary colleges and universities and in response to alterations in the status of academic institutions in modern society. I refer to the first of these newer cultures as the *developmental* culture and the second as the *negotiating* culture.

The collegial, managerial, developmental, and negotiating cultures are often invisible to people who are part of them. Nevertheless, they have as much influence as any other aspect of the institution. As in the case of all cultural analyses, we must evaluate diverse phenomena and tacitly held assumptions, as well as their etiology, if we are to understand the nature and influence of the four cultures.

Overview of the Contents

This book is thus devoted to the examination of each of the cultures in interaction with one another. We begin in Chapter One with an overview of the concept of organizational culture, then provide a summary description of each of the four cultures of the academy. Each is also illustrated in the life of one faculty member and a collegiate institution. In Chapter Two, the institutional aspects of the collegial culture are examined, primarily through an analysis of the origins, myths, and characteristics of institutions that are dominated by it. In Chapter Three we assess the impact of the collegial culture on individual faculty members by looking at their roles, their responsibilities, and the realities of academic life.

Chapters Four and Five contain a similar examination of the

managerial culture, Chapters Six and Seven concern the developmental culture, and Chapters Eight and Nine concentrate on the negotiating culture. We conclude each of these chapters with a case study of a specific collegiate institution or faculty member and relate the case study to the preceding cultural analyses. Each study illustrates one of the four cultures, as well as the interplay between that culture and the three others. These cases speak to the possibilities that the four cultures offer for improving the daily lives of men and women at academic institutions who seek to influence their future direction.

In the final three chapters of the book, I consider the four academic cultures in relation to several other models of organizational life and change. Chapter Ten focuses on three schools of thought within the field of organizational development and on two principles of organizational change. Attention is directed in Chapter Eleven to a model of organizational change offered by Goodwin Watson and a model of innovation diffusion proposed by Ronald Havelock. Each of these is directly related to the four cultural analyses provided in the previous chapters. The models also set the stage for the comparisons made in Chapter Twelve between our four cultural analyses and two recent descriptions of institutional type and organizational frames of analysis: Robert Birnbaum's outline of collegial, bureaucratic, political, and anarchical types of academic institutions (1988) and Lee Bolman and Terrence Deal's four organizational frames (1991).

The interplay among the various models in Chapters Ten, Eleven, and Twelve provides several clues to how collegiate leaders can effectively address some of the problems associated with the interaction among the collegial, managerial, developmental, and negotiating cultures. It is our belief that any efforts to bring about change and increase stability in a chaotic collegiate setting must be based on an understanding of these four cultures and that most of the efforts must be multidimensional in nature, given the coexistence of all four cultures on most college campuses.

This book has been written over a rather long period of time. The four cultures described here were first proposed in a report prepared for the chancellor's office of the California State University and College System during the 1970s. The conclusions reached in

The Four Cultures of the Academy, as well as the case studies used to illustrate the four cultures, have been more fully developed in the two succeeding decades; they are based on more than 150 consultations that I have conducted at 300 colleges and universities. I was privileged to listen to the stories, concerns, and hopes of more than 800 faculty members and academic administrators during that time. I am also fortunate to have served as president of a nontraditional graduate school during the past five years and to have interacted with many dedicated colleagues (faculty members, administrators, students, and alumni) in this exceptional institution.

I wish to acknowledge and express my appreciation to the men and women of the academy. Their comments have been perceptive, gratifying, and reassuring. I have also been a witness to their pain and uncertainty about the future of higher education. I therefore hope that this book may be of value in helping deans, faculty members, presidents, and other campus leaders who face complex organizational settings and situations. Specifically, the book should be of service to academic deans who can use the four cultural analyses to shed light on the particularly thorny and enduring problem of faculty tenure and promotion policies. *The Four Cultures of the Academy* can also provide direction to faculty members who want to gain understanding and guidance in overcoming faculty resistance to new curricular proposals. College presidents developing plans to ensure that their institutions are responsive to new constituencies and student needs will benefit not only from the analyses of the four cultures but also from the discussion of strategies for change reviewed in the final three chapters.

In my presentation of the four cultures to more than five hundred faculty members and administrators at a dozen conferences and workshops over the past ten years, I have repeatedly been told that the cultural analyses have been of tangible value to deans, faculty members, and presidents. I have also found the analyses to be of use to consultants to collegiate institutions. Like college deans, faculty members, and presidents, consultants can draw upon the analyses to discover and understand various sources of resistance and to map out appropriate plans for change—especially when the cultural analyses are used in conjunction with the other organizational strategies presented in the final three chapters of this book.

Acknowledgments

In addition to the invaluable contributions made by the men and
women in academic institutions about which this book is written,
I wish to acknowledge the contributions made by my close friend
and longtime colleague, Nancy Barber. Her keen observations about
academic cultures and higher education have been of great value to
me over the past twenty years. The guidance and support offered by
my other long-term friend and colleague, Gary Quehl, is also acknowledged with great appreciation, as are the wisdom of Bruce
Willats, the clear thinking of Eugene Rice and David Halliburton,
and the dedication of Diane Morrison. The five most important
people in my life during the period when this book was written
(and, for that matter, throughout my life) were my late father, Victor
Bergquist; my mother, Frances Bergquist; my two children, Jason
and Katy; and, in particular, my wife, Kathleen. My new daughter-
in-law, Marybeth, and two granddaughters, Alicia and Julia, add
even greater joy to my life and meaning to my work.

    Having recognized the exceptional contributions made by
each of these men, women, and children, I wish to dedicate this
book to another colleague and friend, a man whose death occurred
much too early: Jack Lindquist. Readers will find ample evidence
of the influence that this gifted teacher, consultant, and leader has
had on my own thoughts and values. Jack and I (we were sometimes
called the Swedish Mafia) worked closely together during the 1970s,
and his ideas and ways of approaching problems continued to influence my own work during the 1980s. In preparing *The Four
Cultures of the Academy,* I wanted to make extensive use of his
ideas, many of which have never received the attention they deserve.
(Also, Jack was often too busy with other matters to fully articulate
his own abundant ideas.) I hope that he would have been pleased
with my efforts and would have recognized his own substantial
contributions to this work.

San Francisco, California   William H. Bergquist
February 1992

The Author

William H. Bergquist is president of the Professional School of Psychology in San Francisco, California. He received his B.A. degree (1962) in psychology from Occidental College in Los Angeles and his M.A. (1963) and Ph.D. (1969) degrees in psychology from the University of Oregon.

During the course of his career, William Bergquist has served as chief consultant to the Council of Independent Colleges in Washington, D.C., and as a consultant in such areas as curriculum, student, faculty, and organizational development to colleges, universities, and state and national associations. He has authored or coauthored more than a dozen books, including *Designing Undergraduate Education* (1981, with R. Gould and E. Greenberg), *Planning Effectively for Educational Quality* (1986, with J. Armstrong), and *Solutions: A Guide to Better Problem-Solving* (1987, with S. Phillips). He is currently writing about life themes for men and women who are between fifty and sixty years of age and about shifts in organizational life that are associated with movement into a postmodern era.

The
FOUR
CULTURES
of the
ACADEMY

1

❖❖❖❖❖❖

Understanding
the Cultural Dynamics
of Academic Institutions

The current interest in the study of organizational cultures is understandable, since they provide a framework for creating order out of the complex and often baffling dynamics of organizational life. In the field of anthropology, culture is the conceptual foundation on which field observers base their explanations of the orderliness and patterning of individual and collective life experience. In organizational theory, culture has assumed a similar explanatory role. The term *culture,* however, is vague and ill-defined, and is hence not yet adequate to provide direction for an organization's managers, researchers, or consultants. More definitive categories must be identified that enable them to focus on and use tangible, observable phenomena.

The current book is informed by three definitions of culture that come from differing eras and perspectives. The first comes from the noted anthropologist and social historian Bronislaw Malinowski (1948, p. 36), who defines culture as: "an integral whole consisting of implements and consumer goods, of constitutional charters . . . of human ideas and crafts, beliefs and customs . . . a vast apparatus, partly material, partly human, and partly spiritual, by which man is able to cope with the concrete, specific problems that face him."

A second definition comes from an analyst of corporate cultures, Ronnie Lessem (1990, p. 8), who offers a developmentally

1

oriented approach: "[An organizational culture] has to cultivate a humanly fulfilling context—a space and time—within which the production and consumption of needed, worthwhile, and quality products and services can take place."

One of the most inclusive definitions of organizational culture has been articulated by Edgar Schein (1985, p. 9), an organizational consultant and theorist: "Organizational culture is a pattern of basic assumptions that a given group has invented, discovered or developed in learning to cope with its problems of external adaptation and internal integration, and that has worked well enough to be considered valid, and therefore, to be taught to new members as the correct way to perceive, think and feel in relation to those problems."

What do these seemingly disparate ideas have in common? Several features are noteworthy. All three definitions suggest that culture provides meaning and context for a specific group of people. The culture holds the people together and instills in them an individual and collective sense of purpose and continuity. As Malinowski pointed out, cultures involve spiritual as well as material and human domains. Collegiate institutions in particular are in the business of conveying and providing meaning to not only their students but also their faculty and administrators—and ultimately society as a whole. Given that colleges and universities are primary conveyers of our society's overall culture (Parsons and Platt, 1973), it is particularly important that we identify and attempt to understand the nature of the deeply embedded cultural properties of these institutions.

All three definitions, furthermore, suggest that a culture helps to define the nature of reality for those people who are part of that culture. In other words, it provides lenses through which its members interpret and assign value to the various events and products of this world. In her superb study of student and organizational life in two liberal arts colleges, Nancy Barber (1984) notes that they present quite different models of reality through their myths, rituals, traditions, and procedures. Barber (1984, pp. 387–388) argues:

> The point of identifying and discussing contrasts between the models of reality presented by St. Anne's

College and Washington College is not to declare a winner by comparison, or even to prescribe for institutional change. The two colleges are fundamentally different in their cultures, deepest values, and understanding of the world: in what they intend to be, and are. . . . The purpose of such contrasts is rather to sharpen the outlines of each institution's culture and customary practice. . . . [I]t is normal to view the perspectives maintained by one's own culture as self-evidently true and obvious reality. . . . [A]ll of us are afflicted with anesthetic insensitivity to cultural features and values unmarked in our own culture. Contrast with other institutions' practices can increase awareness of cultural "markers" and values, and can move such values from the realm of the necessary and obvious to an arena of choice.

Barber's analysis leaves us with the impression that if we are to understand and influence men and women in their daily work inside collegiate institutions, then we must come to understand and fully appreciate their implicitly held models of reality.

The final concept shared by these three definitions is perhaps the most important. It is that the culture serves an overarching purpose—a dimension that is often ignored in cultural analyses. A culture is established around the production of something valued by its members. A culture does not exist for itself; rather, it exists to provide a context, as Lessem notes, "within which the production and consumption of needed, worthwhile, and quality products and services can take place." In our study of any culture, we cannot help being influenced by the culture from which we are making our observations. We cannot reflect on this latter culture without being influenced by yet another set of cultural biases. In this way, the culture of a society or organization remains invisible.

The culture of academic organizations must thus be understood within the context of the educational purposes of collegiate institutions. The ceremonies, symbols, assumptions, and modes of leadership in a college or university are always directed toward the institution's purposes and derive from its cultural base. Precisely because of its subordinate (though critical) role, culture is a phenomenon so elusive that it can often be seen only when a college or university is struggling with a particularly complicated or intractable problem—as is the case with most of the colleges and universities that we will be studying in this book.

The Four Cultures in Higher Education

As we turn specifically to higher education, we find a few preliminary analyses of organizational culture that have set the stage for more extensive and diversified studies. William Tierney (1988, 1990) has done a superb job of surveying existing research in the assessment of academic cultures (and climates) and of identifying some of the critical tasks to be accomplished in establishing a body of literature in this field. Much of the other work done to date has focused either on the tools and concepts that are needed to do an adequate job or on the analysis of the culture that operates in a single institution at a specific point in time—usually in highly distinctive or innovative colleges (for example, Clark, 1970; Riesman, Gusfield, and Gamson, 1970). The present work builds on the Tierney's recommendations, while moving beyond the preliminary, single-institution analyses.

As previously stated, we propose, first, that there are four distinct cultures in American higher education, each with its own history, perspectives, and values. Recognizing that each culture can only be adequately understood in the context of its historical roots, its multiple representations in many different aspects of campus life, and its embodiment in actual ongoing campus operations, we offer these preliminary descriptions.

> *The collegial culture:* a culture that finds meaning primarily in the disciplines represented by the faculty in the institution; that values faculty research and scholarship and the quasi-political governance processes of the faculty; that holds untested assumptions about the dominance of rationality in the institution; and that conceives of the institution's enterprise as the generation, interpretation, and dissemination of knowl-

edge and as the development of specific values and qualities of character among young men and women who are future leaders of our society.

The managerial culture: a culture that finds meaning primarily in the organization, implementation, and evaluation of work that is directed toward specified goals and purposes; that values fiscal responsibility and effective supervisory skills; that holds untested assumptions about the capacity of the institution to define and measure its goals and objectives clearly; and that conceives of the institution's enterprise as the inculcation of specific knowledge, skills, and attitudes in students so that they might become successful and responsible citizens.

The developmental culture: a culture that finds meaning primarily in the creation of programs and activities furthering the personal and professional growth of all members of the collegiate community; that values personal openness and service to others, as well as systematic institutional research and curricular planning; that holds untested assumptions about the inherent desire of all men and women to attain their own personal maturation, while helping others in the institution become more mature; and that conceives of the institution's enterprise as the encouragement of potential for cognitive, affective, and behavioral maturation among all students, faculty, administrators, and staff.

The negotiating culture: a culture that finds meaning primarily in the establishment of equitable and egalitarian policies and procedures for the distribution of resources and benefits in the institution; that values confrontation and fair bargaining among constituencies (primarily management and faculty or staff) with vested interests that are inherently in opposition; that

holds untested assumptions about the ultimate role of
power and the frequent need for outside mediation in
a viable collegiate institution; and that conceives of
the institution's enterprise as either the undesirable
promulgation of existing (and often repressive) social
attitudes and structures or the establishment of new
and more liberating social attitudes and structures.

A second proposal in this book concerns the mixture of cultures in most collegiate institutions and the value of this mixture.
Although most colleges and universities, and most faculty and administrators, tend to embrace or exemplify one of these four cultures, the other three cultures are always present and interact with
the dominant culture. This is a particularly important premise for
readers to consider, given that some analysts of organizational culture believe that hybrid cultures are undesirable or symptomatic of
a fragmented, troubled institution. William Tierney (1988, p. 7), for
instance, states that "strong, congruent cultures supportive of organizational structures and strategies are more effective than weak,
incongruent, or disconnected cultures."

By contrast, we can point to the work of Robert Birnbaum
(1988). Though not specifically a study of organizational culture,
Birnbaum's richly textured analysis of four kinds of institutions
identifies ways in which various types can be effectively integrated.
Like Birnbaum, we believe that differences in institutional type are
important and that variations in cultural composition underlie
them. We further propose that all four cultures exist in virtually
every collegiate institution. They are often at odds with each other;
however, all four must be acknowledged and brought into any dialogue aiming to create a "self-correcting," "cybernetic" institution
(to use Birnbaum's terms).

A third proposal offered in this book involves the nature of
the cultural interaction. We suggest that each has an "opposite" on
which it is dependent and with which it shares many features and
assumptions. Thus, developmental culture, which has evolved
primarily in response to faults associated with the collegial culture,
is nevertheless dependent on it and has in common with it many
values and perspectives. Similarly, the negotiating culture grew out

of faculty opposition to the managerial culture but looks to it for identity and purpose and shares values and perspectives with it.

When efforts are initiated to bring about change (whether by individuals or by institutions), these must take into account that different strategies are needed and appropriate for each culture. Typically, a hybrid of strategies is required. We believe that our ideas about the four cultures of the academy relate directly to and expand on models of organizational analysis and development offered by two specialists in the analysis of collegiate institutions—Ronald Havelock (1971) and the aforementioned Robert Birnbaum (1988)—and two sets of authors that have written more generally about the nature of contemporary organizations and organizational change—Goodwin Watson and David Johnson (1972) and Lee Bolman and Terrence Deal (1991). All six of these organizational theorists have focused on organizational issues at what we have called a second-order level of analysis (see Chapter Ten). These analyses require that we reconceive our organizational problems and goals—that we try doing something new rather than try improving the status quo. An appreciation of academic culture is essential to any effective use of second-order analyses or strategies for change in collegiate settings.

Given the subtle nature of organizational cultures, I have chosen to provide not only a detailed description of such organizational characteristics as values, leadership, assumptions, and criteria for appraising performance in the institution, but also a series of case studies that suggest ways in which each of the four cultures work on a daily basis in academic institutions and in the lives of their faculty members. These case studies illustrate how these four cultures interact and help to produce the often confusing and paradoxical conditions in which contemporary faculty find themselves. We therefore begin our investigation of academic cultures by examining the life of one faculty member who, like most of his colleagues, has inhabited all four cultures at one time or other.

Case Study: Peter Armantrout

Peter Armantrout (not his real name) is a professor of English at a relatively small state college (which I will call Fairfield) located in the western part of the United States. His life story is significant, not because it is exceptional, but because it typifies the lives of many faculty in American and Canadian colleges and universities. Armantrout was forty-six years old when our interview was conducted. He spoke easily, though in a rather depressed manner, about his twenty-two years at Fairfield.

Peter Armantrout was an innovative young instructor during the 1960s. He experimented with various grading schemes (including student self-grading) and introduced many "experiential" activities in his classroom. Much of this experimentation was stimulated by his reading of several humanistic authors—notably Carl Rogers (1968). Armantrout came to realize that the way in which he would liked to have been treated as a student was quite different from the one in which he was currently working with his own students. He tried to bring his own practices as an educator in accord with his newly discovered philosophy of humanistic education. Armantrout's life in many ways resembles that of a faculty member at a state university, Steven Abbot, who was described by Joseph Axelrod (1973) in his study of innovative teaching practices during the late 1960s. Like many of their youthful colleagues, Armantrout and Abbot believed that major shifts in the basic philosophy and practices of higher education were at hand when they entered the field of college teaching during this turbulent era.

While reforming his own classes, Peter Armantrout also became actively involved with campus politics. Initially, he worked extensively with faculty governance at Fairfield. He served as a member and then chair of the curriculum committee and devoted extensive time during the early 1970s to moving a major new general education requirement and program through the Fairfield faculty senate. Later, in 1978, Armantrout served as chairperson of the faculty senate and was successful in establishing a faculty award for excellence in teaching.

Yet as Armantrout became a more mature teacher, he moved toward a more conservative stance—paralleling the changes that occurred in the teaching of Stephen Abbot (as noted by Joseph Axelrod in his 1980 follow-up study of collegiate innovation). Armantrout (like Abbot) himself describes a slow erosion in his educational philosophy and classroom practices. He tends now to blame students for not acquiring the concepts that he is trying to convey. He finds most students inadequately prepared for college and worries about teaching them the fundamentals of critical thinking and expository writing. Armantrout speaks wistfully about the dedicated students he taught during the late 1960s and early 1970s: the Vietnam veterans returning to school, the women who wanted to complete college after raising their children, the self-taught laborers. According to Armantrout, since the mid 1980s, Fairfield is once again attracting "kids right out of high school" who are indifferent to higher education. Armantrout knows that it is his own fault that he fails to make his classroom an exciting place to learn. However, he has grown tired of monotonous courses and unmotivated students.

Armantrout has become similarly disillusioned about his leadership at the college. Soon after he served as chair of the senate, he became very frustrated with faculty governance at Fairfield, in part because of the "petty politics" of his colleagues: "We spend more time debating the appropriate placement of an adverb in a faculty resolution than the U.S. Senate spends in preparing the federal budget!" Armantrout was particularly annoyed about the turf wars that led to the demise of his general education program at Fairfield.

The Interaction of the Collegial Culture with the Other Cultures

Up to this point in the case study, we might conclude that Peter Armantrout and his colleagues are struggling with the traditional collegial culture at Fairfield. As we saw earlier, the collegial culture is one that emphasizes and rewards informal and quasi-political collaboration among faculty, as well as independent research and scholarship. This culture provides an environment that recognizes and values sophisticated thought and education. For Armantrout, early interest in college-level teaching probably came from his perceptions of the character and values of the collegial culture. Certainly, his early interests in faculty governance were encouraged and reinforced by the collegial culture at Fairfield. His enthusiasm for educational innovation, however, flew directly in the face of this dominant culture.

Peter Armantrout has become discouraged about the decreased support for Fairfield (and other state-supported colleges and universities) by the legislature. Armantrout found that his salary increases did not keep pace with the rising cost of living and at the same time resented the demands being made by legislators and members of the Board of Postsecondary Education for greater faculty accountability: "Never has any group of people asked so much of so few and given so little in return." Armantrout is directly confronting some of the harsh realities associated with the emergence of the managerial culture at Fairfield College.

By contrast with the collegial culture, the managerial culture values efficient and effective educational programming. This culture attempts to assess the extent to which specific objectives are being achieved. These relate not only to the educational mission of the institution but also to those financial and operational aspects of institutional life that enable the mission to succeed. Goals are usually quantitative in nature and refer to institutionally based measures of input (such as student enrollment, full-time faculty appointments, or number of volumes in the library) or output (number of graduating seniors, size of state funding allocation, or percentage of retained students). For Peter Armantrout, the managerial culture is evident in the changing attitudes and seeming lack of support on the part of the Board of Postsecondary Education and many administrators at Fairfield. Coming from the collegial cultural perspective, he views the demands for accountability and the emphasis on cost containment, as represented in the reduced salary increases, as intrusive and offensive.

His anger at the managerial culture sparked a new-found interest in faculty unionization and his entry into the negotiating culture. Faculty members throughout the state decided to join one of three unions and demanded that all future salary decisions by the Board of Postsecondary Education be based on negotiations with one or more of the faculty unions. Armantrout became vice president of the faculty union at Fairfield and for two years during the mid 1980s served as Fairfield's representative to the statewide union.

The negotiating culture has emerged in colleges like Fairfield largely in response to the seemingly unilateral and inequitable decision-making processes inherent in the managerial culture. Faculty members perceive their relationship to the administration as primarily adversarial and define their work via formal contractual processes rather than the more informal methods used in the other three cultures. Through his involvement in Fairfield's faculty union, Peter Armantrout fully engaged in this culture during the late 1970s and early 1980s. He eventually found it—and the three other cultures—inadequate, however.

When speaking about unionization at Fairfield, Armantrout becomes particularly introspective. He speaks of deterioration in his relationship with colleagues who now serve as academic administrators at Fairfield. He believes that unionization has produced a formality and coldness that makes the college a rather unpleasant place to work. There was once a close-knit group of young faculty and administrators who shared exciting ideas about student-oriented education; now, according to Armantrout, these men and women have not met together for at least ten years. Though he does not even know if all of them continue as teachers or administrators at Fairfield, he suspects that most are still there, as "no one ever seems to leave Fairfield, except to retire or die."

In seeking to find more community at Fairfield, as well as to fulfill his own commitment to teaching, Armantrout has periodically entered the developmental culture. He has attended faculty development workshops, college-sponsored conferences on critical thinking, and even a recently held workshop aimed at helping men express their feelings (that Fairfield co-sponsored with a local community mental health center). Each of these activities were initially quite satisfying; however, like many aspects of the developmental culture, they seemed to have a short-lived impact and did not really change his life in any appreciable manner.

The developmental culture was established at Fairfield (and many other colleges and universities in the United States) during the late 1960s and early 1970s, largely in response to the lack of systematic planning and formal staff development in the collegial culture. Emphasis is placed on the careful, collaborative assessment of current campus resources and impending campus needs and the formulation of comprehensive strategies for meeting these needs through improvement in the quality and use of existing resources. Assessment tends to be based on more elusive and qualitative measures than in the managerial culture. These criteria often concern student growth and development (stages of student development or the acquisition of critical thinking skills) or faculty development (levels of faculty morale or student suggestions regarding instructional improvement).

Peter Armantrout personally experienced the first stages in the birth and maturation of the developmental culture during the 1960s. His interest in humanistic education shifted during the 1970s and 1980s into a concern for ongoing professional development and the design of educational programs responsive to diverse and shifting student needs, styles, and stages of development. Armantrout's disillusionment with current students at Fairfield suggests his need for this culture. Yet his disillusionment also indicates the inability of this culture to attract or hold the attention of senior faculty members in contemporary colleges and universities.

Armantrout becomes more cheerful when he speaks about his plans and interests in a variety of nonacademic fields. Fairfield State College does not seem to be included in Armantrout's future. He hopes to take early retirement (at age fifty-five) and move to a small community on the Pacific coast. He would like to write, though he worries that he may have little to say that is truly original after years spent teaching the ideas of others. Perhaps he will start his own press. Armantrout chuckles when he hears himself talking about "pipe dreams" and speculates about his more realistic future: retiring to his small house in the nearby mountains, where he can garden, do woodwork, and perhaps teach a bit at a local community college.

When all is said and done, Peter Armantrout appears most interested in disengaging from Fairfield. He feels he has very little left to accomplish or to contribute. He has won and lost many battles at Fairfield, but none of them seem to be worth all of the energy, passion, and sacrifice that he gave to these causes as a younger man. According to him, Fairfield simply is no longer worth the effort. He assumes that he shares his desire for early retirement with many of his colleagues at Fairfield, as well as with colleagues at many other American colleges and universities.

What about Peter Armantrout? What has led him to this rather depressing state of affairs? Even though he may still be a fairly good teacher and wise counselor, he has ceased to be a leader. At a time in his life when he might be a particularly wise and valuable member of the Fairfield community, Armantrout has chosen to look elsewhere for his professional and personal gratification. What seems to be the source of this disenchantment? He identified many culprits: the stingy and insensitive state legislature and Board of Postsecondary Education, the petty faculty members at Fairfield, the often indifferent and ill-prepared students, the timid and bureaucratically obsessive administrators, and an unrealistic president (Chapter Four).

We would propose that Peter Armantrout's dissatisfaction also results in part from the tension between the four academic cultures at Fairfield. The sense of community that he used to find in the traditional collegial culture at Fairfield no longer exists (if it ever did exist). All that is left is the bickering of the faculty. He has also looked for a sense of community within the developmental culture at Fairfield; yet he finds that it exists only sporadically and is usually swamped by the financial and instructional pressures that besiege Fairfield State.

When he looks to the managerial culture, Armantrout finds reality and some clarity regarding purpose and function but feels that he is not part of this culture and that it ultimately betrays or at least diminishes the academic values that first attracted him to higher education. In anger he turns to the negotiating culture. He finds it to be just as irrelevant and bogged down in faculty haggling as the collegial culture.

Armantrout's current disillusionment stems from his vague sense that none of these cultures is adequate to meet either his own personal needs or those of Fairfield State College. In the next eight chapters, we turn to a more detailed examination of these cultures as a means of better understanding and helping Peter Armantrout and Fairfield State College, as well as many other troubled faculty members and administrators in contemporary collegiate institutions.

Part One

The Four Cultures

2

❖❖❖❖❖❖❖

The Collegial Culture

Since American higher education was first inaugurated in the colonial college, faculty members have worked predominantly in a collegial culture. This culture encourages diversity of perspective and relative autonomy of work. It is a "loose coupled" culture—to use a concept from Birnbaum's (1988) analysis—whose members are unable to formulate or state the criteria by which colleagues are to be judged clearly or consistently. Relationships are informal, non-hierarchical, and long term. Changes are made in this culture through quasi-political negotiation—often behind closed doors.

Men and women who are successful in this culture usually are actively involved in the faculty governance processes of their institutions. Alternatively, they hold a position of high prestige, based on scholarly activities, research, or longevity on the faculty. From this position of informal power, they are able to influence the political process without direct or overt intervention. Leadership will thus emerge from committee and deliberative group activities or from autonomous academic activities.

Leadership that is based on scholarships and research became particularly dominant with the emergence of the German-style research university in the United States 120 years ago. Leadership that emphasizes collaboration and quasi-political activities is directly influenced by the original colonial liberal arts college, which in turn is designed after the British universities at Oxford and Cam-

17

bridge. The collegial culture in American colleges and universities is embued with both the British and German models of higher education. Interdependence and collaboration are more actively supported by the British model, whereas faculty autonomy is more prevalent among institutions resembling the German universities.

Origins of the Collegial Culture

When colonial Americans began to establish a permanent society on the new continent, they looked to their homeland, England, for models of how to become "civilized." It is not surprising that they looked to Oxford and Cambridge when designing and establishing the first American colleges. As Frederick Rudolph (1962) has noted in his excellent history of American higher education, the British university contained many elements that continue to influence American higher education, as well as some elements that have gradually been changed or eliminated.

One of the most important characteristics of the British university in the seventeenth century was the dominance of liberal arts. These institutions were directed toward the improvement of young men's minds, rather than the promotion of career aspirations or social status. It was assumed that the young men attending Oxford or Cambridge were already in a social position to obtain work after graduation. Similarly, in the American colonial college, emphasis was placed on liberal education. Though young men were being prepared for specific vocations, such as the ministry, law, or education, they were not given specific instruction in these areas until well along in their collegiate careers.

Another major characteristic of the British university was total control over the environment in which young men lived and learned. Residential living at the university was a given. The extracurricular activities in which students were required, or at least expected, to participate (including fraternal organizations and sports) were considered to be just as important as the formal curriculum of the collegiate classroom. Rudolph (1962) labels this characteristic "the collegiate way" and describes it in the following manner:

[It is] an adherence to the residential scheme of things. It is respectful of quiet rural settings, dependent on dormitories, committed to dining halls, permeated by paternalism. It is what every American college has had or consciously rejected or lost or sought to recapture. It is William Tecumseh Sherman promising to be a father to an entire student body; it is comfort and full tobacco jars in a Princeton dormitory; in an urban university it is counselors helping the socially inept to overcome their weakness. Imported with so much of everything else from England, the collegiate way in America was from the beginning the effort to follow in the New World the pattern of life which had developed at the English colleges (p. 87). . . . Adherents of the collegiate way . . . pointed with satisfaction to the extracurriculum, to the whole range of social life and development, to the benefits of religious influence and orientation (p. 89).

The collegiate way helped to establish the philosophic and historical foundations for many of the nonintellectual purposes of the American college. . . . The collegiate way lent itself to the idea that a college could be a reformatory, a school of moral regeneration. . . . It would account for the fact that no American institution of higher learning can be an institution of learning alone (p. 108).

Faculty members were expected to engage with their students in all aspects of life at the university, for a complete liberal arts education incorporated heart and muscle, as well as mind. According to Rudolph (1962, pp. 136–137), the American colonial college "became an arena in which undergraduates erected monuments not to the soul of man but to man as a social and physical being."

A third characteristic, one that continues to be influential, was the British university's emphasis on complexity of thought and the educational process. Faculty and students were judged on the basis of their manner of thought and discourse, rather than on the basis of any specific body of knowledge. Thus, in the evaluation of academic performance, style took precedence over substance. Quality counted more than quantity. The sciences were considered inappropriate for a liberally educated person, and the humanities (as we now know them) held sway over the curriculum. The faculty was suspicious of any curriculum that was too practical, concrete, or contemporary. Such a curriculum ran the risk of being superficial or ephemeral.

These properties of the English academic culture were appropriated intact by leaders of the first colonial colleges. Several characteristics of these colleges, however, were unique and not specifically borrowed from their distinguished sister institutions in England. The first colonial colleges (notably, Harvard and Yale) were led by strong presidents who dominated their institutions and considered faculty members to be hired underlings. Instructors were usually quite young and given minimal pay. They had very little to say in the formulation of curriculum, let alone in the governance of the college. Typically, the president of a colonial college himself taught the final course in a student's senior year to ensure that the student left with the correct philosophy of life and appropriate ethical standards. According to Rudolph (1962, pp. 164-165), quoting in part from George P. Schmidt's *The Old Time College President* (1930), the president "was in most institutions the dominating influence . . . the greatest single force in college life. . . . the old-time president lived at the college, was not absent for long periods of time, probably taught every member of the senior class, knew most of the students by name, indeed probably made a practice of calling on them in their rooms. For these reasons he was an influence and asserted an authority in the life of the undergraduates that his successor [in the late nineteenth century] never could."

Jencks and Riesman (1968, p. 6) also noted that college presidents in early American institutions were "far more domineering than they are today, carrying the business of the college around in their brief cases or even in their heads, entrusting very little to committees of faculty members or lower level bureaucrats, and imposing their personal stamp on the entire college. . . . In part, this was because the faculty was still quite unprofessionalized. . . . The vision of a college professor as an independent expert with a mission transcending the college where he happened to teach was almost unknown." Thus, in the early history of American higher education, a precedent was set for strong administrative leadership and weak faculty influence. Rudolph (1962) even suggests that faculty in these institutions were extensively exploited by presidents and the boards of trustees that these presidents effectively controlled.

This precedent was soon overturned, however, as the colonial faculty member matured, became more firmly established, and began to influence the curriculum that he was asked to teach and monitor. Nevertheless, the role of a strong administrator, who rules by moral force and even fiat, continues to influence the professional lives of many leaders in contemporary collegiate institutions. There is still room in many colleges and universities for a strong president—especially in those institutions that preserve a strong religious heritage, such as was found in the colonial colleges.

This kind of strong collegiate leader gains authority because of his quality of thought and character. To use Max Weber's (1947) term, the effective colonial leader held "charismatic" power, rather than being a man who attained authority from the presence of specific administrative expertise. Supposedly, an effective academic leader did not need formal background or training in academic administration. He only required the quality of thought and a moral sense from which his colleagues could gain inspiration. Just as colonial college presidents taught the final course, so ideal college presidents, according to the dictates of the colonial culture, led their institutions by educating and serving as an example to fellow administrators and faculty members.

A second important characteristic of the colonial college was its isolation from primary and secondary school education in America. When the colonial college was being established, the only existing educational programs were offered to young men (and a few young women) who needed a rudimentary introduction to reading and writing in order to conduct commerce and read the Bible. The colonial colleges were established for older students, in part to provide teachers for these elementary school programs. There was a major gap in time between the elementary programs provided to children between the ages of five and ten and the college programs offered to young men (and later young women) between the ages of seventeen and twenty-two. Because of this gap, elementary schools and colleges developed independently, with very little interaction and very little need for direct articulation between specific program units.

Only at a later point were new educational programs established to accommodate young men and women who had completed elementary school but were not yet old enough for college. These "college preparatory schools" filled the gap and were the precursors to contemporary high schools and junior high schools. Thus, a major characteristic of the colonial college was its autonomy from lower levels of education. In general, administrators and faculty members in the colonial colleges were not previously employed at elementary or secondary schools. Rather, they were specifically educated and prepared from the beginning (at first through the undergraduate colleges and later through graduate programs) to assume a position in a college or university.

Clearly, certain aspects of the American colonial college have influenced the collegial culture of contemporary American colleges and universities. They have shared this influence, however, with a second model of higher education that was borrowed in the mid-nineteenth century, not from England, but from Germany. Just at the time when the American public, through its federal and state representatives, was expressing an increased commitment to higher education (through the Morrill Land Grant College Act of 1862), the leaders of many American collegiate institutions were becoming enthralled with the achievements of German research universities. Brubacher and Rudy (1958, p. 171) consider this influence to be profound:

> The impact of German university scholarship upon nineteenth-century American higher education is one of the most significant themes in modern intellectual history. Just as the American college has derived its structure from an English prototype, so the American graduate school [and university] has taken its pattern from the Philosophical Faculty of the German university.
>
> The essence of the German university system, which gave it intellectual leadership in the nineteenth century, was the concept that an institution of true

higher learning should be, above all, "the workshop
of free scientific research." This emphasis on the
disinterested pursuit of truth through original investigation led, on one hand, to the development of the
concept that a true university must maintain freedom
of teaching and freedom of learning within certain
carefully defined limits. On the other, it led ultimately
to a stress on the various services which higher learning could render to the state.

This university, unlike the American colonial college, was
dominated not by a willful president but by a willful and autonomous faculty. In their pursuit of knowledge for knowledge's sake,
German faculty members were given great freedom in their selection
of course offerings and their choice of scholarly projects. The German university emphasized not only the liberal arts, but also the
sciences. Paradoxically, the German university (and later the American research university) was both more theoretical and more practical in orientation than either the British university or American
colonial college. The strange mixture of theory and application
became even more pronounced in the American university. The
reputations of major Midwest research universities, such as the University of Michigan, the University of Wisconsin, and the University
of Minnesota, were built on a solid record of technical achievement
as well as scholarly excellence (Brubacher and Rudy, 1958).

Another major characteristic of the German research university was its emphasis on the discipline and work of faculty members,
rather than the education of young people. Whereas British universities and American colonial colleges were expressly devoted to the
education of young men and women, the German research professors often found undergraduate education to be a nuisance. Leaders
of the German research universities typically directed their most
valuable educational resources to upper-division and graduate-level
education. These institutions were particularly interested in the education of young intellectuals in specific academic disciplines. Faculties wanted to produce more researchers and scholars in order to
expand their own influence and that of their particular fields of
study.

In some ways, the German university resembled the British and American colonial institutions. Administrators were valued because of their scholarly record and character, not because of their specific administrative abilities. Typically, only an established scholar or researcher was allowed to preside over these academic institutions. The German university also remained independent of elementary and secondary educational institutions. General education was considered the prerogative and responsibility of these lower-level institutions. In the United States, many nineteenth-century leaders of major research universities actually argued for the adoption of a six-year secondary school plan, such as was found in Germany. Such a plan would eliminate the first two years of undergraduate education at the university. This scheme led to the creation of two-year junior and community colleges (to which we will turn in describing the managerial culture).

Although the British and American colonial college models remained dominant in the small American liberal arts colleges through the mid-twentieth century, the German research university model reigned at most large, state-supported universities and even at the larger, more prestigious, private universities. The prevalent notion of "quality" among American college and university leaders was built on the image of Harvard, Yale, Stanford, and other private universities that converted from the British to the German prototype by the beginning of the twentieth century.

Jencks and Riesman note that the "university college" model, which emulates the German research university and defines its primary purpose as the preparation of students for graduate work, now dominates American higher education, even in those small state-supported and private colleges and universities where such a model is inappropriate:

> Out of more than 2,000 undergraduate colleges, probably no more than 100 today really fit the [university college] description. Yet these are the most prestigious colleges in the country, to which the ablest and most ambitious students usually gravitate. They also attract the ablest faculty and administrators and the most generous philanthropists. And they provide a model

which many of the other 1,900 colleges regard as desirable, even if not immediately accessible. Drawn by
emulation on the one side and pushed by accrediting
agencies on the other, an increasing number of terminal colleges hire Ph.D.s from the leading graduate
schools even though they fear the impact of men who
may not be happy or complacent at a terminal college,
and who may also make others less happy or complacent. . . . New and better-trained faculty recruits in
turn help propel the institution toward the recruit-
ment of students on the basis of academic ability, with
diminished reference to traditional considerations
[such as religious affiliation or family ties] [1968,
pp. 24–25].

Although the leaders of many smaller colleges and universities imitate the British university model, because they are unable,
financially and/or intellectually, to create a first-rate research university, they are inclined to view their institutions as second class.
In his study of eight collegiate institutions (varying widely in size,
programmatic emphasis, and structure), Warren Bryan Martin
(1969) offers convincing evidence about the extent to which the
research university prototype—and, more broadly, the collegial culture—now dominates the consciousness of American faculty and
academic administrators. Martin found that these academicians
shared attitudes about "educational assumptions, values and goals;
the criteria for institutional excellence; and the prospects for professional or institutional change" (1969, p. 206).

With the growing importance of scientific and technical research during the *Sputnik* era, the late 1950s and early 1960s, the
research universities became even more esteemed and imitated. Much
of the growth in American higher education occurred during or
immediately after this era, partially in response to the need for
trained scientists (and partially in response to the baby boom). As a
result, a large proportion of the faculty members who now teach in
American colleges and universities received graduate training during
a time when the German research university model was particularly
prominent. Consequently, many of the tacitly held assumptions

about the role of faculty in a collegiate institution and about the proper place of an academic's discipline, scholarship, and research are based on the German model (Parsons and Platt, 1973).

Taken together, the British, German, and American colonial traditions produce a culture in which faculty are oriented primarily toward their disciplines. As in the British tradition, this orientation may be reflected in the content and scope of the undergraduate curriculum, or, as in the German tradition, it may appear in the nature and purpose of faculty research and scholarship.

The mixed traditions also produce an environment in which faculty members are suspicious and even disdainful of any orderly or obvious program of instruction. Teaching at the collegiate level is conceived of as an art, not a science or technology. One is an effective teacher because one knows his or her subject matter and, usually, because one has sat at the feet of another great teacher. A sense of tradition pervades the collegial culture and provides it with its unique and often quaint atmosphere, as well as with its stability and ubiquitous resistance to abrupt change.

One of the more insightful, though damning descriptions of this culture has been provided by Nevitt Sanford (1971, p. 357), who observes:

> Professors often identify with their discipline or speciality rather than with the role of teacher. They respect norms concerning how much time one may properly spend with students or how much interest in students one may display. . . . One should not in conversation with colleagues or other professionals go beyond the bounds of one's own speciality. Other rules hold that if something outside of one's speciality comes up for discussion he should always defer to other specialists, even though this puts an end to the conversation, and that he should always exhibit a devotion to the highest standards in matters of appointments and promotions and admission of students (let somebody else suggest that a risk be taken in particularly interesting cases).
>
> It all seems pretty grim—as indeed it is. . . .

> [W]e find in our institutions of higher learning wide-
> spread unhappiness and cynicism. Indeed, the aca-
> demic culture seems to decree that it ought not to be
> otherwise. Since the faculty member is devoted to such
> high purposes—the pursuit of which is constantly in-
> terfered with by people who do not understand—it
> would seem almost immoral to take any pleasure in
> what one does.

Sanford believes that this culture must be changed if effective teaching is to take place and if faculty members are to find more meaning and fulfillment in their work. In the early 1970s, Sanford's critique of the dominant academic culture helped to inspire a new developmental culture (see Chapter Four). His analysis, unfortunately, still rings true in the 1990s.

Images and Myths of the Collegial Culture

The historical antecedents of the present-day collegial culture clearly affect the career aspirations of faculty and administrators, their self-image as professionals, and the nature and scope of problems that now face them. Many collegial faculty would like to be successful researchers and scholars or would like to be able to teach some day in a major research university or an elitist liberal arts college. Both of these images of success are informed and reinforced by widespread contemporary cultural images of the successful faculty member.

During the 1930s and 1940s, the *Halls of Ivy* was a very successful radio (and later television) program, starring Ronald Coleman as President Hall of Ivy College. Many contemporary faculty members were young and impressionable children when this series played and have been influenced by its images—even if unconsciously. The typical faculty member's memory of the *Halls of Ivy* blends scenes from the actual program with those from other stock "campus romance" movies.

It is always autumn at Ivy College. The leaves have turned a bright red and yellow. We are ambling down a tree-lined street that winds graciously between old, well-preserved colonial homes.

At the end of the street, we arrive at President Hall's handsome (though not ostentatious) home.

President Hall's well-mannered young son is raking leaves in front of the home. You say hello to him and knock on the door. President Hall's maid (an eccentric but lovable lady in her late fifties) answers the door and invites you into Dr. Hall's living room. A cheery fire always seems to be lit (and in need of minimal tending). You sit by the fire and are offered an inviting cup of tea (or hot cider—something nonalcoholic, of course).

President Hall enters the room. He wears an elegant, though slightly worn, cardigan sweater and carries with him a copy of Shakespeare sonnets, which are familiar friends. A mix of Marcus Welby and Mortimer Adler, President Hall engages us in conversation about literature, modern values, and the intellectual growth of students at Ivy College.

Dr. Hall observes that a liberal arts education is truly valuable in our day and age. Only last week, he was teaching about Socrates and the hemlock in his freshman section of Western civilization. One of the young ladies in the course could not see how studying Socrates made sense in our modern world. Dr. Hall asked this young woman (Susan) about the upcoming senior prom: "Do you have a date to the prom, Susan?" "Yes, of course," said Susan. "Well," said Dr. Hall, "you are probably going to the prom in part because you want to go and because you like the fellow who has asked you. You are also going to the prom, however, because it is expected of you. The prom is a part of the social fabric of our society that keeps our world on an even keel. Things were the same in Socrates' time. Socrates believed that it was important to preserve the rules of Greek society, even if this meant he would have to die upholding these rules." Dr. Hall pointed with pride to Susan's sudden expression of enlightenment and joy. She now understands how philosophy and history can apply to everyday life. Susan has changed her major to philosophy. She talks about living a new life with the classics of Western civilization.

At the end of this reaffirming meeting with President Hall, you bid him farewell. On the way out, you greet Dr. Hall's warm and quietly intelligent wife (who is baking cookies in the kitchen) and walk back down the winding street. You have much to think about and much to be thankful for in this world of stability, serenity, and good manners.

The contemporary academy does not very closely resemble the mythical world of President Hall. Faculty members and academic administrators rarely find themselves working in this type of environment with this kind of accommodating student. Women as well as men now preside over and teach in these institutions. Yet the images conveyed in this story continue to influence the aspirations of faculty members and administrators (particularly if they are male). Administrators are never as wise or as responsive as they could be. Colleagues are never as bright, well read, or articulate as they ought to be. Students are never as appreciative of a liberal arts education as they should be; certainly, they are not as competent and well-prepared as the despairing faculty member would like them to be.

This conflict between what they would like and what they actually confront is particularly difficult for many faculty members to reconcile, for their whole orientation in life is toward the ideal rather than reality—the possible rather than the actual. For example, on the Myers-Briggs type indicator (Briggs-Myers, 1976), which assesses Jungian-based preferences for sensing versus intuition, faculty members typically score very high on intuition. "Those people who prefer intuition," notes Isabel Briggs-Myers (1980, p. 2), "are so engrossed in pursuing the possibilities [the world] presents that they seldom look very intently at the actualities."

A second image that affects the aspirations of many faculty in the collegial culture is that of the scientist or scholar in the sterile but impressive confines of a famous research laboratory or think tank. This image builds on the German research university models, but is influenced by American mass media (much as the *Halls of Ivy* informs the collegial culture image of a liberal arts college designed on the British model). When speaking candidly in an interview, many faculty members note the role of science-fiction movies and books on space travel or futuristic utopias in first whetting their appetites for the sciences. Other academics identify novels and movies in which a reclusive scholar develops a grand, revolutionary theory or penetrates the human soul in some profound manner.

Our protagonist—the ideal scientist or scholar—usually

dwells on some lofty plane. Subsidized by family wealth or secure in a university appointment, he (rarely a woman) seems to be oblivious to the more mundane matters of finance. Personal relationships have a low priority, though the professor may be seduced at the end of the film or novel by an attractive laboratory assistant, reporter, alumna, or daughter of the university president. His requisite apparel is either a white lab coat or a herringbone jacket. He invariably smokes a pipe and partakes of an afternoon sherry. The scientist or scholar is often a former college athlete (the Rhodes Scholar model) but is now physically active only when an emergency occurs (about two-thirds of the way through the novel or movie). His physical prowess emerges only when the monster is invading, when fieldwork is required, or when our protagonist wants to show that he is still an all-American fellow by participating in a pick-up football game being played on the grass in front of the laboratory or library. Our modern-day equivalent to the scholar-athlete is Steven Spielberg's Indiana Jones.

The scientist-scholar's work is usually performed in solitude or with one or two young protégés who provide appropriate respect and encouragement. Neither our protagonist nor his assistants are very interested in the ethical implications of their work until late in the movie or novel. They are concerned with the ultimate impact of their research on the welfare of mankind but are shortsighted about its immediate implications. The work itself is a breakthrough—always on the frontiers of knowledge. In Thomas Kuhn's terminology (1962), this research is never in the realm of "normal science," but is always in the realm of revolution and new-paradigm construction.

The research or scholarship is, of course, always successful. Very little attention is given to problems of dissemination; the new knowledge is immediately available to the entire world. Only early on in the novel or movie is there resistance to the dissemination of our protagonist's findings. By the end of the movie or novel, the scientist or scholar often shifts attention from his own work to broader social or religious concerns. The quest continues on this broader plane.

Like the *Halls of Ivy*, this image of the scientist-scholar is undifferentiated and sexist; yet it nags many faculty members and reduces their satisfaction with their current professional careers. Academics are often disappointed about their inability to conduct major, revolutionary scholarship or research. They are discouraged by the lack of attention to the few articles that they do publish. Many faculty members seem to live with a mythical manuscript of exceptional quality that they are still preparing or trying to get published. Given that the average faculty member publishes no more than one article in a lifetime, the discrepancy between image and reality is often great and a source of distress.

Concern about promotion, salary, office space, laboratory equipment, library holdings, and human subject review procedures often seems to dominate the lives of faculty who do have an opportunity to engage in research or scholarship. A significant amount of time, especially since the early 1970s, must be spent in applying for new funds to sustain a current project or to begin a new one. Members of science faculties speak of the frustration associated with the need to fabricate practical implications of the "pure research" that they wish to conduct in order to receive funds. Members of humanities and social science faculties express anger at not being able to compete with physical scientists for federal or state funding and about the general lack of public recognition or support for scholarship.

In view of these myths and their historical roots, how do institutions function in this atmosphere? Furthermore, how does the collegial culture interact with the other three academic cultures that we have identified? We turn now to a case study of one college to gain some understanding into how the collegial culture manifests itself in the daily life and in the problems of a collegiate institution, as well as how it interacts with the other three cultures.

Case Study: Canon College

The president at Canon College was very pleased to be able to announce that this small liberal arts institution, with a total student enrollment of 650 students and forty-five full-time faculty members, had just received a generous grant of more than $1,000,000 to undertake one of the largest and most ambitious curricular reform projects of its kind ever mounted in the state. Like many small

liberal arts colleges in the United States, Canon College was initially supported by and found its identity in the Catholic faith. In
the late 1960s and early 1970s, the college began to move toward a
secular base and hired more faculty members and administrators
(including a president) who were not members of the sponsoring
religious order. With this transition came shifts in the academic and
organizational culture of the college, as well as new financial pressures (given that higher salaries were expected by the secular faculty
and administrators). Shifts in the academic culture have moved the
college from a classical liberal arts tradition, which emphasized the
humanities and arts, toward a more "practical" orientation, which
emphasizes business and other applied fields, in addition to the
liberal arts. This transition is not unique to Canon College. It is,
nevertheless, painful and difficult.

As a Catholic college, Canon has constantly faced a paradox
that is common to many church-affiliated institutions: the college
is simultaneously impoverished and surrounded by boundless resources. Though its faculty and administrators are poorly paid, the
college sits on beautiful and very valuable property. While the College scrapes for funds to stay open, it anticipates future funding of
a substantial nature from local community foundations. And
though the grant that Canon received is among the largest of its
kind ever given to a small liberal arts college, Canon College has
been considering reduction in the size of its faculty in order to
restore a more viable student-faculty ratio.

For many years this simultaneous impoverishment and
wealth was a source of paradox and frustration for members of the
Canon College community. In the 1970s Canon College received a
major federal grant for its humanities program, just as the college
was facing its first major financial crisis associated with the shift
toward a more costly, secular faculty and administration. Additional funds for faculty development were obtained a few years later
through a generous grant from a large national foundation. This
successful funding record reached its zenith with the massive grant
for curriculum development and continued with the funding of
student development activities through a subsequent federal grant.

Another distinctive and longstanding aspect of the academic
culture at Canon College arises from its location in a region of the

country noted for the quality of its large public and private research universities. Inappropriate and destructive comparisons are made between Canon College and these other local institutions. The tension is increased by the college's practice of often hiring graduates of these higher-status universities.

Thus, although Canon College is clearly committed to teaching excellence and to working with good, if not necessarily gifted, students who can profit from individual attention, there is a pervasive feeling of inferiority at the college, particularly when it is under stress. A longing for the traditional values of the collegial culture—scholarship, high academic standards, extensive faculty autonomy, and support—is intensified when faculty (and administrators) face major budget cuts and diminished prospects for institutional growth.

How then does the curriculum development grant fit into this picture? For some faculty and administrators, the grant was initially perceived as a savior—as the answer to many of the college's problems. With substantial funds, faculty could become both teachers and scholars and could effectively compete in the academic marketplace with colleagues from more prestigious institutions. With the grant money, faculty and administrators could construct a new, more dynamic, and appealing curriculum that would attract more and better students, thus making Canon College a stronger and financially more secure institution.

For other faculty and administrators, the grant was seen as a tempting but disruptive influence. They feared that the availability of substantial funds would enable the college to overlook its deep-rooted financial problems and encourage the faculty to develop unrealistic expectations about the resurrection of a "purer" collegial culture at this small, tuition-driven liberal arts college. In this sense, the grant was perceived as a smoke screen or diversion that made the college's long-term problems even more difficult to address.

In its initial report to the Curriculum Development Committee, an evaluation team from outside the college offered a story, "The Shadow of the Dam," to illustrate one of its major findings and concerns. The evaluation team described a small village that is located directly in front of a large dam, behind which stands a large reservoir of water. Because of bureaucratic confusion or indifference, the village has never had access to this water. As a result, the villagers' crops are wilting, and the town residents are always thirsty. Those who own the dam finally agreed to allocate some water to the villagers—but only if they use the water exclusively to keep the streets of the village clean. The villagers therefore direct most of their energy and creativity to seeing how the water being used to clean the streets can somehow be made to splash on the crops and into the mouths of their thirsty children.

Similarly, in the case of Canon College, the funds have been given for curriculum development; however, salaries at the college are remarkably low (particularly given the socioeconomic level of the community and region in which the college is located). The faculty most requires higher salaries. Yet the new funds expressly cannot be used to supplement salaries, and so the faculty must justify need for the funds to enhance their professional skills and the college curriculum. Like the villagers, Canon College faculty members devoted considerable energy and creativity throughout the duration of the grant to devising various ways to receive indirect compensation from the grant or to engage in activities that they would have done by themselves with sufficient salary (travel, purchase of new computers, attendance at national conferences). The evaluation team suggested that the curriculum development program would always live in the shadow of the dam as long as the college was unable to address the pressing issue of low faculty salaries. The college has been unable to raise salaries to a significant degree over the past five years and cannot expect to do so during the coming two to three years, given its current financial crisis.

During the initial year of the grant, program management and structure were patterned after that of the much smaller grant for faculty development that had just ended. Faculty members applied for funds in several different categories. The most ambitious and visionary faculty members applied for and received funds to initiate several different curricular projects, whereas more reticent or complacent faculty members (or those unwilling to compete with their colleagues) applied for and received fewer funds.

Faculty members usually spoke of this initial year as a period of competition and some estrangement among Canon College faculty members. Members of the Curriculum Development Committee often felt pressure from their colleagues who were applying for funds; at the same time they were concerned about the unmet needs of those faculty members who had not actively sought out funds.

At a retreat held during the fall of the second year, the Canon College faculty chose to abandon this mode of funding proposals and instead inaugurated a Curriculum Development Planning (CDP) process, whereby each faculty member submitted a plan for the use of funds that were specifically allocated to this individual. Once the Curriculum Development Planning process was inaugurated, the sense of competition lessened, though the paperwork and bureaucracy seemed to increase.

Several faculty members at Canon indicated that they thought the program went "downhill" after the initial plans were approved. None of the other aspects of the grant gained as much attention or seemed to hold as much credibility as the Curriculum Development Planning. Furthermore, Canon College is an institution where "programs come and go." Several faculty members noted that several of the most promising new curricular ideas that emanated from the CDP (such as computer science) were in place for only one to three years before being phased out, even though all signs indicated that they were likely to be very successful. Systematic curricular planning at Canon College is not readily apparent and seems to be housed primarily in the Office of the Dean.

In view of the rapid demise of new programs, a summary assessment of the structural impact of the grant on the college's curriculum was rather negative. Moreover, most of the new tools for curriculum planning (including new information about student development) remained in the hands and heads of a few administrators and faculty members. There was little evidence of improved faculty expertise with regard to curricular planning, evaluation, or renewal. Apparently, there were insufficient resources to realize the hopes inspired by the grant and a lack of patience to see through those changes that the grant did support. Curricular change itself seems to have been the goal rather than the means to some collectively shared educational goal or curricular vision. In the eyes of many Canon College faculty, the desire for change in and of itself is part of the problem.

The anger and frustration with the administration and the organizational climate of the college was extensive. Administrators at the college were clearly in an untenable position, as they were forced to slash budgets and suspend virtually all new program initiatives. The grant did very little in a tangible manner to prepare the college for this crisis or to prepare the individual players (faculty and administrators) to cope with the attendant stress and ill-will provoked among members of a once-supportive college community.

The Collegial Culture in Interaction with the Other Cultures

What seems to be at the heart of the problems facing Canon College? Why was it unable to benefit more from its substantial curriculum development grant? We can look to several factors. First, in the past primary concern at the college was for issues associated with the collegial culture: advancement of the discipline and preservation of academic standards. Though the Catholic origins of this college would suggest a more managerial orientation (see Chapter Four), Canon was established in the shadow of and borrowed its culture from more prestigious local universities that have always been saturated with the collegial culture.

In part as a result of the grant, Canon College became more bureaucratic and management oriented, with new emphasis being placed on the specification of program outcomes and the use of new educational technology. The developmental culture also became more prevalent. The perspective of faculty and administrators was more cosmopolitan and individualistic.

A new legal-rational basis of authority was created at the college that placed more control in the hands of middle managers in the institution. Canon College had to become more bureaucratic because it was faced with a different kind of "growth issue"—not increases in numbers of students but substantial increases in the amount of money available for curriculum development activities. Without greater concern for equitable and consistent review of faculty requests (and hence increased paperwork), faculty at Canon College believe that the grant would have become a "snake pit," with some faculty pushing unfairly for special considerations and other faculty being given too little or too much.

Several grant-related organizational studies revealed a corollary reason for the increased bureaucratization: the containment of institutional conflict. New bureaucratic procedures were adopted in many different sectors of the college (not just with regard to the curriculum development program). As in Curriculum Development Planning, most of these procedures sought to ensure that every faculty member (or student, administrator, or staff member) was given fair treatment by the college—a first step toward the negotiating culture. Under extreme financial pressures, however, the college has moved away from this protectionist use of bureaucracy and has instead employed these procedures to dismiss a relatively large number of untenured faculty members. This practice represents a major challenge to the dominant collegial culture of the college and may signal a major shift in organizational processes and procedures toward a more managerial perspective—or eventually toward the formation of a negotiating culture by the faculty in response to the firings.

A second problem concerns the tension between student-centered and faculty-centered instruction at Canon. On the one hand, there has traditionally been a strong developmental culture at the college, with principal faculty attention given to the personal and professional growth of the student. On the other hand, the grant has seemed to encourage at least a short-term diversion of focus from the welfare of students to that of the faculty members themselves. Many faculty members at Canon College took long-delayed sabbaticals during the four-year grant period. As a result, many courses were taught by part-time, novice teachers who knew little about and showed little commitment to the unique academic culture at Canon College. Though students at the college knew little about the Curriculum Development Program, they did experience some of its negating side effects: poorer or at least less experienced teaching, less continuity of academic leadership, and faculty distraction from the dominant teaching-learning mission of the college.

Efforts previously devoted to teaching appear to have become directed primarily toward scholarship. Academics at many other collegially oriented colleges and universities have turned their attention to nonacademic matters (such as campus politics), but those at Canon College generally allocated their new-found time and money to activities and resources related to their disciplines. They often obtained doctorates or served on national panels of their disciplinary associations. Unlike faculty at many liberal arts colleges, they had funds to attend regional and national conventions.

This new interest in and recommitment to the collegial culture and to an academic discipline were very gratifying to many faculty, who had themselves graduated from research universities. Having just returned from meetings where new findings in their fields were being presented and discussed, Canon faculty were able to represent themselves for the first time as up-to-date members of their disciplines. They frequently spoke of a new identity that came with participation in national associations. They were less likely to indicate how this new identity and renewed sense of their disciplines related to their teaching and the development of their students. They expressed confidence that there was a connection between their own professional development and the education of their students; however, like many other participants in the collegial culture, they were rarely able to describe this connection clearly.

Another source of dysfunction at Canon concerns the widening perspectives of its faculty, which have further exacerbated a conflict between the collegial and managerial cultures at this college. Many of the Canon College faculty had come to the college directly from graduate school. Other faculty and administrators were members of the religious order that founded and governed the school for many years. Many of these women had spent very little time away from their convent and the college's campus for the past twenty to thirty years. The grant was seen as an excellent opportunity for these "cloistered" secular and religious faculty and administrators to see more of the world.

For many Canon College faculty, this broadening of perspectives was particularly important. Jack Lindquist's (1978b) superb study of innovation in American colleges and universities suggests that the acquisition of a cosmopolitan point of view by faculty members at small liberal arts colleges may be one of the most important ingredients in their increased capacity to adapt to changing internal and external environments. As one Canon faculty member noted succinctly, "We all grew up." Another concluded, "I now have access to people and ideas that I brought back to the classroom." Canon faculty talked about the empowering role that the new knowledge and experience created. With understanding of alternative collegiate programs and other modes of governance and administration, the Canon faculty became more eager to participate more actively in the leadership of the college. Unfortunately, their timing was not very good: facing a series of financial crises in 1986 and 1987, the administration of the college became understandably less inclined to explore new governance and administrative structures and processes. Thus, the dominant and reenvigorated collegial culture at Canon came directly into conflict with the emerging managerial culture and the financial realities of the institution.

A final grant-related conflict concerns a new emphasis on the individual, as opposed to the community. Many faculty members and administrators have suggested that the personal orientation of the curriculum development program had eroded the collegially based sense of community at Canon College. One faculty member attributed this erosion to the spirit of competition that the grant produced among faculty and staff members, along with the heightened desire to go off campus in pursuit of personal and professional interests. (There was a decidedly moral overtone to this faculty member's observations.) Another faculty member spoke of the grant as serving to decrease faculty identification with the "Canon family." For this faculty member, an advocate of the old collegial culture at Canon, personal identify was embedded in the Canon College community. She grieved the loss of this community spirit and the rise of a new individualism at the college. For other faculty members, pushing for a more negotiative culture, the "Canon family" concept was outmoded and unhealthy. It connoted the faculty's continuing sacrifice and the absence of clear faculty governance. They applauded its demise.

A related observation came from a faculty member who felt that Canon College was changing from an organization in which people "banded together to help each other" to one in which people were paid for their time. This was a direct result of the policy to pay faculty members through the grant for curriculum development work. Although most of those interviewed recognized that payment for services rendered was a healthy alternative to the demand for unpaid labor made of faculty in previous years, they contended that the faculty members at Canon were losing their sense of commitment to the community and were likely to move towards the managerial culture. After further examining the more personal aspects of faculty and administrative life in the collegial culture in Chapter Three, we shall more fully explore the managerial culture, for it has become a dominant force in most colleges and universities—even those (like Canon) with a strong collegial tradition.

3

❖❖❖❖❖❖❖

Living and Working in
the Collegial Culture

The collegial culture has traditionally placed great value on faculty
work that is directed toward disciplinary scholarship and research.
The proponents of this culture also value the inculcation of a disciplinary orientation in students. John Millett, while president of
Miami University, spoke of the dominance of disciplinary special-
izations in his work *The Academic Community* (1962, pp. 70–71):
"It is often said that faculty members have a major loyalty to their
discipline or professional field of knowledge rather than to the college or university in which they practice their profession. To a
considerable extent this observation is valid. The very nature of the
academic profession with its emphasis on specialization promotes
this sense of scholarly rather than local or community identity."

A small group of highly esteemed, elderly faculty on each
campus are allowed the privilege of moving across disciplines to
teach in a related field or to write in an interdisciplinary, synthe-
sizing manner. Most faculty, however, are expected to confine themselves to disciplinary matters. Only the academic administrator and
librarian are allowed to be truly interdisciplinary, and they lose
academic credibility when they assume these roles. In general, interdisciplinary work is tolerated at both ends of the academic pecking order: that is, in the least prestigious (small liberal arts) colleges
and in the most respected (major independent) universities.

41

The collegial culture also values the autonomy of faculty in their work as teachers, scholars, and researchers. This autonomy, in part, reflects the more general and unique autonomy of American colleges and universities in our society (Ben-David, 1972). When academics in the collegial culture are reviewed for promotion and tenure, their accountability rarely extends to direct observation of faculty performance in the classroom, or to assignment of priorities to specific research or scholarship activities.

Many faculty members in the collegial culture would take great offense at being asked, let alone required, to accept an observing colleague in their classrooms. It would be considered an invasion of the essential privacy required by the teaching-learning act. Ironically, even though classroom teaching is certainly a public event, it is considered an intimate interchange between faculty member and student. This interchange might be profoundly disrupted if observed and judged by another faculty member. Faculty members are also given the freedom to choose the area in which they will conduct research, as long as it lies within their disciplinary domain. The major faculty prerogative, called academic freedom, precludes both observation of classroom performance and review of ongoing research and scholarship.

Academic freedom is one of the dominant norms of the collegial culture. It originates, according to Millett (1962, p. 56), in the distinctive role of American colleges and universities as vehicles for social change in our society: "The whole concern in the United States and in the Western world with academic freedom is an effort to acknowledge the unique relationship between higher education and society. Higher education is dangerous. It carries with it at all times the possibility that it may upset an existing power structure in society. It carries with it at all times the possibility that individuals and institutions in society may have to accept new ideas and new ways of behavior." Statements like this are reinforced throughout the collegial culture by the emphasis on "pure scholarship" and reason. If colleges and universities are truly sources of change for contemporary society, not either bastions of reactionary ideas or preservers of history and tradition, then academic freedom becomes essential to safeguard the society as well as the academy. Unfortunately, this freedom and the underlying assumption about the academy as a agency of social change and a moral force in society are upheld at a price. They tend to isolate the academy and its faculty members from the mainstream of American life. Faculty can choose to be either irrelevant or the unwanted gadflies of our society. Neither role is positive, and both perpetuate a destructive isolation of the academic from the nonacademic world.

In the collegial culture major emphasis is placed on independent work. Typically, faculty members labor alone on projects, teach by themselves in the classroom, and plan curriculum and courses in isolation from their colleagues. Millett (1962) describes the strength of this individualism in the collegial culture and relates it directly to the basic mission of the collegiate institution: "The goal of the academic community is to provide an environment of learning, not a product of learning. Knowledge is acquired by individuals. It is not an object to be built and used like an automobile, a piece of furniture, a house, or a pencil (p. 62). . . . The goal of education is realized in individuals. It is conceivable that the learning process could be carried on with just one scholar and one student. Or one scholar could pursue his efforts alone, as might a single student" (pp. 68–69).

For many faculty members, one of the most attractive features of the collegial culture is this tolerance for and even encouragement of autonomous activity. Whereas the other three academic cultures, and most of the other dominant cultures in our society, reinforce collaboration and corporate activity, the collegial culture nurtures the "lone wolf," the "eccentric," and the socially oblivious "absent-minded professor" in a manner that is unique to American higher education. A *New Yorker*-type cartoon from the late 1960s illustrates this autonomy. Two research scientists are seated at two large instrument consoles, facing in opposite directions. One of the scientists remarks to the other, "I see from the latest scientific journal that you and I have been working on the same problem for the past five years."

In his humorous, but thoughtful, book, *The Academic Tribes*, Hazard Adams (1976, p. 13) notes that in American higher education, "eccentricity is not merely tolerated, it is positively admired. The model for the researcher is the genius. Genius is eccentric. Therefore researchers should be eccentric. . . . Eccentricity is a symbol of the scholar's intellectual freedom, to say nothing of his stubbornness. The tolerance of eccentricity, although sometimes puzzling to outsiders, is inevitable in academic life, despite the range of irresponsibility it sometimes protects."

Qualities of Leadership

Academics in the collegial culture still look for charismatic characteristics in the people they allow to lead them, just as they did in colonial, British, and German institutions. They look to personal and ill-defined qualities of character, wisdom, and vision. They also look for political savvy. Hazard Adams (1976) observes:

> Universities [are] more like political organizations [than like businesses] [p. 2]. . . . The fact is that real authority in the university is not hierarchical, as in business or the military; it is not even "separate" as it is in principle in the United States government. There is not a system of checks and balances so much as a diffusion of authority. According to academic mythological history, there was once a pleasant Eden where the university was truly collegial and all administrative chores came about as a result of a division of responsibilities among faculty members. Vestiges of the Golden Age remain. In the best of all possible fallen institutions, the faculty controls courses, curriculum, academic requirements, and the like. The administration controls the budget. Personnel matters exist in the shady area in between. It is not really separation, but diffusion of powers [pp. 4–5].

Faculty members who live primarily in a collegial culture generally assume that effective leadership is exerted through the complex give-and-take of campus politics. General education programs are created that effectively protect disciplinary turf. Negotiations take place inside and outside interminable and frequent curriculum committee meetings. Personnel review of faculty occurs in multitiered, unpredictable committee meetings that incorporate both subtle horse trading and thoughtful discussion about the ultimate merit of diverse activities and accomplishments in a faculty member's portfolio. The successful faculty leader will have learned how to live in and even enjoy these committee meetings and will have gained power by working skillfully within this structure (as well as working outside by meeting individually with colleagues and making artful use of memoranda, agendas, and action-oriented proposals).

These political skills are not easily gained, and a faculty member's credibility is not readily built. As a result, most faculty members do not gain much power until they have been a member of one specific college community for many years. Until the late 1970s, the result was that each college and university had its own built-in hierarchy: old, skillful, and knowledgable faculty members sitting at the top and new, inexperienced faculty members sitting at the bottom. With the decrease at most collegiate institutions in new positions and the severely reduced mobility of most academics, there are few young, inexperienced faculty members. Hence, the hierarchy has disappeared. This situation, however, may change in the late 1990s, as many senior faculty members begin to retire.

Anyone who has survived the quasi-political wars of tenure and has served over a period of time in many committees has gained enough political skills to be effective in influencing the intricate—almost baroque—deliberations of a faculty. Yet the loss of hierarchy seems to have precipitated a crisis in some instances. Older faculty members either try to make the informal rules and norms of collegiate governance even more complicated, in order to confuse or exclude their slightly less experienced colleagues, or they become disillusioned with the whole process and seek to avoid or reform it (and in this way introduce faculty colleagues to the developmental culture).

Institutional Influence and Change

A faculty member who tacitly accepts the norms, values, and rules of precedence of the collegial culture will usually assume that institutional change takes place primarily through—and power resides in—the quasi-political, committee-based, faculty-controlled governance processes of a college or university. John Millett (1962) describes the faculty member's role in the academic community:

> The key element in the academic process and in the academic community is the faculty. There is no other justification for the existence of a college or a university except to enable the faculty to carry on its instructional and research activities. Without a faculty higher education has no reason for being. It is the faculty which realizes or fails to realize the basic objectives of each college or university [p. 65].

> Every faculty member expects that the system of organization and operation in a college or university will recognize the importance of the role of the faculty member and provide him with a status of dignity and consideration. The faculty member does not think of himself as an employee of the college or university. In particular, he resents any suggestion that his relations to a dean, a vice president for academic affairs, and a president involve supervisory authority [p. 101].

Because of the real or imagined power of faculty governance, collegial academics believe that the road to increased influence comes through assuming leadership (usually acting as chairperson) of major college or universitywide committees: for example, curriculum, personnel review, and faculty awards committees; committees overseeing committees; and executive committees. On many campuses, a faculty senate presides over the affairs of the institution; on other campuses, one or more faculty members sit on the president's cabinet as central decision makers of the university.

Millett (1962, p. 75) identifies this faculty involvement in decision making as "direct democracy": "Every person of stated academic rank has an equal voice and vote in the realization of collective action. At the university level the system for decision making may be either direct or representative. The faculty of a university may meet together as a whole and as an academic senate take appropriate actions affecting the general conduct of educational affairs. Except in a very small college or university, much of the actual achievement of an academic consensus rests with committees."

American higher education's unique mode of governance has been described in other works (Perkins, 1973). Even those corporations, social service agencies, and research organizations that encourage the involvement of professional staff in decision-making processes (see Lawler, 1986) typically do not allow as much participation as that found in contemporary colleges or universities infused with the collegial culture. Many trustees of these colleges and universities do not either fully recognize or appreciate the role of faculty influence. Their own background in a managerial culture—whether in a corporate environment or in public service—begins with the assumption of top-down decision making. This background does not prepare them for the collegial culture.

Because of the faculty's understanding of the "real" way in which an institution is influenced or changed, it has little regard for or patience with systematic planning processes advocated by proponents of the "rationalistic" culture. The step-by-step analysis of a personnel or curriculum problem is considered inappropriate. Such approaches are often judged to be quite naive in that they do not take into account the give-and-take of faculty politics. Books about how to run effective meetings and workshops on successful decision-making or conflict-management processes are much less likely to be received openly and used by faculty members than by other professionals in our society. The rationalistic culture will deeply penetrate other aspects of society long before it has a widespread and enduring impact on the faculty and collegially oriented administrators of our academic institutions.

Accountability

Faculty members in a collegial culture judge themselves and their colleagues as effective if they have established a strong publication record in "refereed" journals, if a large percentage of their undergraduate students decide to attend and are accepted into prestigious doctoral programs in their discipline, if they have chaired major institutionwide committees or have wielded informal influence in their deliberations, and if their own teaching is heavily oriented toward advanced undergraduate or graduate courses.

For a faculty member immersed in the collegial culture, academic ranks and the attainment of tenure are quite important. Considerable attention goes into discussions about these matters in faculty review committees. Even though formalized personnel review procedures are usually avoided by these committees, their neglect should not be interpreted as a lack of serious concern for the process itself. Rather, it should be seen as evidence of the collegial culture's suspicion of any systematic procedure that can be "applied" (like a coat of paint) to the subtle art of teaching and research. Though in many ways a proponent of the rationalistic culture, Joseph Axelrod (1973, p. 9) has created an appropriate metaphor for the collegial instructor as a teacher-artist:

> Every teacher-artist, like the artist in any sphere, attacks his task in the only way he can: he develops his own style, and he expresses himself in his own personal ways. Each person's talent, being unique, pushes him or her in a particular direction. What is more, the teacher-artist (again like any artist) is influenced in his own particular way by the hundred external factors that surround his art: the precise nature of his subject matter, the sophistication and motivation of his students, the conditions imposed by his own department, the campus ethos within which he carries out his task as teacher, and—beyond that—the influences of all of the system and supersystems [of which he is a member].

Given this reluctance to use formalized procedures in day-to-day campus activities, it is interesting to note that considerable credence is given to the processes of research review and publication. In many instances, faculty review committees give higher priority to publication records. How many articles and books has this faculty member written that were selected competitively by referecd journals or important publishing houses? Certainly, one of the most attractive features of this performance review criterion is its quantifiability: number of articles of a certain length, number of books of a certain length, and so forth. Furthermore, someone outside the faculty member's own college or university (the editorial board or editor of a journal or publishing house) assumes responsibility for making the difficult decision about the worth of this person's work.

Some faculty members and academic administrators (particularly those from the developmental culture) suggest that publications play a major role in faculty review procedures precisely because they are readily quantifiable and enable a faculty member's colleagues to avoid making qualitative judgments. Thus, though the proceedings of the collegial culture are superficially qualitative and based on peer review, they may in fact be biased toward quantifiable criteria and oriented toward the judgments of outside experts. It is precisely this ambiguity about accountability in the collegial culture that has moved many administrators (and faculty), often under pressure from a demanding citizenry, toward a quite different culture—the managerial culture. In the case study to which we now turn, we will see just such a movement and the conflict it inspired.

Case Study: Jim Herbert

Jim Herbert is a forty-seven-year-old chemist who is teaching at Western State University, located in the Rocky Mountains. Western State has only recently received university status and as a result is undergoing an "identity crisis." In some ways, it is still an oversized teachers college that happened to be located in an energy-rich, growing city. In other ways, Western State can lay claim to a status that is comparable to that of the other two major unversities in the state, for it has a strong engineering and mining school and a respected school of education.

The faculty members at Western State are in general ambivalent about their institution. They respect the work of their colleagues and share frustration about the seeming preference shown to the other two universities in the state (in particular, by the state legislature). Western is located in the largest urban area in the state; however, it receives less support than the two research universities, which are located in smaller urban areas. Nevertheless, the academics at Western State often seem to believe (or at least act as if they believe) the popular image of Western as a second-rate university.

Jim Herbert feels that he lives at the heart of this ambiguity. He hears that he is working in a "teaching institution," where emphasis is placed on the ability of faculty to instruct and advise students. Yet he feels uneasy about his upcoming tenure review, for he knows that his colleagues will look at his publication record—which is scant—in deciding whether or not to grant him tenure. Herbert enjoys teaching. He wanted to work at a teaching institution. He also is aware that he does not have the academic credentials to obtain a job in a research university.

Herbert came to Western in 1971, straight out of a Ph.D. program in a neighboring state. Western State attracted him because it was identified in the state master plan as a place where student growth and development at the undergraduate level would be emphasized. He found this emphasis to be intact when he first arrived at Western, perhaps because most American colleges and universities were stressing "relevance" and "student involvement" in the early 1970s (on the heels of the activist late 1960s).

By the mid 1970s, things seemed to shift at Western. A new emphasis on research emerged at the college. A new president (formerly academic vice president at one of the two research universities in the state) announced the intention of making Western into a university, and, furthermore, into a major research university. Jim Herbert felt betrayed. He had come to Western for different reasons and was not interested in changing the course of his professional career now. Herbert looked around him and became scared. In the 1960s and early 1970s, Western was able to recruit faculty members (like himself) with Ph.D.'s from only moderately good research universities. Because of a tight job market, Western could now hire bright young researchers from renowned universities in the East and Midwest.

Herbert faces a dilemma: he cannot move to another college or university that is oriented toward teaching; he knows that no jobs are available in this kind of institution for a middle-aged chemist. If he is to remain at Western, however, he must begin doing research and publishing, at the expense (he believes) of his own self-esteem and the best interests of his students.

Herbert has given serious consideration to quitting teaching, but he hesitates to move out of the academic world. Not only is it the only world he has known as an adult, but also he has a compelling need to prove that he is a capable, intelligent professional. In his opinion, neither his father nor his mother was particularly successful. His father graduated from college and then joined an insurance agency, which he now manages. Jim's mother went to college for one year but dropped out to marry his father.

Herbert is the first person in his family to receive a Ph.D. Everyone is very proud of his achievement and his current academic position. Though he often is chided by relatives about his "woolly-headed" intellectualism and his "head in the clouds" perspective, he knows that he is respected and admired. If he left the academic world, he fears that this respect would vanish, as would, perhaps, his own self-respect.

Yet he feels the "publish or perish" pressure; furthermore, when being totally honest with himself, he admits that teaching is no longer as satisfying as it once was. Is the reason for his dissatisfaction that he has exhausted his enthusiasm for teaching, or have his students become less interested in learning? As there are currently very few chemistry majors at Western (in contrast to the big expansion of the post-*Sputnik* era), Herbert spends most of his time teaching the basic chemistry course for nonmajors. Although the numerous premed students enrolled in his courses are motivated to get high grades, they do not seem to be really interested in chemistry. Maybe a new job in industry would make sense.

If Herbert does leave his university, however, he sacrifices the flexibility and extra time off accorded by the academic schedule. With two small children, he has been able to be an active father during the summer—a situation that would end if he took a job in industry. Still, he would make more money as an industrial chemist. Herbert could do a better job of supporting his family and securing greater financial stability. But what would the money bring? Now, in his free time, he can maintain the house and plant a garden. He also can engage in his favorite pastimes: canoeing and back packing. These aspects of his life would certainly change if he left the teaching profession. With all of this in mind, Herbert struggles to make a decision. He knows he will have to make some significant alterations in his professional life. But what will they be, and why does he feel so angry about being forced to make them?

The Collegial Culture in Interaction with the Other Cultures

Jim Herbert is caught in two major cultural crises that seem at least partially the sources of his frustration. First, he is one of many faculty members in the sciences who are faced with the loss of *Sputnik*-era optimism and prestige. He was one of many young men and women who were attracted to the extravagant promise of technological miracles, a promise that has gone largely unfulfilled. Scientists like Jim Herbert discovered that the world was no longer asking for more physicists or chemists in the late 1970s and 1980s. Instead, corporations were asking for managers to run the high technology operations that had been created by scientists and engineers. There have been several signs of resurgence in the sciences and technology, but the heyday of the scientific disciplines and engineering professions seems to be past.

The struggles that Jim Herbert faces as a scientist reveals a basic flaw in the collegial culture—namely, its rigidity in the face of shifting societal demands. Faculty members in the traditional collegial culture cannot readily shift to new fields or even different areas within their current fields. Intensive specialization leaves many faculty members unable to respond to the changing career patterns of their students.

The second crisis that Jim Herbert faces is located within the collegial culture itself. Because of decreased faculty mobility and the absence of new faculty members, many college and university communities where the collegial culture is dominant have become stagnant. Faculty members have worked with the same colleagues for more than a decade. Each member of the department has already served at least one term as department chairperson. Each has made at least one attempt at making major revisions in the department's or institution's curriculum. They have all published one or two articles in a respectable journal and have found that only ten to twenty colleagues at other institutions have read the article.

Even though academic rank is valued, most of the faculty members have already reached their highest possible level. If they have a Ph.D. (or comparable professional) degree, then they probably were elevated to the rank of professor by the time they had reached age forty or forty-five. These academics are now in their late forties or early fifties and are wondering what to do next. Their relationships with colleagues are complex, intertwined, and important. In many contemporary colleges and universities, academic departments are beginning to resemble large, close-knit families. The children in these families, however, never leave home. Furthermore, the roles of mother, father, and children keep changing. The dynamics of academic departments have become increasingly difficult for an outsider to understand and hence contribute even more mystery to the collegial culture.

Although Jim Herbert has not yet reached the highest possible rank at Western State, he knows that he must become an active researcher in order to attain this position. Given that he no longer enjoys research, is the effort worth the recognition that comes with rank? His pay would be better but would still not come close to the level he had anticipated when entering the scientific community two decades earlier. He has spent enough time with colleagues who are full professors to know that they feel just as stuck as he does; thus, academic advancement will solve nothing. There is simply little he can do or anywhere he can go as a faculty member teaching in the sciences.

Jim Herbert's story will elicit very little sympathy from faculty members in community colleges or four-year liberal arts colleges. They are usually not as committed to the collegial culture as faculty in the four-year state universities. Moreover, many academics in liberal arts colleges experience less of a crisis in the collegial culture (unless, like Canon College faculty, the institution is undergoing a major cultural change). Ironically, faculty in state-supported universities of intermediate prestige seem to be more committed to the collegial culture than are their colleagues at more elite research universities (private or public), less prestigious community colleges, or small, private, liberal arts colleges.

It appears that those faculty members who are near (but not at) the top of the collegial pecking order are most committed to ensuring the survival of this culture. Robert Wilson and his colleagues (Wilson and others, 1975, pp. 24-25) note, for instance, that academics in state colleges and universities are faced with conflicting goals and expectations leading to "frustrated upward aspiration" and a tendency to see deficiencies in their students rather than themselves.

The mid-level state university is particularly likely to absorb the collegial culture's apparent ambivalence regarding teaching. Though this institution is often assigned a primary undergraduate teaching mission within a comprehensive state higher-education plan, it usually is staffed by faculty members who are recruited from research universities and are committed to their disciplines and to the advancement of knowledge through research and scholarship. Graduate students may be acceptable; undergraduates are not. As a result, the formal institutional mission speaks of teaching and undergraduate education, but the actual reward system in the institution is geared toward research and graduate education.

Because the dominant role of research and graduate education cannot be formally acknowledged in these state universities (in view of a contradictory mandate in the state master plan), a faculty member (such as Jim Herbert) is constantly faced with conflicting messages: "You are being hired to teach, but we really want you to do research." "You will have to teach four courses this semester, but we still expect you to be an active scholar and to keep up in your field." "Be a good teacher, but do not become too popular with your students, or else your status as a serious scholar and caretaker of your discipline will be called into question by your colleagues." "Above all else, never be named 'best teacher of the year' (at least until you have received tenure)."

The contradictory messages are particularly prevalent and destructive in the evaluation procedures employed by many collegial cultures. Faculty members such as Jim Herbert are assessed primarily on the basis of their research productivity; however, as these criteria are not acceptable in a teaching university, other reasons are given for denying faculty members tenure or promotion if they are good teachers but inactive researchers or scholars. The unwarranted assumption is sometimes made that only a good re-searcher or scholar can actually be a good teacher. At other times, research and scholarship have value, supposedly because a teacher is principally responsible for keeping current in his or her disci-pline and best demonstrates this currency through research activity. Neither of these assumptions seems to hold up very well under careful scrutiny. They lead one to conclude that research and schol-arship are considered more valuable than teaching by many faculty in the collegial culture. Jim Herbert is quite accurate in his concern about career advancement at Western State if he is not an active researcher.

Western State University, like most other state universities, is also home to the managerial culture. This culture is dominant in Western's professional schools (which are rapidly growing in size and influence), as well as in the academic administration of the university. The managerial culture is not ambivalent about teach-ing. In this culture, teaching is the most important mission (or product) of an educational institution such as Western State. The managerial culture rewards Herbert's teaching and does not require him to do research, unless formally part of his job description. But with all of his dissatisfaction with the collegial culture, Jim Herbert does not seem to be attracted to the managerial culture. He believes that teaching should be an art and that the managerial culture somehow diminishes the quality and nature of this instructional enterprise. When one is an "instructional manager," what does he or she "love?" Outcomes, not the process of learning, are valued. The student is treated as an "income center" or as a composite of various competencies or specific learning outcomes.

Jim Herbert and others who are unhappy with the collegial culture generally perceive the managerial culture as quite alien and unresponsive to their real needs. Many faculty members at Western are looking to the negotiating culture for guidance and leadership. In many ways, the negotiating culture has been more responsive than any of the others to the changing role and status of faculty members such as Jim Herbert. Academics like Herbert are inclined to view academic managers with disdain and suspicion and are thus likely to find the "we-them" mentality of the negotiating culture much more attractive than the demands for institutional loyalty, sacrifice, and obedience that often seems evident in the other three cultures. Western State University has a very active faculty union. Herbert has joined this union so that he might obtain a better salary and improved working conditions. He does not want the union to negotiate about academic matters (such as curriculum or assignments) because he believes that this responsibility should remain with the academic departments and the collegial culture.

Herbert and many of his colleagues are also quite suspicious of the developmental culture, though he has participated in several faculty development activities at Western State. He dislikes the behavioral jargon of this culture (viewing it as "pseudo-science"); he is skeptical about the real power that this culture holds at Western State: "If I become actively involved in these faculty development efforts or try some new teaching methods in my classroom, what will happen to my research, and how will my colleagues perceive my use of these new instructional 'gimmicks'?"

Herbert seems to be waiting to see what happens with the developmental culture before he makes any major commitments. In his relatively long tenure as a faculty member at Western, he has seen instructional "fads" (programmed instruction, "experiential learning," computer-assisted instruction) come and go. Where are the stability and continuity that are to be found in the collegial culture? Where at Western are the tangible results found in the collective action of the negotiating culture? Yet Jim Herbert knows that something has to change, or he will be looking elsewhere for a job and a career. Perhaps sometime soon the developmental culture will make a difference. Until it does, Herbert will probably remain a constituent of the dominant collegial culture of Western State University.

4

❖❖❖❖❖❖❖

The Managerial Culture

The managerial culture originates in two types of American collegiate institutions, much as the collegial culture is a hybrid of the British and German university models. One of the points of origin for the managerial culture is the Catholic college and university in the United States. The other is the American junior college (recently redefined as the community college). Although the rural, Protestant, colonial college actually preceded (and helped to determine the nature and purpose of) the colonial high school, the urban Catholic college in America was an extension of the established elementary and secondary schools that were being run by various teaching orders of priests and nuns for the sake of city youth from the lower socioeconomic classes. Coming out of the elementary-secondary school tradition and building on the accepted hierarchy of the teaching orders and church, the Catholic college was created under the assumption that lines of authority should be clear and that the formally designated administrators of the institution should have control over the planning and managerial functions of the college.

The junior (community) colleges in the United States similarly grew out of the elementary and secondary school systems of their surrounding communities. They were managed like other educational institutions in the local school system. Faculty members were trained as teachers rather than as scholars or researchers, and administrators were just as likely to have received their advanced

57

degrees in higher education as in a specific academic discipline. Offering courses in areas where clear curricular guidelines could be defined and where the desired competencies of students could readily be specified, these colleges focused on vocational preparation (as did many of the Catholic colleges). First established in the latter part of the nineteenth century, junior (community) colleges have become a major component of American higher education over the past forty years and, together with the Catholic college and university, have been the primary source of the managerial culture in American higher education. This culture, in turn, has become increasingly influential in this country and has generally become almost as prominent as the collegial culture.

In the managerial culture, educational outcomes can be clearly specified and the criteria for judging performance can be identified and employed. Faculty members are effective as leaders if they are successful in fiscal and personnel management—often in the role of department chairperson or division head. Academics in this culture often assume that the best way to influence their institutions is through movement into an administrative position. Typically, these faculty do not bother with faculty governance processes and consider them inefficient and a waste of time. In preparation for a future role as administrators, managerially oriented faculty members argue from the perspective of cost containment, feasibility, and specifiable outcomes.

In their teaching role, faculty in the managerial culture often work with instructional materials that have been prepared by other people. The act of instructional design is often separated from the act of teaching, these two sets of skills often being viewed by the managerial faculty member as distinct. In their broader instructional role, managerial faculty members will often devote considerable time and attention to the specification of educational objectives or outcomes, to the sequencing of autonomous instructional units, and to the selection and use of instructional methods that draw on resources other than the faculty member. The faculty member is usually considered dispensable in the role of teacher and acts instead in the role of instructional systems manager.

Origins of the Managerial Culture

Catholic higher education began to play a major role in America only during the mid-nineteenth century, when many immigrants entered the country and settled in the major cities of the Northeast. "With the massive immigration of the mid-century, the founding of Catholic colleges accelerated," observes Philip Gleason (1967, p. 17). "The single decade of the 1850s saw as many new institutions (42) as had been founded in the previous sixty years."

The Catholic college and university in America was clearly committed from the first to serving the "underserved." As when creating hospitals and welfare agencies, the Catholic Church adopted various paragovernmental functions after it found that the formal governmental agencies of the cities were not serving their parishioners effectively (Jencks and Riesman, 1968). The existing suburban Protestant colleges were not accessible to the impoverished (or even the more well-to-do) Catholic parishioners—more because of geographic location and cost than because of any religious discrimination. As a result, the teaching orders of the Catholic church themselves established colleges and universities for both men and women.

The Catholic college, unlike Protestant institutions, served mainly as a vehicle for the upward mobility of its students. Whereas Protestants initially tended to come to America to escape religious or political persecution, Catholics sought vocational and economic improvement (Jencks and Riesman, 1968). The Catholic colleges of America reflected this orientation. From the first, these institutions directed their efforts at occupational preparation. The traditional, gentlemanly liberal arts of the Protestant colleges never caught on in Catholic institutions, for the skills being taught in the Protestant liberal arts curriculum were meant for young men (and women) whose parents had already guaranteed their place in society. Catholic college students had not found their niche and expected the college to provide an opportunity for social mobility.

Because to a large degree the Catholic college served poor students who lived nearby (in urban environments), there was also less inclination to make the undergraduate experience residential.

Many Catholic colleges had dormitories, but most of these institutions usually or exclusively served the commuter students who lived at home and often worked in addition to attending college. The "collegiate way" that Rudolph describes in conjunction with the Protestant college (and the collegial culture) was simply not experienced by a great majority of students in Catholic colleges.

The *Halls of Ivy* setting was quite another world. *Going My Way* might be a more appropriate image. The early Catholic college more closely resembled an urban rectory than an ivy-covered, rural college. Most of what the Catholic college student learned was acquired in the college classroom, not in extracurricular activities. Even more was learned from the combination of classroom knowledge and experience gained out in the world: from parents without college educations (and often with limited command of the English language), from jobs, and from contemporaries who were not attending college.

The Catholic college also differed from the Protestant one in the extent of clerical control over the academic and nonacademic affairs of the institution. Protestant colleges were run by lay presidents (after the early colonial years, when ministers were often presidents); they also were governed by lay boards of trustees. Laymen were attractive because they had money and were expected to provide financial support to the college. By contrast, Catholic colleges and universities were often led by clerics (priests and nuns); moreover, the boards of trustees at these institutions were until very recent years populated by other clerics from the teaching order that founded and provided funds for the college.

The Catholic colleges have never established a tradition of direct lay financial support; they have relied instead on financial support from the church (which, in turn, elicited funds from the laity). In being directed by clerics, the Catholic colleges, more than the Protestant institutions, embraced the governance and administrative structures of the sponsoring church. Given that the Catholic church was even more hierarchical and authority-based than most Protestant churches of the nineteenth century, the Catholic college became much more hierarchical and authority-based than comparable Protestant colleges.

Another feature of the Catholic college during the nineteenth century is also noteworthy and distinctive. The Jesuits, the most influential teaching order by far in American Catholic higher education, were strongly influenced by the European seven-year curricular model for postprimary education (Gleason, 1967). The distinction between high school and college was not drawn; rather, the first three years were considered preparatory and the final four years more specialized. In view of this curricular orientation, Jesuit educators found the distinction in America between high school and college to be artificial and unacceptable. The blending of secondary and collegiate educational culture was further encouraged.

The educational enterprise was directed toward the welfare of the student, not the promotion of a specific discipline. Whereas undergraduate education in the Protestant college was considered preparatory to real education (graduate school), the undergraduate education of the Catholic college student was considered the culmination of an integrated secondary (high school) and postsecondary (college) educational program.

The emphasis in Catholic colleges and universities on the importance and dignity of undergraduate education helps to account for the relative lack of focus on graduate education in these institutions (Gleason, 1967) and for the failure of the German research university model to affect Catholic institutions. Whereas the Protestant colonial college was forever influenced by the German concentration on graduate education, research and scholarship, and faculty autonomy, the Catholic college was influenced by its major rival: the junior college.

The junior or community college shares several characteristics with the Catholic college, even though the former is a public, two-year institution and the latter is a private institution usually offering a four-year degree program. Like the Catholic schools, junior and community colleges were first formed to serve the less privileged populations in the United States. William Rainey Harper, the first president of the University of Chicago, is usually identified as the father of the junior college movement in the United States (Hillway, 1958). Arguing that the pedagogical distinction between the first and last two years of college is greater than that between high school and college, he advocated the division of undergraduate institutions into "junior" and "senior" colleges (Harper, 1909).

Two junior colleges were established on the basis of Harper's model: the Lewis Institute in Chicago (1896) and the Bradley Polytechnic Institute in Peoria, Illinois (1897). Although several private junior colleges—notably, Lasell Junior College (formerly Lasell Female Academy) in Newton, Massachusetts—were founded during the middle of the nineteenth century (Landrith, 1971), the junior and community college movement is usually considered a public sector and twentieth-century phenomenon.

Any history of twentieth-century junior and community colleges or any historical document that concerns them is filled with growth charts and statistics about increasing access of young, middle-class men and women to higher education. A 1947 report from the President's Commission on Higher Education (Hillway, 1958, p. 3), for instance, offers the following observation: "Only a few decades ago, high school education in this country was for the few. Now most of our young people take at least school work. . . . Until recently, college education was for the very few. Now a fifth of our young people continue their education beyond the high school. Many young people want less than a full four-year college course. The two-year college . . . is about as widely needed today as the four-year high school was a few decades ago. Such a college must fit into the community life as the high school has done."

The community college and Catholic college have other features in common. They are both local in orientation and control. A Catholic college is usually run by the local, autonomous teaching order of the church, with very few directives coming from above. Similarly, the community college is by definition financed and controlled by the local community, usually through a board of elected officials. Both kinds of institutions stress instruction more than scholarship or research and are governed by a hierarchical, clearly delineated line of authority. The community college and Catholic college also share an orientation toward commuter students from lower socioeconomic levels and an image as institutions promoting social mobility, rather than merely acknowledging ascribed status (as does the Protestant college).

The term *innovative* is often used to describe both types of institutions—largely as a result of their shared commitment to educate the underserved and to accomplish their mission through the use of nontraditional modes of teaching and learning. Community colleges, in particular, began purposively as an innovative, alternative structure in American higher education that was designed to serve nontraditional students. By contrast, the Catholic colleges often grew more organically and less deliberately out of a tradition of service at the elementary and secondary school level. As Terry O'Banion (1989, p. 1) has noted, "The community college as an institution is one of the most important innovations in the history of higher education."

Medsker and Tillery (1971) observed in their Carnegie Commission Study entitled *Breaking the Access Barriers:* "American public community colleges came into being near the turn of the last century, being conceived by a few innovative educators of that period as the capstone unit of an integrated system of secondary and postsecondary education. Such two-year institutions were designed to meet more effectively the new knowledge requirements of a society caught in a dramatic shift from a rural-agricultural to an urban-industrial base" (p. 13).

Given that the collegial culture that dominated most academic institutions during the nineteenth century was indifferent or even hostile to the articulation between secondary and postsecondary schools, it was essential that a new kind of institution be formed to provide this bridge. Furthermore, the new urban workers, who could not afford and probably did not need a liberal arts education, had to be given access to an occupationally oriented educational program beyond the high school level.

In their close articulation with the secondary school sector, the community and Catholic colleges also resemble one another. Like Catholic college faculty and administrators, those who lead the junior and community colleges often come out of high school teaching, counseling, or administrative positions (Medsker and Tillery, 1971). Moreover, in many areas of the United States, the community colleges are now (or at least until recently have been) governed by boards that also oversee the operations of primary and secondary school systems. It is not uncommon for gifted high school students to be taking courses in their local community colleges or even for some college remedial courses to be offered by local high schools. Although many community college faculty and administrators prefer to identify themselves primarily with colleagues in four-year institutions, many others are inclined toward reverse snobbery and align themselves with those who serve all of the citizens without "academic pretensions": that is to say, with their high school and vocational-education colleagues.

The similarities and differences that have been drawn between Catholic and community colleges reveal several of the most important and often intractable tensions within the managerial culture. First, there are differing opinions about the source of authority in colleges and universities that are dominated by this culture. On the one hand, at Catholic colleges authority is typically vested in the president, who in turn receives authority from the church or, in modern times, from the board of trustees of the college. This board (like that of the Protestant college) usually is constituted of members who remain for many years and who select most, if not all, of their successors. On the other hand, the community college president is typically beholden to a board elected by the local community. Members of the board and the president must be responsive to other community leaders, pressure groups, and concerns. Faculty members in community colleges normally perceive themselves as employees of public agencies; conversely, academics at Catholic colleges are more likely to see themselves as part of a corporate-type setting, with major control being exerted by an invisible, but powerful, governing board.

The difference between the purposeful innovation of the community colleges and the less deliberate innovative spirit of the Catholic colleges provides, or at least suggests, a second source of tension in the managerial culture. Community colleges have often been a source of disappointment for educators who take the innovative mission of these institutions seriously. Given the power of the collegial culture and the requirement that community college faculty receive advanced degrees from institutions that are often dominated by the collegial culture, it is not surprising that teaching and learning activities in many community colleges are likely to approximate those of four-year institutions. Though the role of faculty member as dispenser of prepackaged materials is still much more common in community colleges than in four-year institutions, most community college faculty members are less supportive of instructional technologies than they were in the 1970s and 1980s. The promising future of computer-based instruction (and, at an earlier time, of programmed instruction and televised instruction) has never been realized, in part because of costs and inadequate support services but also because of collegially based faculty resistance.

With these shifts in faculty experience and attitudes, community college institutions have often become truly "junior": they are simply smaller or less expensive versions of their older brothers (the four-year colleges and universities). Contemporary community colleges are supposed to serve as a bridge between secondary and postsecondary schools, but they are increasingly likely to look like senior colleges and universities. More and more often, their faculties share with their senior college and university brothers and sisters some disdain for high school education.

Catholic colleges, by contrast, are often assumed to be conservative, given the traditional role of the church in contemporary American society. Therefore, when a Catholic college such as Alverno (Milwaukee, Wisconsin) or Marylhurst (Portland, Oregon) becomes a leader in innovative programming, many members of the higher education community are surprised. They often forget that these colleges were founded to provide low-cost and personalized services to underserved populations. Throughout the managerial culture, we find this pull between tradition and innovation. At times we are all impressed by the extraordinary progress that is made in a college or university that is run by a strong president and has clear and consistent lines of authority (Bergquist and Armstrong, 1986). Certainly, effective management can be a key ingredient in successful innovation. Yet collegiate institutions that are dominated by the managerial culture are repressive, uninspired places to work or learn. It is often quite difficult in a managerial culture to determine which events or policies have changed an organizational atmosphere from a state of repression to one of creativity and risk taking.

The repressive features of the managerial culture are often exacerbated by the financial problems of the institution. In both community colleges and Catholic institutions, we find a struggle with finances. Very few Catholic colleges have large endowments,

primarily because donations tend to go to the church rather than
directly to the college. Similarly, community colleges rarely have a
secure funding base; they are always susceptible to the whims of
local politics, shifts in the economy, and, as a result, an uncertain
number of tax dollars available to support the institution.

State universities generally are more secure in their funding
(the current crisis in several major research universities notwith-
standing) because of solid, widespread reputations that make them
less vulnerable to shifting public attitudes and because of the
broader, statewide budget bases for these institutions. Local community colleges have always had to scramble for dollars more than
better known state institutions. Even the introduction in some
places of statewide community college systems has not eliminated
potential financial crisis—a situation that encourages attention to
costs and reinforces the central role to be played by those academic
managers who control the budgets and exhibit fiscal expertise.

In recent years, management and the management culture in
all collegiate institutions have become increasingly important and
visible. With the emergence of multipurpose, multiconstituency,
multilevel universities in the 1960s—signaled by the successful reception of Clark Kerr's *The Uses of the University* (1963)—American higher education felt it had found the answer to many of its
pressing problems. In the same year that Kerr's book on the "multiversity" was published, a second major book, *The Age of the
Scholar* was also published by Harvard University Press. This book,
written by Nathan Pusey, then president of Harvard University,
received far less attention than did *The Uses of the University*. *The
Age of the Scholar* was written much more from the traditional
collegial point of view and warned of some of the dangers of Kerr's
multiversity. Enamored of the prospect of large-scale, efficient universities that could meet a variety of educational needs occasioned
by the coming baby boom, the world of American higher education
was not ready to hear these warnings.

The multiversity depended on exceptional managerial skills.
Budgets were much more complex than in the simpler institutions
of the past. Increased administrative support services were required
to handle the diverse demands being placed on this multipurpose
institution.

In part because of these diverse demands and the inability of multiversity administrators to meet them, the golden age of the multiversity was quite short. With the strident calls of Mario Savio and his followers at the University of California (Clark Kerr's own multiversity), the age of student discontent was inaugurated. Students deplored the indifference of vast educational systems to their unique needs. They complained of complicity between big business, big government, and big university; they demanded a renewed focus on teaching (rather than a preoccupation with research and publishing) and a new emphasis on social values and reform. The student protests did not overturn the multiversities, though they did tarnish them, nor did they diminish the impact of the managerial culture on modern colleges and universities. They did, however, provide fertile ground for the growth of two other cultures: the developmental and the negotiating.

The managerial culture was further enhanced by the rapid growth in the 1960s of higher educational systems that encouraged statewide planning of facilities, the development of sophisticated cost-finding procedures, and the demand for comparability in the description, budgeting, and evaluation of academic programs. Though the new postsecondary commissions (1202 Commissions) that were required in the 1972 Higher Education Amendments of the U.S. Congress never got off the ground, they reinforced the desirability of statewide coordination and monitoring of all collegiate institutions—public and private, proprietary and nonprofit. This large-system emphasis encouraged the development of uniform budgeting practices on the college and university campus (as exemplified by the heavily funded work of the National Center for Higher Education Management Systems), which in turn encouraged the creation of a new generation of educational managers who were versed in the technical language of "induced course-load matrices" and "resource requirements planning models." These were no longer retreaded faculty members serving temporarily as department or division head. They were professional managers of the educational enterprise, who had developed their own language, rituals, and values.

Whereas statewide planning has had a profound impact on the management of budgets within colleges and universities, federal regulations concerning hiring, firing, and performance review have greatly affected personnel management. Affirmative-action guidelines, equal-employment mandates, and related federally imposed restrictions have required administrators in higher education to gain new knowledge and skills in the management of people. Once again, an academic is ill prepared to deal with this new world of legalities and regulations. A specially trained corps of managers is required to keep a college or university out of the courtroom and in the good graces of federal funding agencies.

Another factor that has contributed to the accelerated growth of the management culture in contemporary colleges and universities is reduced federal, state, and private philanthropic support for colleges and universities. As the ideals of higher education in the immediate post-*Sputnik* years were found to be something of an illusion, public discontent with collegiate institutions began to increase. The student protests of the late 1960s also damaged the cause of higher education in many circles of influence and wealth. Colleges and universities have therefore had to do some severe belt tightening in the 1970s, 1980s, and early 1990s. Retrenchment has become an all-too-common condition among many collegiate institutions, which had been characterized by growth and prosperity in the 1960s and early 1970s.

Effective collegiate management does not seem to be as imperative under conditions of growth as it does under conditions of retrenchment and declining resources. New demands for accountability on the part of skeptical publics combine with the new planning that is required of institutions facing scarce resources. Both factors encourage the emergence of strong managerial leadership and discourage the laissez faire collegial leadership that was acceptable and dominant until the mid 1970s.

A final reason for the expansion of the managerial culture is the significant increase in part-time faculty and resulting diminution in the influence of academics in the daily operations of colleges and universities. In many American colleges and universities, part-time faculty members teach more than one-half of the courses being offered. These institutions have become increasingly centralized, with control resting in the hands of a few full-time faculty members and administrators. The collegial culture tends to wither when part-time faculty appointments are prevalent. Part-time academics simply do not have sufficient time or interest to participate in the campus politics, lengthy committee meetings, or informal negotiations that typify the collegial culture. Because many of the part-time faculty are themselves working in corporations that support a managerial culture, they find a strong, top-down managerial structure to be appropriate and feel comfortable in delegating academic administrative matters to a few full-time faculty members who become increasingly involved themselves in management.

Images and Myths of the Managerial Culture

The clearest images of the managerial culture in American higher education emanate from more contemporary sources (television, magazine articles, film) than the 1930s radio programs of the collegial culture. Instead of Dr. Hall and his beloved Ivy College, we have the story of the corporate executive who brings the know-how of business into the troubled world of contemporary collegiate life. The scene opens with a traditional college president, George Herbert (who looks a bit like Dr. Hall—cardigan sweater and a wistful smile), frantically calling the chair of his board of trustees at Tempo College, Mr. Sheppard. The chair, who serves as president of a large textile firm, listens patiently as Dr. Herbert describes how the college is out of control. Budgetary constraints are not working. Faculty members have come to dominate important decision-making functions at the college and are applying unrealistic notions to solving practical, business-based problems. Sheppard suggests that Dr. Herbert might benefit from the sage advice of his number-one vice president, a young man named Jim Creighton, who can be released from his own pressing job for a six-month period to help straighten out the mess. Sheppard generously offers to pay Creighton's salary for this six-month period as a statement of his personal support for Tempo College and the education of young men and women.

Jim Creighton arrives at Tempo one week later. He acts quickly and decisively, collaborating skillfully with Herbert in the establishment of a solid budgetary-control system. He also helps President Herbert set up an effective, low-cost management information system and an accompanying strategic and tactical planning process. He confronts faculty members regarding their destructive behavior and convinces them that some managerial training would be extremely valuable to them in their departmental functioning. The faculty soon realize that a real leader is in charge and no longer feel a need to convene faculty senate meetings. Instead, they meet with President Herbert and Jim Creighton to plan for general curricular reform in the college. Faculty senate meetings are restructured to address matters of intellectual interest to the faculty, rather than dwelling on faculty governance issues.

The next chapter of this mythical story from the managerial culture begins with Creighton encouraging the faculty and academic dean to specify more clearly the nature of the services they are rendering to students. This outcome is best achieved by identifying a series of competencies that each graduating student from Tempo College should possess. The curriculum of the college is restructured around these competencies, and the faculty embraces new educational technologies (particularly, computer-assisted instruction) so that students might acquire the necessary skills efficiently and effectively. The word soon gets out that Tempo College is doing an excellent job of helping students learn what they need to know to get and keep a job, as well as prepare for future career advancement. Student enrollment for the next year doubles, as Creighton prepares to return to the textile industry.

The president, the dean, and the faculty thank Jim Creighton for his generous and wise assistance. They speak of newly discovered respect for the corporate sector and express hope that Jim or his colleagues will soon return to Tempo so that the college community might benefit even further from modern business practices. Creighton reflects on six months of accomplishments and his own satisfaction in aiding an important human service organization with its internal management.

This story is, of course, quite simplistic and overdrawn. Yet many academics, administrators, and (especially) trustees of American colleges and universities have wished that more corporate wisdom could be applied to contemporary collegiate problems and that faculty members would be more appreciative of established business practices. Many Jim Creightons sit on collegiate boards of trustees and long to run the college or university for six months.

Recent years have produced a second story that differs some-what from our first tale of corporate service and rescue. Manage-ment theorists focusing on the less rational processes of corporate life—corporate culture, corporate leadership, and the spirit of en-trepreneurship—have lately received attention. A new image of the collegiate leader emerges from this emphasis on corporate vision and creative enactment of this vision. In describing newly emerging and successful forms of leadership in community and small col-leges, both William Deegan (1989) and Robert Peck (1983) speak of the "entrepreneurial" college presidency. According to Deegan: "During the past few years, primarily because of changing fiscal and demographic circumstances, there has been a growing interest in supplementing community college collegial, political and bu-reaucratic processes with some entrepreneurial and intrepreneurial approaches to solving problems and creating opportunities. Entre-preneurial activities are defined as those that help generate resources (such as contract training programs with corporations or the crea-tion of private foundations to raise funds). Intrepreneurial activities . . . help reduce costs or increase productivity within the organization."

Peck similarly defines the entrepreneurial presidency as one in which "opportunity consciousness" is blended with a clear sense of purpose. The promotion of innovation and creativity is com-bined with intuition and efficient administration. Peck (1983, pp. 39-40) states:

> Successful small college administration looks like a sailboat race. In such a race, there is one objective; namely, to round the mark first. There is no doubt about this objective, but to realize it one must tack back and forth, avoid obstacles, accommodate changes in the direction and force of the wind, adjust to the flow of the tide, and always maneuver within the fleet. No matter how skilled the skipper, he cannot predict his course in detail (a course that appears to the uni-nitiated as pure confusion), but his winning the race

is nevertheless a function of skill—obviously—since
the same skippers keep winning race after race. A
skilled entrepreneurial president skippers his institution toward a clear and definable goal—what the institution is to become in the next five years—but each
tack and maneuver is a creative response to the condition at hand. No action can be described in detail in
advance, but achievement of the goal is nevertheless a
function of skill.

This image of the successful skipper in a managerial culture
does not include someone like a Jim Creighton from corporate life.
Creighton might not be sensitive to the various winds that are blow-
ing. He might not be sufficiently flexible to perform the complex
tacking maneuvers that are required to sail in the treacherous waters
of contemporary higher education. The successful college president,
according to Deegan and Peck, is as skillful and effective as the best
corporate executive. Peck notes that, given the limited resources
now available to many colleges and universities, it is remarkable
how well they are being run.

Clearly, the image of the ideal collegiate manager is now in
transition, just as the collegial image of Dr. Hall and his Ivy College
was in need of updating. In bringing about this renovation, it is
essential to understand the values, leadership qualities, assumptions about change, and criteria for evaluating professional effectiveness that undergird the managerial culture in collegiate
institutions. We turn to these factors in Chapter Five after examining ways in which the managerial culture is manifest in the problems and potential of a single institution, Fairfield College, also the
site of our first case study concerning Peter Armantrout (see Chapter
One).

Case Study: Fairfield State College

When the consultant first arrived at Fairfield State College to evaluate its faculty development program, he immediately felt tired and
eager to return to his room in a nearby motel. Somehow, Fairfield
was particularly fatiguing; perhaps more accurately, the college was

boring and depressing. First of all, the campus seemed lifeless and devoid of any sense of community. Throughout the consultant's stay, students, faculty, administrators, and visitors expressed in words and actions their desire to leave the campus from the moment they arrived. This phenomenon became particularly obvious when the consultant tried to schedule interviews with faculty members. Very few were present. They typically spent only about fifteen hours on campus each week. They often met with students off campus or were moonlighting at other teaching or consulting jobs. Such a commitment to off-campus work is not unusual in a college or university that embraces the managerial culture. Faculty and students adopt a businesslike orientation to their work at the school. The school does not hold their loyalty. Instead, they look outside the school for their sense of identity, their social contacts, and (in the case of faculty) a portion of their income. On the positive side, this outward perspective tends to make instruction in the managerially oriented college realistic and directed at problems; on the more negative side, this perspective discourages a sense of community or continuity.

At a later point, the consultant discovered another reason for the apparent absence of much life at Fairfield College. Originally, the state board of higher education had envisioned that Fairfield would become a major university. The architects and campus planners designed a campus that could grow much bigger. The initial buildings were placed at an appropriate distance from one another so that new buildings might be built in between, rather than on the edge of an ever-expanding campus. This planning exemplifies a frequent bias toward growth in colleges and universities that are dominated by the managerial culture. Bigger is usually considered better, and there often seems to be a tacitly held assumption that the problems encountered by a collegiate institution can be solved by increasing its size (as in the case of Clark Kerr's multiversity).

The growth projections proved false. Fairfield grew no larger. Enrollment never increased beyond an initial level of four thousand students. Furthermore, virtually all of the students commuted from home or apartment, and the dormitories went unfilled. The dorms were eventually turned into additional faculty offices or made available to community agencies. Other managerially oriented colleges and universities have similarly suffered from unmet expectations regarding growth—or they have successfully grown larger but in the process have become cold and impersonal, and have sacrificed the organic integrity of collegially oriented institutions.

The Managerial Culture in Interaction with the Other Cultures

The collegial culture may be subject to unplanned change and political chaos, but it also fosters character and community. By contrast, Fairfield College, like many colleges with a strong managerial culture, seems to be barren, not only because of the absence of buildings but also because of the failure of those who work or attend there to make any commitment to the college.

As the consultant began his interviews with Fairfield faculty members like Peter Armantrout, he was impressed with their consuming interest in activities and future prospects that had little to do with Fairfield College. Most faculty members were like Armantrout in that they had been at the college for at least fifteen years. They were now tenured and had little to gain from any additional contributions to the college. Many of them not only had other jobs but also lived in a nearby mountain community reached by a winding and often crowded road. As a result, they tried to leave Fairfield early. Most of the students, however, lived in the valley, where the college was located. They usually divided their time between classes at Fairfield, a second or even third job, and family responsibilities. Unlike the faculty, Fairfield students are generally ecnomically disadvantaged and are the first in their families to attend college. They exemplify the commitment to equality and access of colleges with powerful managerial cultures. Though the collegial culture tends to encourage elitism and is accessible only to those with family money or outstanding academic records (that attract scholarships and student loans), the managerial culture makes it possible for the "common man" to acquire higher education.

The new president at Fairfield recently spoke of his vision of the college as a center of growing academic excellence. He expects Fairfield to be one of the twenty finest liberal arts colleges in the

United States within the next ten years and envisions a shift from the college's dominant managerial culture to a more traditional and elitist collegial culture. Fairfield College faculty members speak sarcastically about the president's vision and stress how infeasible it is given state funding. They describe the indifference of faculty, students, other administrators, and alumni to the college and to the president's dream. Like those at many contemporary public colleges and universities, faculty members may hope for the restoration of a collegial culture; however, they are realistic about the strength of the managerial culture in their own institution and throughout their state system.

For the Fairfield College faculty, the managerial culture is negatively manifest in administrative and board demands for accountability and their accompanying emphasis on cost containment, as represented in reduced salary increases. Most Fairfield faculty members, who were educated in colleges and universities that were more collegial in their orientation, see these managerial initiatives as intrusive and offensive. These academics see little hope of change or of increased local support in the near future; their community seems indifferent to the educational programs and goals of Fairfield. One faculty member observed that the college "could sink into the ground, and no one in this community would even notice!" All that the local people want is a convenient school that their sons and daughters can attend in order to get a better job and more money.

Sadly, no one either inside or outside the college seems to notice or celebrate the fact that Fairfield already provides an invaluable service to the community through its delivery of low-cost, "liberating" education to working-class men and women. This college may not be able to achieve the goals of its current president, but it does do a good job of expanding the vision of its students and preparing them for more useful citizenship in a changing community and world. This is a distinctive and essential ingredient of the managerial culture and at least one characteristic of Fairfield State College that makes it worthy of community support.

5

❖❖❖❖❖❖❖

Living and Working in
the Managerial Culture

In the managerial culture, the highest value is assigned at the instructional level to the learning of students—particularly learning
that can be assessed quantitatively and attributed specifically to a
planned educational event. We find the strong influence of Catholic
and community college education in the managerial emphasis on
tangible educational goals that are primarily directed toward the
student's vocational roles and responsibilities as a citizen. A second
instructional value, however, seems to contradict the first. Teaching
is supposed to be fiscally efficient. Bowen and Douglass (1971, p. 6)
articulate this value when they speak of "efficiency in liberal education" and list various instructional strategies that can reduce costs:

1. It may substitute low-cost labor for high-cost labor, e.g., by replacing faculty time with assistant
   time or by increasing the proportion of junior
   members in the faculty.
2. It may increase intensity of labor usage, e.g., by
   raising teaching loads for faculty.
3. It may substitute student initiative for faculty supervision, e.g., by making study more independent.
4. It may substitute capital for labor, e.g., by using the
   library or television in place of lectures.

5. It may intensify utilization of capital, e.g., by using buildings and equipment more fully.
6. It may substitute low-cost capital for high-cost capital, e.g., by employing temporary buildings, reducing standards of construction, or cutting down on expensive library acquisitions.
7. It may change curricular mix, e.g., by increasing enrollment in low-cost subjects (sociology) and by reducing it in high-cost subjects (physics).
8. It may reduce noninstructional services.
9. It may spread overhead costs by increasing the scale of operation [p. 6].

This list of cost-cutting strategies not only specifies the managerial culture's priorities, it also defines the nature and scope of the clash between the values and goals of the collegial and managerial cultures and suggests many of the points of contention among faculty who have embraced the negotiating culture.

Qualities of Leadership

The key word in the managerial culture's concept of leadership, just as in its notion of effective education, seems to be *competence*. The successful leader is one who is a competent administrator, teacher, or student. The criteria for judging competence in administration tend to be borrowed from corporate settings, whereas those used to define competent instruction are often derived from the miliary and from high technology. Definitions of student competence come from several sources, primarily corporations, the military, and technical training fields. We shall briefly examine each of these sets of definitions.

The competent administrator is an effective manager of people and money. As an effective manager, the administrator is expected to employ modern corporate management theory. Two of the most influential managerial theorists from the corporate sector, Robert Blake and Jane Mouton (Blake, Mouton, and Williams, 1981), have applied their "grid management" theory to the academic set-

ting. Though they acknowledge that "to attain excellence a college
or university must develop an organizational model for itself" and
"cannot be led or managed like a business" (p. 29), they perceive the
chief responsibilities of academic administrators in traditional corporate terms:

1. Establishing and implementing an implicit or
    explicit mission and administering the activities
    that result;
2. Supporting the teaching and learning process;
3. Establishing and supporting the curriculum;
4. Creating a climate for high-quality research;
5. Encouraging service to the university and com-
    munity and beyond;
6. Acquiring and distributing financial resources
    through budgetary management;
7. Managing the academic personnel function;
8. Coordinating student affairs;
9. Managing external relations in order to secure
    and maintain the allegiance of various outside
    groups; and
10. Maintaining the physical plant and basic op-
    erations to provide necessary support services
    [p. 30].

Faculty from the collegial culture would probably take no
exception to the last three of these responsibilities, but they would
have serious reservations about most of the first seven. External
relations and maintainance of the physical plant have traditionally
been viewed by faculty as outside their purview and as appropriately
administered according to the norms and rules of the managerial
culture. Unfortunately, faculty in the collegial culture are often
indifferent to student services and view the general welfare of students (other than their mental development) as someone else's
worry; hence, most faculty members feel comfortable about the
managerial culture's also embracing student services.

When it comes to mission, teaching, curriculum, research,
service, and the management of finances and academic personnel,

we find a different story. Many, if not most, academics from the collegial culture would be profoundly offended by the statement that administrators are responsible for "establishing and supporting the curriculum" or "managing the academic personnel function." They believe that the faculty should control the curriculum and the hiring and firing of other faculty members and support staff (departmental secretaries, instructional service personnel). These faculty members would undoubtedly also wonder what Blake, Mouton, and Williams mean by "supporting the teaching and learning process" and "creating a climate for high-quality research." They would be suspicious of administrative infringement and insistence on accountability. Collegial-culture faculty would just as vigorously fight the idea that administrators are the caretakers of the institution's mission. They would argue that faculty have traditionally been the principal architects of the mission, or at least central parties in deliberations regarding the mission, usually in conjunction with the school's governing board.

Blake, Mouton, and Williams clearly have not offered a model of academic administration that is geared toward the collegiate institution; otherwise, they would have at least noted the probable opposition of many faculty to this list of responsibilities. Blake, Mouton, and Williams are not alone in failing to account for the collegial culture when transferring corporate management theory to colleges and universities. Other attempts to transfer procedures from corporate settings to colleges and universities have often been similarly insensitive and, as a result, have been received with hostility—except for those institutions, particularly community colleges, where the managerial culture is pervasive. Our fictitious hero in Chapter Four (Jim Creighton) would not be welcomed with open arms by most collegially oriented faculty. Tempo College may exist only in the hearts and minds of members of the managerial culture.

A successful faculty member in the managerial culture is a competent teacher. Since administrators (or faculty in administrative roles) are given responsibility for management and since the primary product of a college or university is supposed to be education, then a faculty member should exhibit leadership primarily in his or her classroom performance. One is able to influence the ed-

ucational outcomes of an institution first and foremost through
teaching, rather than by serving as a member of a faculty committee
or as chair of the faculty senate.

In his insightful analysis of the community college culture,
Howard London (1978) has noted that a faculty member who works
in an institution infused with a managerial culture is likely to find
intellectual identity primarily through teaching, rather than
through either independent research and scholarship or interaction
with fellow faculty members: "Teaching in the community college
[is] seen [by faculty members] as a way to maintain both the intellectual commitment and the accompanying self-image" (p. 39). Unfortunately, many of the faculty members studied by London find
very little intellectual stimulation in the classroom; they feel com-
pelled to "popularize" their concepts and to entertain rather than
instruct. Put succinctly, "teachers [have] to preserve or acceptably
modify their identities as intellectual beings in the face of an un-
receptive, skeptical audience" (p. 115).

According to London (pp. 52-53), the faculty member in a
community college is faced with a dilemma:

> Having internalized the value of disinterested inquiry,
> whether in the classroom or through research or schol-
> arship, [community college faculty find] themselves
> organizing, preparing, and teaching in reference to
> the popular functions. The collision of the two func-
> tions [disinterested inquiry and popularized teach-
> ing], for which most faculty were unprepared, . . .
> threatened self- and role definitions; in a subtle yet
> critical way these were assaults on the teachers' iden-
> tities, and as such, had to be repelled. . . . the manner
> in which this was done [through highly rigid and
> punitive modes of teaching] was, for some of their
> students, like salt in an open wound: It challenged the
> very sense of worth and ability [that the students] al-
> ready doubted.

Ideally, competent instructors are able to specify the educational objectives or outcomes of the courses they are teaching and

are able to implement an appropriate, instructional design. Furthermore, the competent instructor can and will use an instructional method that most efficiently and effectively conveys a body of knowledge related directly to these objectives. Robert Diamond and his colleagues at the Center for Instructional Development at Syracuse University (Diamond and others, 1975, pp. 11–12) speak of this new managerial role for faculty:

> A teacher is not the most effective and efficient presenter of information per se, and yet it is his lecturing that consumes the greater part of his instructional time and effort. For quality instruction, the teacher must devote most of his energy to motivating, evaluating, and counseling. Unfortunately, in many courses, countless hours are wasted preparing and giving lectures or demonstrations that are already available in more effective packaged forms. However, changing the role of faculty is not a simple process. Few are prepared to design new materials and to manage complex instructional programs involving large numbers of students. In addition, few have had formal training in generating group interaction or in test construction, evaluations, and data interpretations.

Borrowing from the work done in military education regarding the use of criterion-based instruction (for example, Popham, 1978), competent faculty are expected to design programs that move all students toward competence rather than setting up competitive ("grading-on-the-curve") systems that require some students to succeed while others fail.

In contemporary higher education, the managerial culture generally encourages faculty members to be acquainted with new instructional technologies that have recently become available at relatively low cost: computer-assisted instruction, television, and telecommunication (electronic blackboards, telephone conferencing). The technological revolution has occurred; its benefits should be exploited by competent managerial culture instructors. As the source of many modern educational technologies (from the blackboard to the overhead transparency and simulator), the military has successfully demonstrated that faculty instruction can be significantly enhanced (in other words, students can more readily acquire specified competencies) if supplemented by technologies that allow for low-cost, individualized instruction.

Successful students in the managerial culture are competent learners. They have demonstrated a high level of achievement with regard to specific skills, knowledge, and attitudes. Rather than attempting to influence school policy by means of student councils (let alone petitions or demonstrations), competent students in the managerial culture are aware of the existing lines of authority and do not seek to move from a student role to that of administrator or member of a decision-making body within the academic setting; rather, they look for a role outside the academy as a breadwinner, management trainee, or professional.

Typically, students in a managerial culture are not "trouble makers." They learn to be patient and respectful of the institutional and instructional processes through which they must pass in order to obtain a degree and increased economic prosperity. Students attracted to or accepted by colleges and universities dominated by the managerial culture usually come from middle- or lower-middle-class backgrounds. They are more likely to be vocationally oriented (and less intellectually inclined) than students in colleges and universities where the collegial culture rules (Medsker and Tillery, 1971). They firmly believe in the role of academic institutions as vehicles for upward mobility. In this way, these students are more readily absorbed into large, complex corporate structures that discourage attempts at influencing policy by those employees who are near the bottom of the organizational ladder.

In his case study of a junior college, Burton Clark (1960) describes this myth of upward mobility; he notes that all democratic societies must provide certain institutions that not only hold the myth of upward mobility, but also provide the mechanisms for "cooling off" those who discover that the myth will never be realized for them. According to Clark (p. 151), community colleges are in the business of building mechanisms to "deflect the resentment and mollify the disappointment of those to whom opportunity is denied [in order] to induce them to take less rewarding work

. . . through the gradually accumulated evidence (achievement tests, vocational aptitude tests, course grades, teachers' recommendations, counselors' advice) that they ought to change to a terminal vocational curriculum rather than transfer to a four-year institution."

Since an increasing number of community colleges now function as the first two years of a four-year collegiate program, this analysis is now a bit dated, but it does accurately identify an emphasis in community colleges on skills and the assessment of competence. This emphasis gives the appearance of democratizing the classroom. On the one hand, each student is given an opportunity to succeed and to move ahead with career aspirations, regardless of background or status. On the other hand, as Clark states, the managerial culture becomes a repressive setting in which old socioeconomic distinctions are reinforced rather than broken down if the desired skills are very difficult to acquire in the community college.

In essence, in the managerial culture we find a quest for competent administrators, faculty members, and students who respect and work within a formal, hierarchical structure; this structure in turn encourages clarity of communication, specificity of roles and outcomes, and careful delegation of responsibilities. The goal of leadership is attained when a competent person fills a clearly specified role. General and somewhat vague notions about charisma and leadership by example are more likely to be found in colleges and universities that emphasize the collegial or developmental perspectives.

Assumptions About
Institutional Change and Influence

In the managerial culture, one influences and changes things by being skillful in managing people and money. It is in the careful attention to the regular administrative duties of a college or university that one has an effect on the institution's operations. Elaborate, often esoteric, discussions by faculty in committee meetings and senate hearings are viewed with disdain by those in the management culture. These are the "games" that grown faculty members must play to "massage their egos," "avoid work," or "delude themselves" about the amount of influence they really exert on the life and goals of the college or university.

Members of the managerial culture believe that one becomes more influential by moving up through formal lines of authority. A faculty member becomes department chair, then division chair or dean, then academic vice president, and finally president. The ability to move up through the organization is assumed to be based at least in part upon a rational appraisal by superiors of one's managerial competence: "Can I work effectively with people?" "Can I manage a budget?" "Can I successfully plan for and implement a new program?" Robert Diamond (1976, p. 102) speaks of this assumption when he writes about the way to establish a successful instructional development program: "Without top administrative support in time, talent, and appropriate funding, change will not occur." Grass-roots movements are not viewed with much favor or optimism by those who work within a managerial culture.

One also gains the capacity to influence and control events by acquiring and using valid and useful information. The management of information is a critical ingredient in all contemporary organizations, but it takes on special importance and meaning in the managerial culture. Information is not only needed to make a thoughtful decision; it is also required if one is to receive much attention from peers and superiors. If managers are not in control of the facts, they will not be heard. Data—not charisma—seems to play a critical part in this culture.

Institutional research has become increasingly important in many colleges and universities for this very reason. The administrator or faculty member who has received and can understand budget reports, student attrition figures, and employment projections commands more respect than the administrator or faculty member who has no access to this information or does not understand it. Agencies such as the National Center for Higher Education Management Systems, which specialize in the development of sophisticated information systems, have often offered training programs that are attended only by college and university administrators. Faculty members rarely attend these seminars, even though decisions that have a profound impact on academic life are made on the basis of information generated with procedures and tools introduced at these seminars. When faculty members in the managerial culture have access to these techniques, they usually exert greater influence in their colleges or universities.

In addition to the influence gained through organizational role and access to information, a major source of power in the managerial culture is conveyed by the mentor or sponsor. Although rational review processes are assumed, members of the managerial culture also recognize that they need sponsorship in moving up through an organization. In the past, old-boy networks have been prominent. A young man could move up through the collegiate organization by working with and knowing the right people. In recent years, with attempts to bring more women and minorities into collegiate administration and with greater concern for equity and impartiality of performance reviews, these support and sponsorship networks have tended to go underground. However, they are still present and influential.

In this one way, the managerial and collegial cultures seem to overlap. Both require the operation of an informal network if new leaders are to be groomed and nourished. The networks differ, however, in both composition and function. Collegial networks are generally based on discipline, longevity, or positions taken on critical campus issues, whereas networks in the managerial culture are founded on similarity of functions or levels of authority and responsibility. Thus, faculty members in the social sciences often form relationships, regardless of their role in the school. The head of a psychology department, for instance, might associate with faculty members in sociology even if the sociologists are not in managerial positions in their own department. In a managerial culture, however, department heads are more likely to associate with other heads of departments than with men and women within related disciplines.

In both the collegial and managerial cultures, of course, a faculty member's primary affiliations are with others in the same discipline. Furthermore, in both the collegiate and managerial cultures, women and minorities often find themselves unable to penetrate the influential circles or to gain support and acceptance from superiors. As a result, though women and minorities are being hired with increasing frequency into mid-level managerial positions at

American colleges and universities, they are rarely promoted to higher positions and often find themselves isolated and powerless.

Accountability

In the managerial culture, the criteria of evaluation must be clear, operational, and related to goals. Instruction that is judged according to its fulfillment of certain standards demands this clarity and provides operational definitions for the assessment of student performance. Management-by-objective processes demand a similar level of clarity and also provide operational methods for evaluating administrative performance.

Institutional research once again plays a key part in this aspect of the managerial culture. Classical experimental designs are employed to determine the impact of a specific project and to persuade appropriate constituencies (president, board of trustees, funding agency, community) that it is worthy. Evaluations are often summative in nature (Anderson and others, 1976; Scriven, 1972)— that is, they focus on quantifiable outcomes. By contrast, formative evaluations are characteristic of the developmental culture. Formative evaluation often involves "soft" research and employs anthropological methods (see, for example, Parlett and Dearden, 1977).

A classic example of summative evaluation is found in the work of a center to which we have already referred when illustrating characteristics of the managerial culture: the Instructional Development Center at Syracuse University. During the 1970s and 1980s, the leaders of this center were faced with the challenge of maintaining a viable program in a private university that was faced, like many others, with major financial problems. Robert Diamond and his colleagues at the center built a solid data base that demonstrated that their work was effective in improving classroom learning. They obtained positive results in studies comparing learning in courses taught by faculty that the center had assisted with learning in courses taught by faculty who had not been assisted. These results apparently influenced the university administration's decision to continue funding the center even under difficult financial conditions. Other college and university project directors from the managerial culture hope that their programs will also receive support from rational, management-culture-oriented administrators who are impressed by systematic summative evalutions.

Thus, just as the myth of upward mobility tends to color the ideas of students in the managerial culture, so does the myth of rationally demonstrated effectiveness dominate the views of faculty and administrators advocating the use of quantitative program evaluation: "If we can only show that this program works, the money and support will be there for us." As we shall discuss more fully in Chapter Ten, this research-and-development myth is prevalent in higher education (Lindquist, 1978b) and is attractive to many members of the academic community—even some from the collegial culture. Proponents of both the developmental and negotiating cultures, to which we turn in the next chapters, often join with many of their colleagues from the collegial culture in debunking the managerial culture-based myths of equity, accessibility, and rationality. These simply do not square with the reality of making decisions and setting priorities in many collegiate institutions. Certainly, for Ellen Vargas, the focal point of the case study to which we now turn, the promise of equity, access, and rationality is often seen as a delusion.

Case Study: Ellen Vargas

Ellen Vargas is a youthful thirty-five-year-old business professor at Midlands Community College, a suburban two-year college with four thousand students. Vargas received her M.A. degree in education from a major university in Ohio. She returned to school at age twenty-eight to receive her master's degree because her seven years of work in a Chicago accounting firm were not very rewarding. Vargas wanted more variety in her job. She also appreciated the free time that comes with teaching, as well as the informal contact with students. In her own words, "The students here at Midland keep me from beginning to grow old. . . . I can continue to have a good time and enjoy life as long as I remain in contact with these kids."

Ellen Vargas is five to ten years younger than many of the other faculty members at Midland and does not have the doctoral degree that is held by 55 percent of the faculty. However, she receives one of the highest salaries at the college because of the field in which she is teaching: accounting. The college is unable to attract competent instructors without offering salaries that are at least comparable to the lower end of the salary range for skilled accountants in the corporate sector. Vargas's colleagues resent this disparity in salary, though they also recognize that the business program attracts many students to the college and thereby raises student enrollment and tuition revenues.

Faculty members at Midland also seem to dislike Vargas's easygoing manner and her seeming indifference to faculty affairs. As a former corporate employee, Vargas appears much more at ease in the managerial culture than in the collegial one, though one reason she came to Midland was to be part of a collegial atmosphere. She rarely attends general faculty meetings and when she does often seems to side with the administration rather than fellow faculty members. Vargas has established an open relationship with students taking her courses and often meets with them off campus (at parties and recreational activities).

In contrast to her relaxed off-campus style, Vargas becomes rather stiff when she enters the classroom. She usually lectures to her students and, in keeping with the managerial culture, operates from a clear, well-structured set of instructional objectives and lesson plans. Vargas's students greatly appreciate her approach, especially given the subject matter; accounting, after all, also requires precision. But Vargas is becoming a little uneasy with her teaching. She would like to enjoy it more and to make accounting "more interesting," though she herself left the field because it had become boring. Thus, in Vargas we have a potential convert to the developmental culture—provided she found instructional improvement programs to be appropriate to the factual material she teaches.

Of even greater concern to Vargas is her upcoming tenure review and consideration of her promotion from assistant to associate professor. The college needs business faculty (and more female faculty members) and cannot easily recruit another accountant with her experience and interest in teaching. The Midland faculty has been known, however, to take out its envy and frustration regarding the business program on young business faculty members who are up for review. Vargas also suspects that many of her male colleagues are basically uneasy about her gender. If she does not receive tenure (a definite possibility), then Vargas believes that she should get an additional degree. An M.B.A. would be helpful in moving her back into the corporate world, but Vargas continues to like the world of higher education. She would therefore like to get a Ph.D. in economics or, if she really had a choice, history. She awaits the decision of the tenure committee.

The Managerial Culture in
Interaction with the Other Cultures

Ellen Vargas brings the managerial culture to Midland College through her past experience as an accountant outside an academic setting. When colleges and universities expand the size and scope of their professional programs (business, allied health, law, social work, criminal justice), they create a movement toward the managerial (and negotiating) culture as well as a new population of students and faculty. Many colleges and university administrators may be attracted to expanded professional programs not only because of the increased revenues that might result but also because of the support they expect to receive from these new managerial faculty and students. These professionally oriented faculty and students seek or arrive with a background in work environments that sustain the major elements of the managerial culture: top-down decision making, specification of desired outcomes and objectives, and attention to the most important product of the educational enterprise (teaching and learning).

Administrators may often hope to increase support for the managerial culture through professional programs, but faculty members in the traditional collegiate disciplines (particularly the humanities and sciences) often look with disfavor upon this intrusion. Ellen Vargas exemplifies the threat to traditional faculty members. She exhibits little interest in the prerogatives and politics of the traditional academic culture and frequently finds administrative perspectives more compatible with her own. Unfortunately, decisions about employment and rewards continue to be controlled by collegially inclined faculty members. Vargas is thus likely to be denied tenure, given her managerial bent and her gender.

Ellen Vargas is teaching in a community college. As a result of this affiliation, she may receive a fairer hearing than in most four-year collegiate institutions. The mission and goals of the community college are certainly compatible with her concerns and style. Yet even in this setting, the collegial culture plays a dominant role; most of the faculty in community colleges, whether vocational or academic, received their own educations in a four-year college or university saturated with the collegial culture.

Furthermore, vocational (and professional studies) instructors are often drawn to community college teaching precisely because of their attraction to the traditional academic (or collegial) culture. Otherwise, they would be making more money and finding more job security working in the trade about which they are now teaching. Even when vocational faculty members are not attracted to the collegial culture, they are often intimidated by the verbal dexterity and the credentials of their colleagues in traditional academic fields. Hence, in many community colleges, the collegial culture continues to influence faculty review procedures, faculty morale, and the vocational-academic pecking order.

A second point is illustrated by the Ellen Vargas case. For the faculty members who embrace the managerial culture, there are disagreements over the degree of flexibility and precision that should be incorporated into college-level teaching. To what extent and in what ways should college teaching differ from that at the elementary and secondary school level? Are lesson plans really necessary or appropriate when teaching students who are supposedly more mature and intelligent than high school students? The collegial culture began with the assumption that college-level teaching was distinctly different from high school teaching. As a result, this culture must confront the difficult issue of articulation between high school and college. The managerial culture, by contrast, began with the assumption that college-level teaching is an extension of high school teaching. This culture must therefore confront the issue of differentiating between the educational purposes and appropriate instructional styles of high schools and collegiate institutions.

Ellen Vargas struggles with many of the doubts that other managerially oriented faculty also experience. A distinction is often drawn between education and training. The former concept is associated with academic disciplines and is a central part of the collegial culture. The latter is evident in vocational disciplines and allied with the managerial culture. Typically, education is judged to be more prestigious than training, the latter often being dismissed as inappropriate to postsecondary education. Training is instead often assigned to proprietary schools, inservice programs, or on-the-job supervision. Though many educational theorists and philosophers (for example, John Dewey [1916] 1944, and Michael Polanyi, 1969) have argued against the distinction between education and training, community college faculty members often are convinced of the difference and readily label specific courses and instructional methods as directed toward one or the other. This distinction frequently discourages productive dialogue across academic and vocational fields, as well as reinforcing barriers between the academic and nonacademic world.

Ellen Vargas perceives herself as a member of the managerial culture, but she is somewhat out of place even there, for both the managerial and collegial cultures are generally dominated by men. In many ways, the developmental culture is more compatible with Vargas's concern for students, with her thoughtfulness about alternative teaching strategies, and with her indifference to or annoyance with the political features of the collegial culture. A disproportionately large number of female faculty members are attracted to the developmental culture, perhaps because it is predominantly concerned with interpersonal relationships and contextual understanding. These are areas in which women and many developmentally oriented men are particularly interested (Gilligan, 1982; Belenky, Clinchy, Goldberger, and Tarule, 1986). Yet if Ellen Vargas is to survive in the collegiate community, she should probably stay away from the developmental culture. Even greater concern about student life and an exploration of alternative instructional methods are likely to further hamper Vargas's attempts to receive tenure and a promotion. In general, female faculty members have wisely waited until after receiving tenure before becoming actively involved in developmental activities.

Like many other faculty members who leave the business sector in order to begin teaching, Ellen Vargas is antagonistic to faculty unions. In part, she became a college instructor in order to become a professional (with the status and respect that accompany this role). Participation in a faculty union is contrary in her mind to professionalism. Her attitude is like that of some community college instructors who enter teaching from specific trades (electronics, plumbing, and carpentry) and want to have nothing to do with faculty unions, because they began teaching not to become "union" or "management," but "professional" instead. Other vocational instructors become immediately involved in faculty union activities because of their own extensive backgrounds in trade unions.

Ambivalence about union involvement is to be found among many community college faculty, who (like Ellen Vargas) have not come to terms with what it means to be a faculty member in a collegiate institution. Thus, though Vargas might have recourse to the grievance procedures of her faculty union at Midland if she receives a negative tenure decision, she probably will not avail herself of the opportunity. She would prefer to make herself more acceptable to the collegial faculty at Midland by obtaining a doctorate in a traditional academic discipline. At this point, her own advocacy of the managerial culture is likely to fade, and she herself will become a proponent of the collegial culture.

6

❖❖❖❖❖❖❖

The Developmental Culture

For all its strengths—specifically, its encouragement of deliberation and open communication—the collegial culture suffers from a lack of organization and coherence. These deficiencies are particularly important for a collegiate institution that is faced with limited financial resources and a changing student constituency. In response to these problems, some collegial faculty members have advocated a more deliberate mode of planning and development that retains faculty authority and a democratic spirit, while avoiding the political infighting of the collegial culture. Under the banner of faculty development, curriculum development, and long-term institutional planning, these faculty (and some administrators) have created a new culture during the past ten to twenty years. We have called this culture developmental.

Rationality is particularly important in this culture. Organizations and procedures are redesigned to accommodate more effectively the particular needs of the institution ("form follows function"). Institutional research is brought to bear on issues of institutional planning. Faculty are asked to examine their own assumptions about teaching and learning, student needs, and so forth, in order that they can better make decisions and plan programs. Members of this third culture tend to be relatively naive about the political process of a college or university and often are viewed by

93

managerially oriented faculty and administrators as too idealistic
and ill equipped to implement a carefully conceived program.

Origins of the Developmental Culture

During the student movement of the late 1960s, there was a growing
sense among many faculty and academic administrators that traditional collegiate institutions (and the dominant collegiate culture)
were not responsive to the needs either of students or of society.
Student life and its improvement required greater emphasis. Furthermore, collegiate institutions needed to be more committed to
and clear about many of the less tangible domains of human growth
and development (for example, moral development and critical
thinking) that often seemed to be lacking among contemporary
citizens. The work of Nevitt Sanford and his colleagues in the classic *The American College* (Sanford, 1962) pointed the way to specific strategies directed at addressing these needs. Sanford focused
not only on the classroom, but also on the extracurricular aspects
of student life. He and his colleagues also offered new concepts of
teaching and learning and directed the attention of faculty and academic administrators to areas of student life that previously had
been considered the exclusive domain of student counselors and
directors of student service programs. Academicians such as Joseph
Katz (Katz and Associates, 1968) and Dick Martin (1969) began to ask
what role colleges and universities should play in a more complete
development of students.

The research of Arthur Chickering on student growth in
small colleges and his description of central aspects of student development drew attention from scholars as well as those working
more directly with students. Along with Sanford's *The American
College,* Chickering's *Education and Identity* (1969) became a best-
selling book in American higher education. The work of William
Perry (1970) on the stages of students' intellectual and ethical development also was conducted in the late 1960s and published in the
early 1970s, though it was not to have a major impact until the late
1970s and early 1980s.

The new, intense attention directed at students and their specific needs required an equally forceful statement about the teach-

ing skills of collegiate instructors and their growth and development. It also drew attention to the requirement for new forms of institutional research aimed not just at readily quantifiable items like finance, student enrollment, and resource allocation, but also at the more elusive aspects of student learning and campus morale. As students are affected by all aspects of campus life, each of these initiatives in turn produced the need for a more comprehensive program of organizational change and development. We will briefly consider all three kinds of these initiatives: faculty development, institutional research, and organizational development. Our attention will turn first to the origins and characteristics of the faculty development movement.

Faculty Development in a Time of Retrenchment (Astin and others, 1974) was a highly influential monograph that sparked many conversations about the failure of American colleges and universities to respond to the needs of either students or faculty. The authors of this book suggest (p. 14) that faculty development might be an appropriate, though partial, response to these concerns:

> In their roles as chemists, literary critics, or psychologists, professors often show painstaking care for method; but with regard to teaching, the academic culture is remarkably unreflective. In part this reluctance derives from the dreary record of many educationists who do profess to train teachers; in part, from the tendency of every profession to cloak its own processes in mystery as a way to achieve status; and in part, from the notion that an academic is valuable for what he knows, rather than for what he can help other people learn. As a result, professors may describe teaching as so straightforward that it requires no special training, and yet as so complex and idiosyncratic that mere training could never meet its extraordinary demands.
>
> Helping professors to teach more effectively may, as some would argue, be unnecessary, impossible, or both; but the first view is not wholly sustained by the response of students and the second appears to

violate a premise of the academic profession itself. Be-
side, the issue is not only training; the practice of any
art generally benefits from colleagueship, knowledge
about the effects of the art, rewards for good work,
support for special projects, arrangements for collaboration, a knowledgeable audience, and so forth.

The field of faculty development emerged in part from this
growing academic concern for student development. As Jack Lindquist (1978a, p. 12), a major figure in this field, has commented: "In
the early 1970s, many of the same developmentalists who had urged
attention to the person of the student urged institutional attention
to the person of the professor. Professors are developing adults who
face such strains as a very tight job market, classrooms too full of
extremely diverse students, institutions rife with adversarial clashes,
and personal transitions which raise serious questions about identity and future directions."

New attention to faculty concerns and welfare also emerged
from demands that collegiate institutions do a better job. The authors of *Faculty Development in a Time of Retrenchment* (Astin
and others, 1974, p. 17) remarked:

Despite cycles of anti-intellectualism, resentment at
the soft life professors are thought to lead, and suspi-
cions of political unreliability, large parts of the
American public have long been enchanted by higher
education. They have regarded it as the path to economic and social mobility, as a source of culture and
of knowledge valuable to society, and in the case of
many nostalgic alumni, as the pretext for the best
years of their lives. To some extent, the enchantment
has recently been shaken. . . . the suspicion has grown
among taxpayers and alumni that professors are not
very effective as teachers—except on behalf of political
or cultural radicalism. People suspect that even when
effective, education no longer necessarily leads to a
good job and that professors enjoy a measure of free
time and autonomy denied to most of those who pay

their keep. For these and other reasons, people are asking that professors, like others, be held accountable for doing a good job—in this case on behalf of students and of society.

In one of the first books written on the topic of faculty development, Bergquist and Phillips (1975, p. 3) observed: "Institutions of higher education face the harsh realities of decreased funding, steady or declining enrollment, and limited faculty mobility, together with demands for accountability voiced by students, parents and state and federal officials. Since the teaching enterprise is central to higher education, faculty in particular are being asked to reexamine their personal and professional attitudes toward classroom instruction and toward their relationships with their students. Many faculty are also being asked to consider training in new classroom procedures, as well as possible reorganizations of departmental structures and governance systems."

Later in the 1970s, faculty were faced with certain harsh realities: not only were many forced to learn new teaching methods and modes of relating to changing student interests and needs, but others were obliged to consider changing disciplines or at least shifting attention to other areas of their current disciplines. Thus, the words *retraining* and even *retreading* were added to the growing vocabulary of the faculty development field—much to the chagrin of many faculty members and practitioners of faculty development who had begun their involvement under more positive and humane circumstances.

By the mid 1970s, faculty development had become quite large and complex and was offered in some form by approximately one-half of the colleges and universities in the United States. Several major foundations (most notably, the Kellogg Foundation and the Lilly Endowment) were supporting major faculty development initiatives. A national association (the Professional and Organization Development Network in Higher Education) had been initiated to provide a forum for discussion of new approaches to the field. Newsletters and workshops were prepared and disseminated by many colleges, universities, centers, and consortia. A major series of handbooks on faculty development were produced by the Council for the Advancement of Small Colleges (CASC, now the Council of

Independent Colleges) (Bergquist and Phillips, 1975, 1977, and 1981), and several national interinstitutional projects were conducted by national higher education associations, such as CASC and the Association of American Colleges (Gaff, 1978).

In the area of instructional improvement, the faculty development practitioner, a product of the developmental culture, diverged significantly from the practitioner of instructional development, a product of the managerial culture. Instructional development practitioners have concentrated specifically on student learning and often advocate instructional methods that eliminate the need for a faculty member's physical presence or even instructional materials that are "faculty-proof." By contrast, those in the faculty development field have generally focused more on the faculty member than on the student, although the field emerged in response to student needs and concerns. By enhancing a faculty member's skills (through training programs) and encouraging renewed interest in teaching and student advising, the faculty development practitioner believes that the quality of learning for students is ultimately improved. Many practitioners, in moments of candor, also admit that they are ultimately more interested in the faculty member than the student as a learner. As sophisticated, adult learners, faculty members offer the faculty development practitioners greater challenge and sense of shared goals than traditional college-age students.

Because of this primary interest in faculty learning and because of the developmental field's retention of the collegial culture's skepticism about quantifiable evaluation, the outcomes of faculty development projects have often been less than satisfactory for funding agencies and the general public that had expected faculty development initiatives to benefit students directly.

Several major funding agencies (such as the Fund for the Improvement of Postsecondary Education) were never supportive of faculty development programs in and of themselves; they were always more interested in faculty development as integral to some other purpose (usually related to the improvement or expansion of student learning opportunities). Other agencies (such as Kellogg and Lilly) that had initially funded faculty development activities also soon became less inclined to do so unless they supported some other end (such as curriculum reform). Thus, a basic assumption in the developmental culture about the inherent compatibility of personal and institutional welfare was called into question by those who could most influence institutional priorities from outside (namely, the funding agencies).

Accompanying the emerging emphasis on faculty development was an intensified interest in institutional research. This interest was not limited to the budgeting devices of the managerial culture; rather, attention was directed more broadly toward the generation of information about institutional climates and culture, student learning styles and stages of development, and institutional goals and priorities. The Educational Testing Service (ETS) developed a series of institutional research tools (an educational environment scale and institutional functioning inventories, for instance) that provided an overview of institutional life for a college or university. ETS also developed an institutional goals inventory that assessed perceptions about the desired state of the institution and the extent to which the institution was successfully moving toward this desired state. Comparable instruments were developed at other institutions and by other testing organizations (see, for example, Bergquist and Shoemaker, 1976).

Other instruments were developed in the early 1970s to assess student learning styles. Riechmann and cedGrasha (1974) devised a means of evaluating the interpersonal preferences of students within a learning environment; Joe Hill (n.d.) from Oakland Community College (Michigan) developed a cognitive mapping method to analyze the appeal of certain media (as well as numerous other factors), and David Kolb (1976) provided a learning style inventory that measured preferences for certain cognitive functions. By the late 1970s, much more elaborate instruments were developed to assess students' generic skills in such areas as critical thinking, writing, and problem solving (such as the COMP-ACT battery of tests created by the American Testing Corporation). Through interviews with students, an assessment of both developmental stages and tasks was possible (Chickering, 1969; Perry, 1970; Knefelkamp, Widick, and Parker, 1978).

Much more important than the proliferation of testing procedures and instruments, however, was the linkage made between these efforts at institutional research and those at planned institutional change. Harold Hodgkinson (then of the Center for Higher Education at the University of California) led a group of nationally known consultants in proposing that institutional research be coupled with action plans that furthered the systematic movement toward institutional goals and that kept in mind institutional climate and style.

The largest and most extensively documented of the combined work on research and planned change was mounted by Arthur Chickering and Jack Lindquist in their project called Strategies for Change and Knowledge Utilization (Lindquist, 1978b). Working intensively with seven colleges (and less closely with about a dozen others), Lindquist effectively demonstrated that knowledge about an institution's life and culture that has been systematically acquired can enhance the quality and success of institutional change efforts (Bergquist and Shoemaker, 1976).

Much of the interest in these new approaches to institutional research seems to have died down during the 1980s. Most colleges and universities continue to conduct institutional research, but it is usually focused on finance, student enrollment and attrition, and resource allocation. The shifting of institutional research back to former areas of concern may be short lived, however, as more states and regional accrediting agencies begin to push for the assessment of student-learning outcomes on an institutionwide basis. We are likely to see substantial resources being devoted during the 1990s to the development of instruments and procedures that are appropriate and sensitive to a wide variety of outcomes.

Faculty development and efforts to bring about institutional change in the early 1970s were complemented by organizational development initiatives. Borrowing heavily from the lessons learned by corporations about organizational change and development, Ron Boyer and Tony Grasha at the University of Cincinnati and Walter Sikes of the Center for Creative Change (NTL Institute) in Yellow Springs, Ohio (Sikes, Schlesinger, and Seashore, 1974), began to conduct workshops, provide consultation, and write about the need for effective organizational functioning (decision making, problem solving, conflict management) in collegiate settings. Several major faculty development practitioners (such as Bergquist and Phillips) and advocates of institutional research (such as Lindquist) urged that organizational development be closely linked with other developmental efforts. They also proposed and were actively involved in the formulation of administrative development efforts that would further strengthen these initiatives.

Thus, by the late 1970s, a relatively sophisticated and unified set of concepts had been developed regarding the ways in which development might effectively take place in all aspects of collegiate life: in other words, student, faculty, administrative, organizational, curriculum, institutional research, and, ultimately, comprehensive development (see, for example, Bergquist and Shoemaker, 1976).

Myths and Images of the Developmental Culture

The myth of healing seems to dominate the developmental culture. Behind it lies the notion that one can take the best from the collegiate culture (namely, its values) and the best from the managerial culture (namely, its procedures) and blend them together to create a healing and positive influence in the life of an institution and its people. Somehow the collegial and managerial cultures can be made one. The rift between them can be mended by the developmental physician.

The developmental culture can also bridge the gap between the needs of individuals (students, faculty, and administrators) and the requirements of the institution itself. Members of the developmental culture believe that they can always discover a point of compatibility between personal and organizational well-being. They may even believe that the welfare of individuals and that of the organization are truly one and the same. The developmental practitioner can match what is good for the individual with what is good for the institution through professional growth contracts or developmental plans (Bergquist and Phillips, 1981). The formality of a contract or plan smacks of the managerial culture; yet the idea is quite collegial in its emphasis upon the distinctive features of each contract or plan (reflecting the specific needs and relative autonomy of each faculty member).

The developmental culture is not only supposed to heal the rifts between the collegiate and managerial cultures and between personal and organizational well-being. It also is based on the belief that this reconciliation must occur before any other genuine growth or development of faculty, students, or administrators can take place. An emphasis on individual growth (particularly of faculty), irrespective of the institution's welfare, is reminiscent of the collegial culture's unsuccessful attempts to promote faculty growth and development through sabbaticals, travel funds (to attend academic conventions), and so forth. Little evidence exists to indicate that these efforts were ever of much long-term benefit to either the faculty member or the institution. Similarly, the managerial culture's apparent indifference to the individual welfare of faculty members leads to isolation and professional exhaustion that are also detrimental to both the individual and institution. Somehow, according to advocates of the developmental culture, the concerns of individuals and organizations must be brought into harmony.

What is the source of healing? For developmentalists, it is often the application of rationality to personal and organizational life. Planned change is possible. The irrational can be overcome, primarily through the application of behavioral science principles and techniques to the life and welfare of collegiate institutions. The behavioral sciences, according to developmentalists, have something to say about all aspects of campus life—not just student services. One might go so far as to say that the developmentalists are advocating that the behavioral sciences replace the physical sciences as the major mode of inquiry in collegiate settings (much as the physical sciences replaced philosophy in the nineteenth century and philosophy earlier replaced theology) (Czesak, 1984).

One of the strengths of the developmental culture is its reliance on basic behavioral science principles. Although the collegial, managerial, and negotiative cultures tend to offer a mixture of often confusing or even contradictory theories and concepts regarding personal, instructional, and organizational life, the developmental culture provides a clear and coherent theory that can readily be articulated by most members of this culture. Yet this very coherence and uniformity are also a source of weakness. It is a culture that attracts a small number of advocates but remains inaccessible to many faculty and administrators who are oriented to one of the other three cultures and who are alienated by the developmentalists' jargon and their pat answers. The judgmental (even moralistic) tone that is found in much of the developmental literature leaves those outside the camp with the sense that in some way they are perceived as a little less bright or a little less motivated than their dedicated developmental colleagues. The case study that follows illustrates just how difficult it is for developmentalists to introduce their values and perspectives into a collegiate institution that is saturated with one or both of the dominant (collegial and managerial) cultures.

Case Study: Mountain State University

Three outside members of the Mountain State University consultation team arrived at the local airport on a Saturday afternoon in late summer. Windsor, the southern town in which Mountain State University is located, was seasonably hot and humid. It is a medium-sized town of eighty thousand citizens, a population that seems about right for a university of nine thousand students. Many of the students at Mountain, however, do not live in Windsor; they commute each day from a radius of about one hundred miles. Those who attend Mountain do not fit the traditional demographic patterns—but then very few universities nowadays are filled with white young men and women who enroll in college straight out of high school.

At Mountain State University, more than one-half of the students are more than twenty-five years of age. Seventy percent are women, many of these returning to school after more than ten years away from any formal educational training. For the returning women at Mountain, education is often very costly; it means not only time away from job and family, but also the stress they experience as a result of unsupportive husbands, demanding children, and unforgiving bosses. For women at Mountain, the cost is sometimes domestic violence resulting from their unwillingness to remain the silent and compliant mate. Education has had an impact upon the lives of Mountain State University students—of that there is no doubt.

These factors were all known to the outside consultants as they flew into Windsor. One of the major reasons they wished to work at this university was their respect for this student population and their wish to support populist forms of higher education. The three consultants, however, were not prepared for the full implications of this populism.

They began their consultation by meeting during the evening with members of the curriculum committee at Mountain for final review of the evaluation questions that were to guide the campus visit. On Sunday, members of the consulting team (the three outsiders, plus three members of the Mountain State University faculty) met to create an interview protocol that would be responsive to the questions selected by the committee. The team decided to conduct interviews with at least thirty faculty members, students, and administrators, as well as to observe a variety of events at Mountain and to review several written documents. The six-member team conducted forty-two interviews, observed six different kinds of events (ranging from a faculty social gathering to informal campus life at Mountain), and examined more than a dozen reports, memos, brochures, videotapes, and announcements.

On Thursday morning, the team members distilled the data they had collected and formulated an oral report that was presented to members of the curriculum committee on Thursday afternoon. This report was received with considerable interest and enthusiasm by members of the committee. Immediately after the oral report was completed, the external leader of the team was asked to summarize the report to the academic vice president, a request with which he complied.

Following an evening of celebration and mutual congratulations, the outside members of the team prepared to fly back to their home towns. At the airport, the team leader received an emergency phone call from an assistant to the academic vice president. The assistant informed the team leader that the report was very controversial and that if it found its way to the Mountain State University president, the academic vice president and anyone else associated with this ill-founded venture would undoubtedly be fired. Furthermore, the videotape that was made of the oral report was to be burned (not merely erased). The team members' euphoria about this consultation evaporated rapidly, and Windsor began to feel like a place to be avoided in the future.

What was in the report that so jeopardized an administrator's future? Why were several of the leaders of this university so fearful of their president's reactions? Why were the evaluation team's developmental concerns met with initial acceptance and then intense resistance? Some of the findings reported by the team members provide answers to these questions.

First, as the consultants knew even before coming to Windsor, populism seems to pervade the mission, history, and current operations of this university. It exists to serve the underserved, probably more than any other university in the state. Faculty, students, and administrators speak of upward mobility at Mountain, based on initiative, integrity, and competence. This emphasis on "bootstrap" achievement seems to be important to both faculty and students. At Mountain State University, if students do not work hard, then they do not deserve to succeed.

On the one hand, this populism and emphasis on self-motivation mean that faculty and students benefit from their own individual actions. It also means that members of the Mountain community often perceive a major disparity in faculty rewards, recognition, and morale. One of the chief academic leaders spoke of the "yellowed notes" used by faculty who spend little time in preparing for class. Apparently, these faculty are no longer interested in their own careers or their own professional renewal. This administrator felt that these faculty deserve heavier teaching loads and that they would not be helped much by professional development programs. On the other hand, he spoke quite favorably of the "motivated" faculty, who were not only good teachers, but also found time to do research, write, participate in campus activities, and work actively with students: "These faculty should get lower teaching loads, so that they can devote even more time to research and new course development." Thus, to those who were productive, more should be given; to those who were not, less. As is typical of many administrators who themselves come from the elitist, collegial culture, this person believes that there are some people who are worthwhile and others who are not. Developmental activities would be of little value for either group.

A second problem at Mountain concerns the powerful role of the university president. There is a high level of respect for and recognition of the accomplishments of the president ("he has made us what we are today"), but a sense of paternalism pervades Mountain State. Actions tend to be based on personal negotiation, and there are unclear guidelines for the consistent implementation of institutional policies and procedures. Emphasis is placed on trust in individuals rather than in formal policies and procedures. In this sense, the president contributes to the collegial culture at Mountain State University.

Having previously served as a state legislator, the Mountain State president also brings a political and legal orientation to the university. The president never says no to a request; he makes effective use of delay and deliberation. He tends to respond to the "squeaky wheel" and to managerial concerns rather than to the educational needs of the university. Though his style was appropriate during the expansion years at Mountain State University, it may be less appropriate to a mature institution.

Another aspect of presidential authority at Mountain is related to centralization. Decisions are made at the top of the organization, and communication usually comes from or goes to the top. There is very little lateral movement of information. This system was appropriate and did not pose a problem when Mountain was a small teachers college; however, faculty and administrators now feel they have diminishing access to the president. It is difficult to manage a centralized system in an institution that is growing rapidly. A bit more of the managerial culture and perhaps some managerial training might be needed (especially if they go hand in hand with the emergence of the developmental and negotiating cultures).

At the present time, the president has a rather parochial view of the school and its place in the state's educational system. His opinion is, of course, important, for (in the words of one faculty member at Mountain) the president "knows this state"; he has a high level of influence and contact with state leaders. Nevertheless, the president and other leaders at Mountain are sometimes unaware of general trends and practices in American higher education and hence have little knowledge of or appreciation for either of the newer academic (developmental and negotiating) cultures.

A third problem with organizational life at Mountain concerns the simultaneous freedom and powerlessness that faculty members experience. One faculty member explained, "I can do what I want in my classroom." This is a strong, pervasive, and valued aspect of the organizational culture at Mountain State University. It is based directly on the collegial culture. There is an accompanying sense of autonomy among faculty and support for individual innovative practices—if a faculty member is willing to pay for required resources or if additional resources are not needed. Strong support is also to be found for flexibility, openness, and risk-taking behavior.

However, as one Mountain faculty member noted, "I must do what other people request outside the classroom." Administrative reports take precedence over classroom preparation and are often requested at the last minute (a situation that suggests the preliminary and ineffective entrance of the managerial culture into faculty life at Mountain State). Faculty indicate that they feel "manipulated" or "tricked" by the administration. Decisions are made first, and then information is requested from faculty to reinforce the decision. At other times, the information supplied by the faculty is ignored. A lack of clarity concerning how and when decisions are made throughout the organization creates a feeling of impotence among many faculty at Mountain. This then leads many faculty to complain about the university, without doing much about their grievances. The fact that only the complaints are heard has contributed to a perception at Mountain State that some faculty are "whiners."

A fourth difficulty springs from the diversity found among the schools, departments, and individual faculty members at Mountain. As one member of the consulting team indicated during the middle of the consultation, it was "hard to believe that this is the same institution when visiting different parts of the school." Faculty have varying degrees of access to the president and dramatically different rates of success in getting their ideas heard and accepted by administrators and other faculty. There are also both radically different resource needs and levels of access to those resources. These variations in access, rates of success, and resource needs lead to status distinctions among academic departments at Mountain. Several faculty members talked about a strong pecking order at the university—a common state of affairs at colleges and universities with strong collegial cultures.

These status differences are further heightened by the range of quality and demographic characteristics (age and socioeconomic level) of students and the proportion of men and women enrolled in various departments and programs. Departments with the highest status (and a dominant collegial culture) attract the brightest and more traditional (young, white, well-educated) students. The insularity of departments and department heads enable myths to grow about "other" students who are enrolled in low-status departments and programs (which typically are more managerial or developmental in their orientation). Faculty members and department chairs are often unaware of the actual differences between departments and the differences in their needs and resources.

A fifth issue relates closely to the fourth. Mountain State University is filled with faculty territorialism. There is extensive win-lose competition among departments for limited resources. The general education program at Mountain exemplifies this destructive competition. The only viable discussion about general education at Mountain centers on the distribution of required general education units among academic departments. It is assumed by faculty that this is the only appropriate model for general education, a situation that suggests that the Mountain University faculty may be just as parochial as the administration and may be strongly imbued with the values and quasi-political perspective of the collegial culture.

In one area, however, the university has exhibited a potential for cooperation and for acceptance of the developmental culture. A pilot test in critical thinking was initiated several years ago by the Business Department, using a grant received from a local corporation. Even though they must share their resources, business faculty members have encouraged the expansion of this program to other departments at Mountain. Furthermore, the Philosophy and English Departments at Mountain are very supportive of the critical thinking program and have allowed faculty from outside their departments to teach in areas usually reserved for English and philosophy instructors.

The final problem identified by the consulting team concerns change and crisis. Several faculty members spoke of the university as a "changing institution." The university had just expanded its graduate offerings and begun a number of innovative programs for returning students and men and women working at a nearby military installation. As a result of this growth, faculty and administrators expressed considerable optimism and enthusiasm. They also showed support for the president in his endeavors to find additional funding for the school's expansion (and perhaps his growing recognition of and respect for aspects of the developmental culture).

Nevertheless, the faculty and administrators lack sufficient preparation for the changes being made. Change itself is thus part of the problem at Mountain State University, as manifest in the crisis management that seems to be present in many different sectors of the university. Decisions are not being made, are being delayed, or are unclear even when made. Though the crisis mentality at Mountain provides justification for centralization of information and control, the faculty, administrators, and support staff feel over-worked, underfunded, and unappreciated. The result is often lethargy: "I am expected to do as much as possible, with as little money and time as possible." In these crisis conditions, expectations of work performance and accountability are minimal. Lethargy is also evident in the skepticism and weariness of the faculty. As one faculty member noted, "Our best people—our 'fighters'—are getting burned out." The ground is fertile at Mountain State University for the emergence of a negotiating culture.

The Developmental Culture in Interaction with the Other Cultures

Is Mountain State University really very different from other contemporary American universities? Mountain was selected as a case study because it typifies the problems and potential of many academic institutions. There are really few differences between mid-sized universities of low to moderate status. Christopher Jencks and David Riesman (1968) found a common, dominant paradigm in their analysis of the academic revolution. Can we conclude, then, that a report like the one prepared for Mountain State would receive a hostile reception in other American universities? What was so controversial about this report? Was the reaction due to nothing more than the president's sensitivity to negative comments? Or did the findings touch some other nerves at Mountain University? We will more fully examine the four cultures at Mountain State to get a better sense of the threat represented by the report.

In essence, Mountain State University exemplifies the paternalism (Sennett, 1981) of many American colleges and universities strongly influenced by the collegial culture. Mountain State is a populist institution. As we said earlier, many of the students at Mountain are the first in their families to attend college. Their education and degree will enable them to break out of their current socioeconomic status and to bring them and their families a new more affluent lifestyle. Jencks and Riesman (1968) speak of the role this myth of upward mobility plays in the collegial culture in American colleges and universities. Like Mountain, they remain conservative and obsessed with standards because they are essential vehicles for lower-class men and women to become admitted to the middle class.

Similarly, many of the faculty and administrators at Mountain State University are themselves first-generation college graduates. They are the stars of their families: the ones who were bright and ambitious enough to become college professors and deans. These men and women come from families where career advancement and job security are critical. They are therefore strong advocates of academic teaching as a career and are not inclined to risk their own jobs for any principle or cause. These faculty members often view their main job as preparing ("cloning") students for careers in their own academic disciplines (and see professional training as inappropriate and a retreat to their former status). The faculty become surrogate parents who will guide or at least cajole lower-class students into a new lifestyle and set of values—much as their parents (or other relatives) pushed them toward achievement.

These faculty members look to the president of their institution as the source of their own continuing upward mobility. Academics at Mountain State University want their school to move from lower ranking to a middle- or upper-class status, much as they made their own way to the top. They look to the president of Mountain to make this happen. Just as the hope of upward mobility pervades the faculty's faith in the value of higher education, the myth of upward institutional mobility influences faculty members' belief in the potential of their own collegiate institution and in the need for a strong, competent leader to bring about this advancement—usually single-handedly.

The president of Mountain State University embodies the personal and institutional aspirations of Mountain State faculty members—and their idea of paternalistic authority. He is the source of all power in the school, which he generally exerts through the granting or withholding of favors. Some departments and individuals are blessed with his favor; others have been cast out, often without quite knowing why. He attains authority through his expertise and credibility with the outside world, much as a father "brings home the bacon" and is thereby granted respect and authority by his spouse and children.

Mountain State University would not enjoy its current position without the president, so he must be treated carefully. What would happen if he became disappointed or discouraged and left Mountain? A common fear among many children in traditional families is that father will leave them for good: "After all, doesn't he leave us every day to go to work? With him we must be particularly good. Mom will never leave us, so we can be a bit naughty and rude with her." Paternalism fosters dependency, which in turn engenders a fear of abandonment and a strong institutional consensus against confronting or disagreeing with the paternal figure. Such behavior would not only risk one's own career and livelihood, but would also threaten the welfare of the institution.

If we examine in this light the reaction of the Mountain State administrators to the consulting team, it becomes much clearer and more justifiable. In many ways, the consulting team represents the developmental culture. The members of the team were all individual devotees of this culture. They believed that this university (and all colleges and universities) required a heavy dose of reasonable curriculum planning. They felt that the "provincial minds" of Mountain State University should be liberated by new ideas about how students develop cognitively and affectively. In addition, the faculty should find new ways of collaborating with one another. Decisions made through consultation would produce not only a better curriculum, but also one that the faculty could control. Faculty would feel freer to release their creative energies and direct these energies toward the generation of new program ideas. The team members wanted to protect new ideas and programs from sabotage by foes on the university's faculty.

The premise of the consulting team and of all participants in the developmental culture is simple: if they tell the truth based on data created by, or in conjunction with, other faculty, administrators, and staff, it will be accepted and used by these reasonable men and women. As noted previously in this chapter, advocates of the developmental culture are indifferent or antipathetic to the politics of the collegial culture. Given that the president of Mountain is a political creature, it is not surprising that the consulting team devalued his work and strategies for running the institution. The authority exerted in a developmental culture is much more likely to be based on autonomy rather than paternalism. According to Sennett (1981), autonomous authority is based on the possession of skills and character rather than formal position (as would be the case with a real or quasi-parental figure). The autonomous authority that Sennett describes relies heavily on rational judgment and on clarity of policy and procedure.

The paternalistic president of Mountain State University was obviously concerned with the welfare of some members of the faculty and administration and seemingly opposed to others on the staff who were not supportive of his leadership. The autonomous, developmentally oriented leader, by contrast, may treat everyone the same and, in doing so, may appear to care little about anyone. Sennett suggests that a leader who is indifferent often arouses the desire of subordinates to be recognized. We want our leaders to demonstrate (or at least feel) that we matter enough to be noticed. Thus, although the autonomous leader may seek to reduce his or her control over the behavior of subordinates, that individual in fact continues to exert profound, though subtle, influence. Those working for the autonomous leader try to identify ways to overcome their boss's indifference and rationality.

At Mountain, the movement away from a developmental culture and toward a more paternalistic collegial culture was particularly strong. First, the consulting team never met with the president: he remained a strong but unknown figure. Even consultants assign such a figure a great deal of power in any organization. Faculty members, administrators, or consultants at Mountain have only two possible responses to the ruling paternal figure. They can be respectful of the president's accomplishments and control over the organization, or they can be very critical. In the case of the Mountain State faculty (and the consulting team), reactions to the administration was a mixture of respect on the one hand and disapproval or even indignation on the other.

What is the response of campus leaders and faculty members in this highly paternalistic, collegial culture to the intrusion of a developmentally oriented consulting team? First, those who bring in the outsiders are justified in being fearful of their own jobs. They do not have the protection of those who are part of institutions that embrace a negotiating culture. Second, and even more important, the entire campus is worried about the president's reaction to this report. Might he become so angry or discouraged that he will choose to abandon them? Even those members of the faculty most supportive of change and development at Mountain expressed their fears about the possible loss of the president's leadership in future years. At some level, the entire Mountain State University community is concerned about the president's continuing role at the school. One can predict that presidential succession at Mountain will be traumatic—though perhaps essential to the further maturation of this institution.

Third, most collegiate institutions seem to be reluctant to abandon the paternalism that is so deeply embedded in the fabric of the institution, as well as in its collegial culture. Colleges and universities like Mountain State were founded to protect young men and women and to offer them a responsible surrogate parent for their first years away from home. This mission is no longer appropriate to most collegiate institutions. It is definitely irrelevant to a university such as Mountain State that serves mostly mature men and women. Nevertheless, this paternalistic mission continues to overshadow more contemporary statements of purpose.

Faculty at Mountain, for instance, continue to place greatest value on the teaching that they offer to young men and women. The highest-status departments are those that serve younger students. Departments that serve older students are devalued because they are "practical" (such as business and nursing) and also because they are in some sense betraying the collegial culture at Mountain State University by offering evening courses, allowing students to miss class when their children are ill, or encouraging students to bring their immediate job-related concerns into the classroom. Even a traditional academic department at Mountain (for example, English literature) that tries to be responsive to the needs of adult learners is viewed with considerable contempt by many faculty in other departments.

Similarly, when these same traditional, collegial faculty members look to their president for leadership, they expect to be treated as children. They may complain vehemently about this treatment and may grumble incessantly about the president's arbitrary style. But even in this defiance, they are colluding with the president in the preservation of a paternalistic and collegial culture. They speak of a new leader who would come to Mountain and save them from their current state. They tend to discount their own faculty leaders ("prophets without honor in their own land") and become quite fearful when outsiders come in to tell them about a faculty-governed curriculum project. It is certainly much safer to observe consultants from outside Mountain receive the wrath of the president than incur it directly. Thus, the consulting report and the potential reaction of Mountain State's president to it created extended and emotional conversations among Mountain faculty members. It provided good theater and played well at Mountain State University. The developmental culture at this university, at least for the moment, is just about as welcome as the videotape that the vice president wanted to burn.

7

❖❖❖❖❖❖

Living and Working in
the Developmental Culture

The institutional values inherent in the developmental culture focus on three different aspects of institutional life: (1) teaching and
learning, (2) personal and organizational dynamics, and (3) institutional mission. All three of these sets of values link the developmental culture more closely to the managerial than to the collegial
culture; those in the managerial culture are also particularly concerned with teaching and learning (as they relate to student-
learning outcomes), with personal and organizational issues (as
they affect ongoing institutional operations), and with the mission
and goals of the institution. Yet like all aspects of their culture, an
attempt is made by the developmentalists to address these values
from a perspective compatible with (or at least not offensive to)
faculty in the collegial culture.

Those in the developmental culture generally believe that
teaching and learning should be at the heart of the academic enterprise—rather than research or scholarly pursuits. They generally
advocate an interdisciplinary, problem-solving, or theme-oriented
approach to curriculum development, as a result of their belief that
the collegial culture's preoccupation with disciplines ill prepares
students for a world of complex, systemic issues. Faculty who represent the developmental culture often identify themselves as
teachers rather than as psychologists or historians. They read higher
education literature and research in other fields, rather than sticking

strictly to their own disciplines. They are particularly inclined to read the behavioral sciences (change theory, organizational theory and research, student development theory and research) and philosophy of education (philosophers and interdisciplinary scholars such as Dewey ([1916] 1944), Polanyi (1969), and Bateson (1972) who generally advocate experience-based learning, systemic thinking, and reorganization of human knowledge).

The second set of values, focusing on personal and organizational dynamics, has generally been borrowed from the literature on organizational development in corporate settings. An excellent summary statement regarding these values or "meta-goals" is to be found in Edgar Schein and Warren Bennis's *Personal and Organizational Change Through Group Methods* (1965). One idea that has been adopted by representatives of the developmental culture concerns the role of science in human endeavors. Developmentalists believe that a rational approach to understanding and planning for human interaction is imperative and inherently valuable. Similarly, the spirit of inquiry that pervades the sciences is assumed to be appropriate and desirable in working with people: "The first meta-goal or value is an attitude of inquiry most often associated with science. It is a complex of human behavior and adjustment that has been summed up as the spirit of inquiry and includes many elements. . . . The first may be called the hypothetical spirit, the feeling for tentativeness and caution, the respect for probable error. The second ingredient is experimentalism, the willingness to expose ideas to empirical testing, to procedures, to action (Schein and Bennis, 1965, p. 31)."

This hypothetical spirit is generally compatible with the collegial culture's skepticism about pat answers and programs but is incompatible with the managerial culture's emphasis on decisiveness and clarity. Conversely, the experimentalism of the developmental culture tends to be positively received by the managerial culture, with its emphasis on action and innovation, but is incompatible with the collegial culture's dislike of learning by doing rather than by deliberation and observation.

Another organizational concept concerns choice and ownership. Representatives of the developmental culture inevitably seem to appreciate expanded choice and "consciousness" in the people with whom they work. They wish to provide other people (and themselves) with valid and useful information about possible alternatives (Argyris, 1970). In addition, they respect the process of collaboration, whereby those with whom they work gain a clear sense of having made the decision to select a particular option. A developmentalist might suggest five different ways in which a course could be taught and then help a faculty member collect pertinent information upon which to base a rational choice among them. The choice is always in the hands of the faculty member rather than the developmental practitioner. Within organizational settings, developmentalists strongly advocate that decisions be made by people who have the maximum amount of information that is relevant to the decision. These people are not necessarily at the top of the organization (Beckhard, 1969).

Information is inherently valuable to individuals and organizations, according to the developmentalists. They believe that only through the introduction of new information that somehow calls into question an individual's or organization's current self-perceptions will "unfreezing" take place, as a precondition to real learning and change (Lippitt, Watson, and Westley, 1958). Information is similarly required to preserve authenticity in relationships. Developmentalists encourage direct, open, and clear feedback: the reactions, perceptions, and expectations of others about an individual's behavior. Information about one's own behavior, according to the developmentalists, is essential if one is to continue to mature and become more successful in organizational settings.

Two other concepts of personal and organizational life are espoused by most members of the developmental culture. These are a commitment to inclusiveness and an emphasis on conflict resolution through rational means. Both of these relate to a more general endorsement of democratic goals. Traditional authoritarian relationships between students and faculty are discouraged. Student participation, involvement, and autonomous control are encouraged. Students and staff are free to question the decisions made by faculty or administrators and to take part in the reformulation of plans, in the aforementioned spirit of inquiry, testing of hypotheses and experimentation.

Conflicts are regarded in the developmental culture as a

symptom of unmet needs, lack of information, or inadequate planning:

> What does a problem-solving orientation or conflict mean? First, it implies that if conflict does exist, it must be recognized and confronted as such instead of being denied, suppressed or compromised. Then, once recognized, conflict must be managed and resolved through understanding its causes and consequences fully and then bringing to light all data relevant to further understanding. Finally, the conflict must be resolved by consulting with all relevant individuals and groups and by exploring under conditions of trust and confidence all the possible alternatives for a solution. If these conditions are satisfied, then we can say that conflict resolution was managed and resolved through rational means [Schein and Bennis, 1965, p. 34].

In these last ideas, we often find the greatest incompatibility between the developmental culture and the other three. Each of the others has different ways of working with conflict and generally views the highly rationalistic model of the developmentalist as simplistic and minimally helpful in politically charged and complicated collegiate settings demanding quick and decisive decisions.

The third category of values associated with the developmental culture concerns institutional mission. A faculty member or administrator in the managerial culture often desires clarification of goals and more specific objectives to serve as a basis for program planning and evaluation. By contrast, the developmentalist, frequently asks, "What are we really doing in this college and university, and is it what we should be doing?" "Are our goals directly related to our essential mission?" "What difference would it really make to our students and to our society if these goals are never met?"

It is at this point that the developmentalist, now more of a philosopher than a behavioral scientist, finds the greatest compatibility with those in the collegial culture (though the developmentalist will be more assertive about these issues). But developmentalists will be much less satisfied with the collegial culture's reliance on precedent and disciplinary goals; they believe that the use of precedent does not enable a college or university to change in response to shifting societal needs and values and that disciplinary goals leave a college or university fragmented and isolated.

Much as the railroad companies in the early part of the twentieth century had to decide whether they were in the business of running railroads or of providing transportation, so must colleges and universities in the 1990s determine whether their goal is to teach or to furnish a basis for research and scholarship. The railroad companies chose (implicitly if not explicitly) to run railroads rather than provide transportation; thus, when air travel began, they did not use their expertise in scheduling and passenger service to compete, but sat back and let more entrepreneurial companies provide air transportation. According to many developmentalists, contemporary colleges and universities must continually reexamine their mission if they are not to go the way of the railroads. In this sense, the developmentalists echo the sentiments of many modern-day critics of traditional management practices (for example, Kanter, 1984; Peters, 1987) who complain about the lack of clarity in the purpose and goals of contemporary corporations.

Qualities of Leadership

Faculty and academic administrators attracted to the developmental culture usually prefer a different mode of leadership than that found in the other three cultures. Leadership in the developmental culture tends to be exerted in complex and nontraditional ways. Using Max Weber's analysis of power and authority (1947), we can postulate that the developmental leader tries to make use of "expert" power, rather than the managerial culture's "rational-legal" power (or authority derived from position). Developmentalists also attempt to avoid the paternalistic power that is so common in the collegial culture and choose instead a more collaborative or (as we noted in Chapter Six) autonomous form of authority.

Although they do not usually acknowledge it, developmentalists often make just as extensive use of a much less rational mode of power that Weber labels "charisma." This authority springs from the ability to persuade and motivate other people. It is typically found among particularly skillful advocates of the developmental culture.

Stated in another way, leadership is manifested indirectly in the developmental culture. Whereas leadership in the managerial culture is exerted through the authority of formal line relationships, developmental leaders often serve in a staff role—influencing rather than controlling, suggesting rather than demanding, informing rather than directing. The political maneuvering of the collegial leader is replaced by the developmentalist's provision of service. Rather than attending faculty meetings on curricular change, the developmental leader conducts or attends (with colleagues) workshops on processes of curricular reform or on alternative curricular designs. Instead of struggling through a departmental discussion of alternative tenure review systems, the developmental leader will begin working with individual faculty members to prepare career plans (so that they can be prepared for either a positive or negative decision).

This notion of servant as leader is perhaps best articulated by Robert Greenleaf (1970, 1972, 1974, 1979, and 1980) in his series of books on the servant-leader in higher education:

> The idea of The Servant as Leader came out of reading Herman Hesse's *Journey to the East.* In this story we see a band of men on a mythical journey, probably also Hesse's own journey. The central figure of the story is Leo who accompanies the party as the servant who does their menial chores, but who also sustains them with his spirit and his song. He is a person of extraordinary presence. All goes well until Leo disappears. Then the group falls into disarray and the journey is abandoned. They cannot make it without the servant Leo. The narrator, one of the party, after some years of wandering finds Leo and is taken into the Order that had sponsored the journey. There he discovers that Leo, whom he had known first as servant,

was in fact the titular head of the Order, its guiding spirit, a great and noble leader.

> To me, this story clearly says—the great leader is seen as servant first, and that simple fact is the key to his greatness. Leo was actually the leader all of the time, but he was servant first because that was what he was, deep down inside. Leadership was bestowed upon a man who was by nature a servant. It was something given, or assumed, that could be taken away. His servant nature was the real man, not bestowed, not assumed, and not to be taken away. He was servant first [1970, p. 1].

Like negotiative leaders, developmental leaders reside outside any formal role or lines of authority in the collegiate institution. However, unlike negotiative leaders, developmental leaders do not seek to change the institution through collective force; they prefer to encourage increased collective awareness of the problems facing the institution and joint recognition of alternative solutions to these problems. In this way, the assumption of organizational rationality enters a developmentalist's strategy for effective institutional leadership. In order to redirect the attention of colleagues to the basic teaching and learning mission of the college or university, the developmental leader constantly asks, "What is it we want to do in this organization?" Conversely, the developmentalist often directs attention away from the personal issues and power struggles that preoccupy the attention of faculty and administrators in the other three cultures.

In this abiding concern for teaching and learning and use of service to gain influence, the developmental leader is frequently perceived by others as idealistic and ineffective. In recent years, however, advocates of the developmental perspective have begun to enter positions of formal leadership in American colleges and universities. Leaders in the field have become college presidents, deans, and directors of major programs in higher education. Will these men and women have to abandon or at least modify their developmental perspectives (as Warren Bennis apparently did in moving from extensive work as an organizational development consultant to the presidency of the University of Cincinnati)? Or will they be able to influence their colleagues rooted in the managerial or collegial culture? What about the relationship between the emerging leaders of the developmental and negotiative cultures? Will these leaders be able to collaborate on future plans for change in higher education— as representatives of the two cultures that have arisen in reaction to the inadequacies of the dominant cultures? Given the short history of the developmental culture, we will have to wait some time before we have any answers to these questions.

Accountability

One of the first proponents of the developmental culture, Mervin Freedman (Freedman and others, 1979, p. 8), noted in his study of academic cultures: "Very few faculty members can define the basis on which they evaluate themselves or can offer any rationale for what they do in the classroom. . . . Not only does traditional academic culture ignore basic educational issues, it does not even possess the concepts necessary to address them. With no concepts for describing student development, without means to evaluate one's teaching, without even a perspective from which the student may be seen as a person, the professor is denied the most elementary satisfaction of professional activity—seeing desirable things happen as a result of planned action."

Freedman's critique of current, collegially based evaluation systems for college and university faculty reflects the dominant attitude of developmentalists. These men and women are pushing for new, more sensitive ways of evaluating the complicated and often elusive performance of faculty inside and outside the college classroom.

Certainly, the emphasis placed during the 1980s and early 1990s on the assessment of student learning as a means of judging both student performance and teaching effectiveness was based on the developmentalists' initial descriptions and categorizations of basic cognitive, affective, and behavioral outcomes (for example, critical thinking and interpersonal competence). In general, during the 1980s the developmentalists have not concentrated on this area; they have been much more interested in using student-learning outcomes to guide curriculum and faculty development efforts. Instead, proponents of the managerial culture have led the way in making use of the developmentalists' work to improve faculty accountability with regard to student learning. This is one example of the way in which words and concepts created and nurtured in one academic culture are borrowed and employed in a quite a different manner by faculty and administrators from another culture.

When developmentalists do get involved in the evaluation of faculty performance, they are much more inclined than those from the managerial culture to involve faculty actively in the review process. Furthermore, they often look to other fields for ideas about how the evaluation of faculty performance might occur. From the arts they have borrowed the documentation and portfolio procedure, whereby faculty members under review collect evidence (written work, videotapes of classroom presentations, letters of recommendation, and student evaluations) of their achievement in specific areas of responsibility (for instance, lower-division instruction, departmental service, and applied research) or areas of required competence (lecturing, advising, and curriculum design). The extent to which each of these is important is negotiated with the review committee, which indicates the amount of documentation needed in each area (Bergquist and Phillips, 1977). Other developmentalists have borrowed from the social sciences in formulating sophisticated, multidimensional assessment techniques for faculty performance. The Instructional Development and Effectiveness Assessment system, developed at Kansas State University's Center for Faculty Evaluation and Development in Higher Education (Bergquist and Phillips, 1977), exemplifies such an approach, as does the Mutual Benefit Evaluation system, developed by William Genova and his colleagues (Genova and others, 1976) for academic institutions in Massachusetts.

Most importantly, the developmentalists believe that the evaluation of faculty performance must be tied directly to developmental effort: "Do not evaluate anything that you cannot help improve or develop" is a common motto. Through the use of professional development contracts (Carlber and others, 1978), a developmental consultant helps faculty members identify their areas of strength and weakness, particularly as they relate to emerging or anticipated changes in role, responsibility, or career direction. A faculty member works with colleagues, first in conducting this self-assessment and later in formulating plans to enhance strengths and overcome weaknesses. These tools for career planning and professional development may be particularly valuable for faculty members who confront the difficult and changing demands of both the academic and nonacademic worlds, as well as for those who struggle for more equitable treatment of faculty (as representatives of the negotiative culture). We will turn to this fourth culture after examining how a senior faculty member at an elite research university grapples with the developmental culture.

Case Study: Kevin Reynolds

Kevin Reynolds received his Ph.D. in the history of Western thought from a large West Coast university. His accomplishments as an interdisciplinary scholar since this time have been remarkable, especially given the limited educational background of Reynolds's parents. His mother has a B.A. degree; however, his father went to college for only two years and is now a postmaster. Reynolds did not come by his position on the faculty of a major Western university easily; he has always worked hard, first as a graduate student, now as a scholar and researcher.

Reynolds is impatient at being confined to one discipline. His colleagues at Durant University support his interdisciplinary interests, though only because he has established an excellent publication record in his own discipline. Even with this support, Kevin feels some constraint in having to identify himself as a historian at Durant and to devote considerable attention to departmental issues.

Kevin Reynolds is also becoming increasingly frustrated with American higher education. Along with most other members of the developmental culture, Kevin believes that institutions of higher education in this country should become less disciplinary and more oriented toward themes and problems in society. He is tired of fighting the battles of academia and is looking into consulting opportunities in industry and social service agencies.

As a teacher, Kevin Reynolds is noted for his leadership of advanced seminars and his one-on-one advising and dissertation supervision. When students are bright and highly motivated, they will find in Reynolds an excellent source of ideas and stimulation. Less capable students will find him somewhat aloof and threatening. Reynolds is worried about his declining interest in the intellectual growth and development of his undergraduate and graduate students, even though these are among the brightest in American higher education.

Kevin Reynolds looks forward to working with mature, adult "students" in various industrial settings. He has found his involvement with faculty from various community colleges and liberal arts colleges (through faculty development programs) to be among the most gratifying and intellectually stimulating experiences of his recent professional career. These men and women demand his utmost, even though they do not have the academic status of the graduate students that he works with on a daily basis. Reynolds wonders whether the quest for the ultimate academic credential (the Ph.D.) is disruptive of real learning. Are bright and curious human beings made dull and dependent when this degree becomes their goal?

Kevin Reynolds is currently debating a career change. He certainly does not want to leave his respected position at Durant University, but he does desire more job latitude so that he can pursue nonacademic interests. If he does so, would his colleagues at Durant still support him? Would his work outside academia increasingly sour his attitudes about higher education and, more specifically, teaching at Durant? Is he wasting his talent by trying to compete with consultants, "experts," and researchers who are now working in the nonacademic world?

Reynolds's many possibilities represent an embarrassment of riches. Nevertheless, decisions are still hard. Kevin Reynolds comes from the discipline-oriented collegial culture, but (as previously noted) he himself is strongly committed to interdisciplinary and developmentally oriented education. Many other faculty members who are interested in interdisciplinary studies are not as fortunate as Reynolds. They are perceived by their colleagues as being too eclectic or are even accused of being dilettantes who play with ideas rather than work with serious disciplinary-based intellectual issues.

The Developmental Culture in
Interaction with the Other Cultures

In James Watson's *The Double Helix* (1968), the candid and often disturbing account of Watson and Crick's discovery of the DNA structure, the disdain for faculty members (especially researchers) who cross over disciplines or even areas of specialization was vividly conveyed. The King's College, Cambridge, researchers (in particular, Maurice Wilkins and Rosalind Franklin) were highly critical of the ideas of Watson and Crick, essentially newcomers to the field. Though they barely spoke to each other, Wilkins and Franklin agreed on one thing: true scientific advancement came from the patient and competent accumulation of evidence, the systematic elimination of alternative hypotheses, and the eventual emergence of a firmly established, fully documented theorem. Only when this established course was followed would the scientific enterprise be properly served.

Neither Watson nor Crick fitted this model. They showed little interest in acquiring the laboratory skills associated with research in this field. They preferred instead to use the laboratory data collected by other people (mostly that of Wilkins and Franklin) in constructing theoretical models of DNA. The discovery of DNA structures was probably only possible because of this blending of traditional "normal science" (to use Thomas Kuhn's term), as conducted by Wilkins and Franklin, and the more inferential, paradigm-breaking science of the two generalists Watson and Crick.

Of course, a few exceptions to the general rule about specialization are allowed in the collegial culture. One is Linus Pauling. A man of his intellectual stature is allowed to cross fields, as well as to create new ones. His fellow scientists even permit him to leave science completely in order to address issues concerning world peace and nutrition. The interdisciplinary work of other extraordinary scientists, such as Albert Einstein, Jacob Bronowski, and Michael Polanyi, has been similarly tolerated by their colleagues.

Is Kevin Reynolds in the same class as Pauling or Einstein? Obviously not. However, as a professor at a major university and the author of several respected books of considerable intellectual depth, Reynolds can move across fields. But it is not clear that he can venture outside of higher education altogether without alienating himself from his academic colleagues. Reynolds is the classic example of the new American scholar: one who wishes to break down the artificial barriers between the academic and nonacademic worlds. Will he be successful in this endeavor, or must he choose one or the other?

A second important issue is raised by the Kevin Reynolds case. The developmental culture to which Reynolds is attracted often seems to lure good teachers away from traditionally aged undergraduate and graduate students to work with older and more demanding learners: fellow faculty members, academic administrators, and nonacademic professionals. As we saw earlier, he finds a new, exciting challenge in working with more experienced people who wish to apply the concepts they have learned to immediate "real life" problems and jobs.

Reynolds has discovered new ways of influencing change in his own university, as well as in other collegiate organizations. He finds that the political strategies of the collegial culture can be supplanted by the more rational, service-oriented, and sensitive processes and strategies of the developmental culture. Reynolds may be overly optimistic about the long-term impact of these developmental processes and strategies; nevertheless, he is pleased that his analytic skills can be just as useful in designing a new curriculum as in examining a philosophical tract and that the communication skills he perfected while teaching and counseling students can be just as effective with other faculty members.

Third, the Kevin Reynolds case study points to an important relationship between the developmental culture and the managerial and negotiating cultures. Reynold's developmental concerns have led him outside the academy, where he finds that the managerial and negotiating cultures flourish. As Reynolds begins to work more extensively outside the academic realm and to appreciate the challenge of working with corporate executives, allied health professionals, and union officers, he finds the managerial and negotiating cultures to be more understandable and more attractive than before. Clarity of purpose and meaning is demanded. The reality of salary inequities and politics becomes even more apparent.

Reynolds might not like a steady diet of objectivity, pragmatism, and realism, but he finds it a refreshing diversion from the subjectivity and pedantry of departmental politics. Perhaps a bridge linking the collegial, managerial, developmental, and negotiating cultures will eventually be built by faculty members like Kevin Reynolds who seek work outside the academy as well as within it, and by nonacademics who venture inside the academy to do teaching and research on a part-time basis. Scholars such as Reynolds may be among the first people to appreciate fully the need for a creative integration of the four cultures that currently exist in our colleges and universities.

8

❖❖❖❖❖❖❖

The Negotiating Culture

The fourth culture emerged in response to the inability of the managerial culture to meet the personal and financial needs of faculty and staff. If administrators act as though they are responsible for the formulation of institutional policy, then faculties will have to reestablish their influence through collective action. Although faculty unions and collective agreements about salary, job security, and working conditions have been present for many years in American higher education, the movement toward faculty unionization and collective bargaining grew stronger during the 1970s in those sectors of American higher education that had been bastions of collegial and managerial culture (the four-year universities). The movement toward unionization diminished during the 1980s, but it remains an important fact of life in many contemporary colleges and universities.

A faculty member in the negotiating culture believes that change takes places through confrontation and the effective use (or, more often, withholding the use) of prized resources. Collective bargaining negotiations have usually focused on compensation and personnel issues; however, faculty have borrowed from their fellow teachers in elementary and secondary schools the notion that curricular and teaching-learning issues can also be negotiated. Hence, an entire culture, with its own philosophy of education, performance standards, and status criteria, is coming into being.

Origins of the Negotiating Culture

Just as the managerial culture originated in the community (and Catholic) college setting, so also did the community college prove to be fertile ground for the negotiating culture. The close connection between these two-year collegiate institutions and elementary and secondary education systems undoubtedly contributed to the early interest of community college faculty members in collection bargaining. Many of their colleagues in elementary and secondary school systems had already established collective bargaining agreements with their institutions.

Among the four-year collegiate institutions, collective bargaining was a much less welcomed arrival. Not until the late 1960s was collective bargaining established in any of these bastions of the collegial culture. In their study of collective bargaining at four-year college and university campuses, Carr and Van Eyck (1973, p. 17) observe: "Faculty collective bargaining made its appearance at four-year institutions on a scattered, somewhat spotty basis. The starting point might be marked as September 1969, for on that date agreements took effect between the City University of New York (CUNY) and the two units into which its instructional staff had been divided for bargaining purposes."

Since this landmark initiative at CUNY, collective bargaining has grown rapidly in both two- and four-year institutions. Frank Kemerer and Victor Baldridge note that, as of 1975, one-eighth of the colleges and universities in the United States had faculty bargaining agents. At that time, "nearly 12 percent of all professional staff and over 20 percent of the full-time teaching faculty in American higher education [were] represented by unions" (Kemerer and Baldridge, 1975, p. 1). By 1979, Johnstone (1981) reported that faculty at 116 four-year institutions, representing at least 258 campuses, had approved collective bargaining. The number of bargaining units and participating faculty continued to grow in the 1980s, but not as much as before. By 1986, however, over 208,000 faculty were covered by collective bargaining agreements and were represented by collective bargaining agents at 458 institutions (Douglas, 1988). Eighty-three percent (381) of the institutions were public; of these, 88 were four-year and the remaining 293 were two-year colleges and universities. Of the 1,501 campuses in the public sector, 61 percent were unionized; approximately 5 percent of the 1,830 campuses in the private sector were unionized as of 1986. These statistics suggest that the negotiating culture is now prevalent in public institutions, whether two- or four-year, but has not yet made significant inroads in private colleges and universities, where the collegial culture is often entrenched.

The shift in attitude among faculty members regarding collective bargaining is perhaps even more impressive than the statistics. Ladd and Lipset (1973, p. 11) found that, as of 1969, nearly 60 percent of all faculty members gave general endorsement to the principle of collective bargaining. The total amount of support for collective bargaining as a reasonable approach to solving conflict in American higher education appears to be greater than just that found in the formalized faculty unions. We have used the term *negotiating* rather than *collective bargaining* precisely because of this broader base of support.

What are the sources of the negotiating culture? What forces could have led to the eventual acceptance of this seemingly alien culture in the traditional academic setting? Ladd and Lipset (1973, p. 4) suggest that one of the factors is economics: "Academe has gone from two postwar decades of relative boom (1945–1965) in which enrollments, research funds, public and private support, and salaries more or less steadily increased—to a period of retrenchment. As the job situation shifted from a seller's to a buyer's market, and states and private universities were faced with more limited resources, salaries either ceased increasing or raises lagged behind the rise in prices. And as universities tried to make do with less funds, some turned to reductions in staff size, accompanied by efforts to increase teaching and other work loads."

Johnstone (1981) identifies an additional reason as the bureaucratization of colleges and universities in recent years. In this book we have associated increased bureaucratization with the spread of the managerial culture beyond the Catholic and community colleges. Ladd and Lipset (1973, p. 4) also point to growing organizational size and complexity as a factor: "Accompanying the rapid growth of higher education in the postwar era has been an increase in size of institutions and the development in the predominant public sector of gigantic multicampus universities, with central administrations often directly responsible to state authorities. Inherently, such developments led to bureaucratization and reduced the sense of collegiality between faculty and administrators. Professors found that important decisions were being made off campus."

The alienation that often seems to be associated with major growth in the size and complexity of any institution may be a related contributing factor; another one may be increasing academic specialization and professionalization that are associated, ironically, with both bureaucratization in the managerial culture and isolation in the collegial culture (Johnstone, 1981). Clearly, the accompanying decline in collegiality not only contributes to the rise of unionization, but also portends the deterioration of both the collegial and developmental cultures during the 1990s. When faculty members find that they have in common only their contempt for management and are consumed by administrative "atrocities" rather than teaching, research, or scholarship, there is little reason to believe that any academic culture other than the negotiating one will find sufficient nourishment to thrive (or even survive).

Carr and Van Eyck identify still another reason for the rise in collective bargaining: widespread faculty dissatisfaction with the governance systems that are employed by collegiate institutions. In this sense, the negotiative culture is directly confronting the primary domain of the collegial culture. Carr and Van Eyck (1973, p. 57) relate the rise of collective bargaining directly to:

> The desire to improve working conditions other than compensation—in particular to alter [faculty roles] in institutional governance. . . . If the governance system is weak or nonexistent in terms of faculty participation, faculty members of all ages and viewpoints may unite in favoring collective bargaining as a means to counter the authority of trustees and administrators and to gain an appropriate faculty role in running the institution. Their dissatisfaction may, however, reflect conflict and tension within the faculty over the power structure that underlies an existing role in governance. Collective bargaining is then seen as a way of

altering the status of, or equilibrium among, such governance agencies as the departments, faculty committees (in particular, those that handle faculty personnel and grievance matters), the faculty council or senate, and the new faculty "labor organization" necessitated by a turn to collective bargaining.

Thus, increasingly bureaucratized institutional structures may contribute to faculty concern about governance systems.

Collective bargaining is also being used, according to Carr and Van Eyck, in part to confront yet another enemy of some faculty members: established faculty power. It is not just administrators that faculty accuse of being indifferent to their needs and interests; it is also fellow academics who have attained very powerful roles on campus that must somehow be confronted through collective, negotiating action. Akin to this confrontation, believe Carr and Van Eyck (1973, pp. 57-58), is the ongoing war between the "Old Guard" and the "Young Turks" that has recently centered on issues associated with collective bargaining:

Tension and conflict can take shape out of an Old Guard, Young Turk division within the faculty. For example, at a former teachers college, vocational school, or experimental college which had a limited purpose and program, but has been undergoing rapid growth and development into a college of arts and sciences or a regional university, a movement toward collective bargaining may be led by older faculty members who find themselves competing for salary increases and program support with aggressive young faculty members. This tension can be exacerbated where the young faculty members identify themselves with an enterprising new president (or vice versa), rather than with department chairmen and senior faculty members. In such a situation, the decision to turn to collective bargaining is not necessarily the work of young faculty members, although they may attempt to influence or even to gain control of the faculty's labor

organization and the negotiations at the bargaining
table, once their more conservative colleagues have
supplied many of the votes making up the majority in
favor of collective bargaining.

Though most of the sources of collective bargaining seem to
reside in the emergence of newly dominant managerial cultures,
this Old Guard–Young Turk conflict as a source of collective bargaining finds its origins in the collegial culture. Kemerer and Baldridge (1975, pp. 64–65) suggest that faculty unions appeal to two
different faculty groups:

Those who are "preservation" oriented and those who
consider themselves "deprived." The first are essentially high-status professors who, like their skills
counterparts in the industrial sector, have realized that
their rights and privileges within the institution can
no longer be safeguarded by tradition alone. The second—the "deprivation" group—are those who view
collective bargaining as a means to gain power and
benefits previously denied them. Like the semi- and
unskilled workers in the industrial sector, they view
collective bargaining as a means of enfranchisement.
On some campuses, professors seek to preserve past
gains (preservation); on others, they aspire to achieve
parity with the more privileged (enfranchisement).

Preservation-oriented faculty tend to move toward collective
bargaining from a collegial culture—often in an attempt to somehow secure the future of this culture. Those faculty members who
feel deprived generally have long before abandoned the collegial
culture in favor of a managerial (or antimanagerial) attitude that
emphasizes personnel and fiscal concerns more than issues of an
academic nature, such as teaching, research, or scholarship. Both
the preservation and deprivation faculty are driven to collective bargaining from the pressures of a dominant managerial culture. However, the bases for their reaction against the managerial culture are

quite different. As a result, preservation and deprivation faculty members often make strange bedfellows in a faculty union.

As Kemerer and Baldridge (1975, p. 65) have remarked, "Collective bargaining has primarily fulfilled the second [deprivation] function." As a result, collective bargaining has not been very successful among many faculty members who are primarily concerned with academic issues, and it has failed to attract the attention of most who work in elite institutions, embrace a traditional collegial culture, and are attracted to collective bargaining only because of its potential preservation function.

Another factor identified by Ladd and Lipset (and also by Johnstone, 1981), is legislation from the 1960s that has enabled faculty (and other public officials) to strike. President Kennedy issued an executive order in 1962 that provided representation for federal employees. This order served as an impetus for a majority of state legislatures or governers to devise similar regulations covering their employees. "Though some unions were able to secure representation rights prior to the passage of such legislation," note Ladd and Lipset (1973, p. 4), "on the whole, full-fledged collective bargaining has occurred only after states have passed enabling legislation."

A final reason for the growth of collective bargaining is found in "the events of the sixties," according to Ladd and Lipset (1973, p. 4):

> The sudden growth of militant egalitarian movements among the intellectually oriented strata—including college students—related to the Civil Rights movement, and particularly to the opposition to the Viet Nam War, stimulated support for objectives identified with liberal-left ideology, such as student participation in institutional governance. Although this goal . . . has been supported by those with more liberal orientations, faculty and students, even of left persuasion, quickly came into conflict with each other. The thrust for student power challenged many traditional faculty prerogatives. And ironically, unionism in academe, though supported disproportionately by the more left-

inclined faculty, became a conservative force vis-a-vis
student power. Concerned with extending or preserv-
ing faculty power and privilege and with resisting
changes that might undermine them, professors found
the need to organize against pressures from students, as
well as from administrators and state officials.

Like Ladd and Lipset, Carr and Van Eyck (1973) speak of
faculty uncertainty over the student role in governance, whereas
Johnstone (1981) traces the issue of activism back to the faculty: he
finds that faculty (as well as students) have grown increasingly dis-
enchanted with institutions of all kinds and wish to find more
forceful and permanent ways to ensure their voice in the ongoing
operations of the school. The more conservative forces of the 1980s
and the post–Persian Gulf patriotism of the 1990s may have helped
academic leaders put to rest, set aside, or perhaps contain anti-
authority or antistudent attitudes from the 1960s; however, we
should not overlook the lingering effect of these early adulthood
experiences. Vietnam, the civil rights movement of the 1960s, and the
feminist movement of the 1970s and 1980s continue to play an important part in the collective memory of many academicians. They
continue to fuel the fire of student and faculty discontent and assure
the continuing presence of some form of the negotiating culture.

As this analysis suggests, the negotiating culture seems to be
firmly established in American colleges and universities—especially
the public ones. It serves not only as worthy adversary to those in
the managerial culture, but also as an alternative source of influence
and power for those faculty members who feel disenfranchised by
the established collegial culture. Some tension seems to be present,
however, about what the appropriate attitude of collective bargaining leaders should be toward the developmental culture. In
some colleges and universities, collective bargaining units have demanded the inclusion of development resources in faculty contracts;
they consider these resources to be part of the benefit package that
should be available to faculty members for their own career advancement and job security. In other institutions, the administration has argued for faculty development, whereas the collective
bargaining unit has fought against it, either as an administrative

ploy to retrain faculty in a new field or as an implied criticism of the existing levels of competence among faculty. Developmentally oriented faculty members often find themselves caught between these two positions. They would like their faculty, curriculum, or student development activities to remain outside the negotiated contract and propose that development should be a resource that benefits all parties. The developmental culture is advocating the establishment of joint union-management planning and cooperative programming in specific domains that do not represent problems for the vested interests of either party. In this way, the developmentalists wish to replicate the joint union-management "quality of work life" programs that have become popular in many corporate and public service organizations (Lawler, 1986).

The ambivalent attitude of many advocates of the negotiating culture about the developmental culture is quite understandable, given the claim by both that they offer the most reasonable response to the stressful conditions of contemporary higher education. Both the negotiating and developmental cultures grew out of a reaction against a dominant force in higher education. Yet they are fighting against different adversaries and in many ways have more in common with the adversarial culture than with each other. Eventually, faculty members oriented toward the negotiating and developmental cultures must come together to formulate common plans and integrate complementary assumptions about influence and change in higher education. Otherwise, both cultures will fail to provide needed corrections to the dominant collegial and managerial cultures.

Images and Myths of the Negotiating Culture

The real characteristics of the faculty member who is most attracted to the negotiating culture may not coincide with the images and myths of the general public about this culture. Kemerer and Baldridge (1975, p. 67) conclude from their study of institutional and individual determinants of faculty unionization:

> The faculty member most inclined to join a union . . .
> in general . . . will (1) teach at a two-year community

college or four-year public institution with no tradition of strong faculty participation in institutional
governance; (2) have a degree short of the doctorate
and be nontenured; (3) teach in the humanities or social science field; (4) be less than 40 years of age and
male; (5) have a greater teaching load and lower salary
than academics at four-year/graduate institutions; (6)
have a record of little participation in a campus senate
or similar body; (7) have low trust in the campus administration and be dissatisfied with working conditions (i.e., have low morale); (8) be conscious of the
benefits of unions on other campuses and of the nonacademic level on his own campus.

This archetypal faculty member comes from a discipline
closely affiliated with the collegial culture (in other words, the humanities or social sciences) but is estranged from this culture and
receives none of its benefits. One might expect faculty in vocational
fields to be most attracted to unionization, in view of the fact that
collective bargaining is found in many trades that are taught in
higher education (like electronics or auto mechanics). These fields,
however, are not the primary sources of faculty leadership in the
collective bargaining movement. Faculty in these areas may not
carry enough weight with their colleagues in academic fields, or
these faculty members may believe that they have left their trades
and their collective bargaining traditions behind in order to move
into the more "respectable" or professional (though often less prof-
itable) sphere of college-level teaching.

In the case study that follows, we will not see the direct
relationship between academic and vocational faculty, for this college's state system of higher education has separate community
colleges and vocational schools. Nevertheless, even with this segre-
gation, there are major differences within the college between those
from the traditional liberal arts and sciences and those from other
more professionally oriented schools. Furthermore, there is a pervasive sense of second-class citizenship among the faculty here
about the college's role in the state system—especially with regard
to competition for funds with other state universities and colleges.

Such a setting, as we shall see, provides ample opportunity for the creation of a strong and persistent negotiating culture.

Case Study: Plainsville Community College

Plainsville is a medium-sized institution (seven thousand students) located in a midwestern state. Students at Plainsville are usually of a more traditional age and socioeconomic level than one finds in most contemporary community colleges. A visit to Plainsville feels like a throwback to the 1950s. Students are young, white, and well behaved. Everything is orderly, even the request for an outside review of change processes at Plainsville. Like most "middle-class" institutions, however, the tranquility at Plainsville is only skin deep. This is a troubled institution.

A five-person consulting team was invited to conduct a study of organizational change at the institution. The team consisted of two outsiders and one representative each from the Plainsville faculty, administration, and staff. The team completed more than fifty interviews over a two-day period and reviewed many documents that had accumulated over the twenty-five-year history of Plainsville. Members of the consulting team reflected on their overall experiences in conducting the study while preparing an oral report for the Plainsville College community. The most common impression was one of competence and commitment. The personnel at Plainsville were of high quality and demonstrated a deeply felt concern for the welfare of the school. This general impression was contradicted, however, by an image of the college as a "smoldering fire."

After interviewing colleagues all day, one member of the team (who comes from the college) had a dream during the first night of the consultation in which he was coming to campus, only to find that the college was covered with a thick blanket of smoke. As he approached the campus, he noticed that the smoke was emanating from a series of fires that seemed to be continually burning. The fires were not large enough either to burn down the campus or to exhaust the available fuel supply; they just kept smoldering and in this way continued to obscure the campus. Long-term conflict and grievance appear to exist as a way of life on the Plainsville

College campus. Off-campus members of the study team often were confused about the dates of documents that they reviewed, as the problems of the college seem not to have changed over the past ten to fifteen years.

Men and women who have been at Plainsville for fewer than ten years indicate that it is hard to become accepted at this college. Inclusion takes place slowly, over a long period of time. A series of ongoing jokes at the college center on someone's being called a "new faculty member" or a "staff newcomer" even though they have been at the college for six or more years. There is apparently some truth in these humorous comments, for these people often feel like outsiders.

Faculty, staff, and administrators indicated that they "learn the game" at Plainsville primarily by trying to change something. They had to make a mistake and then understood what not to do in the future. Faculty members spoke of feeling embarrassed and even "set up" to make these mistakes. This dynamic seems to be present, for instance, in the assignment of responsible positions to new or uninformed members of the Plainsville community. Although formal power is given to the newcomer (as chair of a committee, for example), the person who formally or informally assigned this power remains offstage "pulling the strings." In this way, the old-timers remain insulated from negative reactions. Newcomers sometimes feel like "front men" who are being manipulated by those who are truly in charge at Plainsville. According to one faculty member, a "culture of shame" is prevalent at Plainsville. Several faculty members spoke of being accepted at the college only after making a fool of themselves at least once. The "game" requires the admission of ignorance and the willingness to throw oneself on the mercy of those who are more knowledgeable.

A longstanding pattern of interaction exists among faculty, administrators, and staff who have been at the college for many years. Several of those interviewed observed that after a person crosses over the barrier of acceptance, they behave the same as the old-timers toward new arrivals. Each of the old-timers seems to play a designated role vis-à-vis each campus constituency, and there is little room for any change in these designated roles.

Plainsville College faculty belong to a statewide faculty

union. This union is very active at Plainsville, and the faculty is often in conflict with the Plainsville administration. Mistrust between the opposing faculty and administrative factions at Plainsville exists at two levels. At worst, opponents are viewed as not to be trusted; they are seen as strong and able but in some manner evil or intent on accomplishing an unacceptable goal. A milder reaction is that opponents are "nice" but ineffective; their intentions could be trusted, but not their competence. These two levels often seem to shift at Plainsville. Members of the study team heard men and women described one minute as incompetent and the next as skillful but manipulative, or even malicious.

The study team came away from the interviews and observations with the general impression that both new and old members of the Plainsville community tend to be "de-skilled" by the organizational dynamics of the college. People who enter the campus quite competent and well intentioned must soon either make a mistake (in order to gain acceptance) or become threatening to (and isolated from) others on campus. In either case, faculty members or administrators have become less valuable resources to the college. They have either colluded with others to fit into a specific role and to join a particular faction, or they remain "newcomers" for many years, thereby avoiding any real engagement in the college community.

Few of the people who were interviewed indicated that they wanted to be more extensively involved in the community at Plainsville College. Yet their lack of interest appears to have much to do with the nature of this involvement. They would like to participate more if they did not feel like outsiders, if there were less conflict and contentiousness, or if their participation would elicit the more creative, esthetic, interpersonal, or intellectual sides of themselves and their colleagues.

The current lack of involvement by many faculty members and staff at Plainsville seems at least partially a function of the structure and formal policies of the school. Classes taught by the full-time faculty are usually held in the morning. In the afternoon, most full-time faculty leave campus to prepare lectures, grade papers, or read books. Some full-time faculty hold other jobs or have assumed major family (child-rearing) responsibilities (though these seem to be declining as faculty grow older).

Administrators and staff usually remain on campus all day. They often express some resentment toward faculty members' lack of commitment, as exhibited through their short days on campus and involvement in collective bargaining. It is difficult for full-time faculty to meet with each other or with administrators or staff because they are always teaching, holding office hours, or working off campus. Part-time instructors teach at the college in the evening and as a result have little contact with other faculty (full- or part-time), administrators, or staff. Plainsville faculty experience a lack of community due to the simple logistical problem of getting people together in one place at one time.

Administrators, faculty, and staff members at Plainsville speak of the "black hole" phenomenon at the college. Ideas are either lost "up the ladder" or are placed on hold for a future review that never occurs. This situation creates a serious communication problem that fuels faculty mistrust of administrators and subsequent reliance on collective bargaining safeguards. Faculty members note the failure of other faculty, as well as administrators, to answer their requests. Staff members speak of a similar lack of response from both administrators or faculty. Administrators describe the same failure of faculty or staff to provide information or commentary on recommendations they have made.

Faculty (and administrators) can accept the fact that their ideas will be turned down at times and appreciate the thoughtfulness of someone who gives them a detailed rationale for the negative decision that has been made. What angers them is the absence of any response at all. They prepare a carefully written personal request or serve on a committee that prepares a thoughtful proposal; they then send it to the proper authority or constituency. They wait for an answer. It is usually not forthcoming, and there appear to be no formal or informal rules on the Plainsville campus to ensure that receipt of a proposal is at least acknowledged.

A related communication issue concerns the failure to take the statements of others seriously. Faculty members and administrators talk about proposals offered by people whom they judge as "not serious." Their proposals are intended only to thwart their enemies. "How," asks one faculty member, "can I tell someone that I'm serious about a proposal and not trying to get back at him?" An overlapping problem is the presence of a loud minority and silent majority. In the privacy of personal interviews, faculty members, administrators, and staff talk of not agreeing with many of the colleagues who supposedly represent their interests. But they feel uncomfortable about expressing their disagreement, either because it would be viewed as a sign of disloyalty or because it would lead to conflict with and potential alienation from a community that was hard to enter in the first place. Men and women who are relatively new to the college or somewhat less forceful than their colleagues complain about committees consisting of the same old faces (whether faculty or administrators) and discussions composed of the same old arguments, without the input of alternative, unpolarized perspectives.

Plainsville College is filled with castes and cliques that discourage any form of communication, whether it be upward, downward, or lateral. The Plainsville caste system seems to have been formed by several of the organizational forces at this college. As previously noted, there is fundamental mistrust of people in other camps, which leads to unsubstantiated rumors and self-fulfilling prophecies. Moreover, there is little turnover among leaders of the various constituencies. The cliques are also the result of two other factors: the problems that people experience in being accepted by the college community and the alienation of the different constituencies from each other. All of these factors make genuine and productive communication difficult.

The processes and relationships of the personnel at Plainsville obviously interfere with the formation of community. The only sense of community comes from opposition and conflict. Faculty strikes are an occasion when people feel a bond with colleagues on their side of the issue. Faculty and administrators indicate that they have never experienced any kinship with all members of the campus community but have sometimes felt close to those who believe they have been similarly misunderstood or abused. In a few instances, faculty and administrators or faculty, administrators, and staff have met together to work on a project of common interest— for example, a joint faculty-administrator evening seminar on instruction. These meetings have been particularly vulnerable to dispute. Typically, one party has misunderstood the actions or motives of another party, and the joint venture has come to an abrupt halt. These undertakings have only worked when everyone has abandoned their traditional roles and "college business" is kept out of the discussion.

A lack of community might also be attributed in part to extensive commuting at the college. At Plainsville, as at Fairfield State College (see Chapter Four), people (in particular, the students and faculty) spend as little time as possible on campus. There is currently nothing that holds them there. Both faculty and students consider the absence of any demand for involvement or commitment one of the college's most attractive features. They can remain autonomous and have time to attend to other important commitments in their lives (family, work, avocation, community service).

Plainsville Community College also manifests an atmosphere of "grief." Members of the community feel hurt and betrayed by others and have found no expression for this grief, other than through conflict and litigation. These actions result in our dreamer's smoldering fires, which are never allowed to rage and therefore never fully burn themselves out. Rather than tears or gestures of support, the disappointment of Plainsville men and women is shown through anger and detachment. Some members of the college realize that they and their colleagues must find a different way of handling their pain. Although their anger is often justified and appropriately expressed, it is usually ineffective when expressed without an equal dose of compassion and understanding.

The Negotiating Culture in
Interaction with the Other Cultures

The pain and alienation felt by Plainsville's faculty and administration are not unusual. An analysis of the negotiating culture at Plainsville and its interaction with the other three cultures helps us better understand the nature of these feelings and perhaps enables us, in the developmentalist tradition, to ameliorate some of them.

Each of the four cultures exists at Plainsville. The collegial culture is to be found among the old-timers. They represent the spirit and hopes of the college. Many of these old-timers helped to found the college and develop its initial mission and curriculum.

Suburban community colleges in the United States were often established by collegially oriented faculty members who wanted to provide predominantly young, white, middle-class men and women with two years of solid academic programming. These faculty members (and their colleges) normally contrast quite dramatically with the institutional cultures and faculty of urban community colleges—especially those with vocational orientation. In the case of Plainsville Community College, there is general antipathy for (or no better than benevolent indifference to) the faculty and programs of several nearby vocational training institutes.

The collegially oriented faculty at Plainsville also create and maintain the complex and often dysfunctional political environment of the school. It is rather typical in American colleges for those most immersed in the collegial culture to be the guardians at the gate, both for students and for faculty entering the school. These faculty are likely to advocate high standards for student admissions, to be particularly critical of any efforts to reduce academic requirements, and to be fearful of admitting any students who might not enhance the reputation of the college. In a parallel fashion, they are likely to be just as reticent about inviting new faculty into their homes and into their inner circles at the college.

The managerial culture at Plainsville Community College is particularly evident in the treatment of part-time faculty by the administration and in administrative attitudes regarding collective bargaining. Many of the academic administrators at Plainsville spoke quite favorably about part-time faculty. Initially, they identified the substantial cost savings associated with hiring an instructor to teach a specific course at a particular time of day. They also often suggested that these part-time faculty members were better teachers, because they were connected with the "real world" and had not yet lost their enthusiasm for teaching and interacting with students. The part-time faculty, unlike the full-timers, were willing (even eager) to teach in the evenings and on weekends. The full-time faculty wanted to teach during the morning, when many students at Plainsville (regardless of age or socioeconomic level) are working. Courses taught by full-time faculty are often half full or are canceled (and by union contract are not replaced by other courses).

Even with all of these advantages, the major reason that academic administrators at Plainsville seem to like part-time faculty is that these men and women (often coming out of corporate settings) are willing to be treated as employees and subordinates and to acknowledge the authority of administrators over curricular matters at the college. Part-time faculty members consult administrators about what is to be taught in a course and about how to teach it. They are open to suggestions made by academic administrators and often are willing to adjust their schedules or course content to accommodate other faculty, courses, and institutional priorities. They get their grades in on time and rarely complain about working conditions or salary.

The full-time faculty members, by contrast, tend to think of academic administrators as reluctant staff to the faculty. These faculty do not see themselves as subordinate to the administrators and deeply resent any attempts by them to influence course content or scheduling. As we have seen, they perceive any interference as a violation of academic freedom. Whereas most part-time faculty members are accustomed to a managerial culture in their own daily work environments, full-time faculty members have often grown up in and never left behind an image of an academic institution dominated by the collegial culture.

Yet there is one group of full-time faculty members who do acknowledge the role of academic administrators as the authority figures at Plainsville Community College. These faculty members are imbued with the spirit of the negotiating culture and perceive the administrators at Plainsville to be their enemies and the source of misunderstanding and conflict at the college. As noted in the first section of this chapter, many of the leaders of the faculty union at Plainsville, and at other American colleges and universities, are disaffected members of the collegial culture. They have often served for a few years in the Plainsville faculty senate and have a long history of work on collegewide general educational requirements, student advising, departmental leadership, or institutional self-studies (for regional accreditation). However, having found them to be worthless or, at best, short-term, ameliorative solutions to the basic problems of the college, these academics have been inactive in these areas for many years.

For faculty union leaders at Plainsville, the central problems are created and perpetuated by the inadequate and insensitive administrators of the college. They speak derisively and with bitter sarcasm about their "good-hearted" president, who on the one hand formally encourages faculty and academic excellence but cuts academic budgets and attempts to fire tenured faculty members on the other. They speak of an academic dean who will not stand up for their rights when negotiating with the president or when meeting with the chancellor and vice chancellors of the state system. For these faculty members, the only way to exert influence and protect personal and collective rights is through the organization of a faculty union and through absolute obedience to this union on the part of all full-time faculty members at the college.

Individual faculty members in the union will speak candidly about the stereotyping that is done by faculty (and administrators) at Plainsville and will admit to differences of opinion with their colleagues about academic matters. This is a remnant of their old allegiances to the give-and-take of the collegial culture. These faculty members also emphasize, however, the critical role played by unity of purpose and opinion when confronting the administration at Plainsville. They speak of specific members of the administration who try to break up the faculty's alliance by befriending individuals or by offering grants, rewards, or professional development opportunities to specific faculty members.

Thus, any attempt by academic administrators at Plainsville to make overtures of support and conciliation to individual faculty or small groups of faculty members is viewed by union members as a strategy of "divide and conquer." Furthermore, any efforts by individual faculty members to bring academics and administrators together to share perspectives or to solve problems are judged to be collusive and self-serving and an act of betrayal.

Those faculty members who joined the consulting team for this project were viewed with considerable suspicion and anger by many members of the faculty union. The team and the faculty members (and administrators) who brought in the team were not, however, representative of the managerial culture, as members of the faculty union suspected. Rather, they represented the developmental culture. These developmentalists, both inside and outside the culture, would (to paraphrase Shakespeare) place a curse on all the three other houses: collegial, managerial, and negotiating. None of these three cultures at Plainsville supports rational problem solving, systematic planning, or constructive conflict management. According to the developmentalists at Plainsville, each of these cultures has encouraged misperception, manipulation, and disorganization.

For representatives of the developmental culture, there were simple and straightforward solutions to the problems at Plainsville Community College. These solutions involved the encouragement of more direct confrontation among various constituencies (particularly faculty and administrators), with the assistance of outside mediation. Members of the consulting team also called for clearer and more consistently applied policies and procedures at the college and for identification of areas in which faculty and administrators could work on shared problems and mutually beneficial projects (Lawler, 1986).

Are these really appropriate answers to the problems that face a college such as Plainsville, given that this college is controlled by the negotiating culture? Are those in the developmental culture not just as blind as others to the realities of the college and its negotiating culture? Perhaps the developmentalists at Plainsville hold a false assumption that there are areas of shared interest and concern at the college. In their attempt to bring various parties together, they may fail to acknowledge that there are major, unavoidable, and unresolvable differences between the faculty and administration—particularly with regard to the distribution and use of authority and to the allocation of scarce resources (including salaries, benefits, and departmental budgets).

The consulting team at Plainsville was not very successful in convincing members of the institution about the value of the developmental culture or in persuading them that any of their rational problem-solving, planning, or conflict-resolution strategies were viable. Moreover, the developmental culture was no more helpful than the other three in responding to several perplexing and lingering problems related to the four cultures, (in particular, the negotiating culture).

At the heart of the matter lies the question: why do the fires at Plainsville continue to smolder? Why does the negotiating culture remain so powerful? After all, it has been ineffective in either reducing or bringing much administrative attention to the sources of tension on campus or in building a sense of community for all faculty (old and new). One answer may be found in the ambivalence of faculty and administrators at the college. Plainsville faculty and administrators tend to embrace all four cultures themselves. They believe in the collegial culture. Yet what about planning and organization? What about building a rational data base? They all hate the administration–faculty union conflict but feel a need for accountability and for protection from excessive accountability. Even if they come from management, they are usually politically liberal and believe in the principle of unionization. Yet both faculty and administrators at Plainsville are paid adequate salaries; many are established in the community and wish to avoid upsetting the status quo. Neither faculty nor administrators want to define themselves merely as workers or wage earners.

Furthermore, each culture has a tendency to feed off its opposing one and needs to be viable. At Plainsville, advocates of the strong negotiating culture (in the form of the faculty union) require worthy adversaries among the administrators representing the managerial culture. A vigorous negotiation culture requires the presence of a major enemy. Only then can significant sacrifices (such as the loss of friendship with members of the enemy camp) be justified. Only with a worthy enemy can one require that internal differences of opinion and individuality be set aside or repressed for the sake of unity and ultimate victory over the other group (Bion, 1974).

A second perspective centers on stagnation at the college. There is no staff turnover or much upward mobility at Plainsville. Many of the faculty and administrators began their careers at the college when it was newly formed or still young. They have been in the same job for more than fifteen years. No one really matures in this collegiate family, and no one leaves home. As we saw earlier, they remain in the same old roles to continue fighting the same battles for years. One is reminded of an episode from the original *Star Trek* television series in which the protagonist chooses to spend the rest of eternity struggling with his double, who is endowed with the same amount of strength and knowledge. The protagonist decides to enter this "livng hell," like most people who enter the negotiating culture, in order to save the universe. (In the real world, of course, one's foes probably have intentions that are just as admirable as one's own.) Though neither our *Star Trek* protagonist nor his double will ever succeed, each must continue to struggle forever. At Plainsville people take their places within fixed, antagonistic positions, which lead to the solidification of the negotiating (and managerial) cultures and affiliations with specific cultures. Old stories are rehearsed and repeatedly told, thereby reinforcing the status quo.

A third possible reason for Plainsville's difficulties is the lack of support for newcomers at the college. These men and women often come to the college with loyalty to the collegial, managerial, or even developmental culture. We have seen that they often make the mistake of trying to bring different parties together—an error that is the initiation rite of the college. The faculty member who convened the consulting team is a "newcomer" (having only been at Plainsville for six years). At a minimum, her action was somewhat naive. According to many people on campus, however, her true blunder consisted of bringing together men and women who represent different factions and cultures. She "made a mess of things," remarks one of the old-timers, by asking faculty and administrators to listen to one another's perceptions of the college's pressing problems and by suggesting that no one constituency is to blame for those problems. Alternative cultures and the ideas associated with them are stifled at Plainsville and at many other colleges and universities when newcomers are discouraged from taking risks or providing fresh perspectives.

A fourth reason for the lingering conflict at Plainsville concerns the "black hole" at this college. As noted earlier in the chapter, people's ideas are rarely accepted or even acknowledged. One possible explanation for the black hole has to do with distorted communication between advocates of the negotiating culture and those who originally come from either the collegial or developmental culture. Though supporters of the negotiating culture can understand (if not agree with) many of the terms and principles employed in the managerial culture, they are often confused by those of the collegial and developmental cultures. Sometimes phrases mean something different in all four cultures (for example, "academic freedom"). Miscommunication that occurs in this way often leads to misunderstanding.

What are the possible responses to these questions and problems for the faculty, staff, and administrators of Plainsville? How might the plot of this long-running play be altered and their long-standing roles and positions be altered or even exchanged? How might the new words be heard, understood, and acted upon? This is clearly one of the major challenges associated specifically with the negotiating culture. If it is to serve a constructive role in higher education, then it must be ready to work more cooperatively with the other three cultures of the academy. Like many other troubled academic institutions, Plainsville's complex and seemingly unyielding problems can be addressed effectively only if all four perspectives are brought to bear on their solution.

9

❖❖❖❖❖❖❖

Living and Working in the Negotiating Culture

Two major values dominate the negotiating culture: equity and egalitarianism. These values are often antithetical to those held by representatives of the dominant collegial culture. Carr and Van Eyck (1973, pp. 265–266) comment that in the traditional (collegial) culture of higher education:

> Every profession commits itself to quality. Practitioners must meet certain basic standards of performance in order to gain admission to and (in theory at least) to remain in the profession, and, beyond the basic standards, the individual is challenged to make a unique contribution to the total effort and achievement of the profession. Every useful definition or description of a profession stresses the importance of the individual in the life and work of the group. . . . Indeed, the line between the professions and the so-called semiprofessions is said to depend in significant degree on the replaceability factor. . . . The academic profession clearly places a high value on individuality—on the belief that at least the best of its practitioners are not readily interchanged or replaced. In the main it believes that there are different levels of quality and excellence which individuals can aspire to and reach.

152

Carr and Van Eyck suggest that this tradition of individuality runs contrary to the collective bargaining tradition of egalitarianism. Collective bargaining agents favor policies and procedures that treat all faculty members alike. Such an approach tends to homogenize the distinctive features and differing levels of quality among faculty members. Although, as Carr and Van Eyck observe (1973), there is not strong evidence that collective bargaining has a leveling effect on faculty performance, the values of individuality and egalitarianism seemingly come into immediate and inevitable conflict in the interaction between collegial and negotiating cultures. The developmental culture shares with the negotiating culture its commitment to both equity and egalitarianism, but they support quite different strategies for achieving these values.

The issue of academic freedom is also controversial in a negotiating culture. Carr and Van Eyck (1973, p. 276) conclude that "academic freedom and tenure are clearly 'conditions of employment' and are thus negotiable at the bargaining table," whereas in the collegial culture, the concepts of academic freedom and tenure are givens that are never negotiable in any setting. The issue is further exacerbated by the problem of required membership in a faculty union that has won collective bargaining rights (Carr and Van Eyck, 1973, p. 281): "What is to be done with the faculty member who refuses to join the faculty union, or even to pay dues or a 'fee' to the union without joining it, because he objects to the compulsory arrangement either on principle or for more practical reasons? The law would require that he be dismissed from his position, yet . . . [no] recognized formulation of the principle of academic freedom condones any such reason for the dismissal of a college teacher, tenured or probationary."

Thus, though the negotiating culture was initiated in reaction to the managerial culture, it shares with it the belief that anything with regard to educational programs and priorities is negotiable. Both the collegial and developmental cultures, by contrast, are based on the belief that certain features of the academic enterprise are not negotiable. The developmental culture, in particular, views the compromise inherent in quasi-political negotiations as offensive and inappropriate in an academic institution.

Qualities of Leadership

Kemerer and Baldridge (1975) note that collective bargaining affects both the formulation of organizational rules and the interpretation and adjudication of these rules through grievance and arbitration procedures. As a result, the power of formal managerial leadership in the institution, in one sense, is reduced. Upper-level academic administrators are prevented from making arbitrary decisions and must always keep in mind the welfare of faculty (at least as interpreted by leaders of the collective bargaining unit) when formulating institutional plans.

The presence of collective bargaining on a college or university campus also complicates the roles of mid-level academic administrators. Collective bargaining is particularly troublesome for the department chair or head. On which side of the bargaining table should this person sit? Usually the chair has been selected by colleagues within the department and will return to a regular faculty position within several years. The position of department chair in most collegiate institutions is not even full-time; the chair spends at least one-half of his or her time teaching and doing research. Yet department chairs do have to make personnel decisions, work with budgets, meet regularly with the dean, and supervise secretarial and clerical workers in the department—managerial functions in most organizations. Thus, the department chair often gets caught in the middle during collective bargaining.

Even when managers (or heads) of academic departments have been selected by a dean rather than by department colleagues, they are caught in the middle, along with deans, assistant deans, budget officers, and others in middle management. As Kemerer and Baldridge (1975, p. 189) have observed: "In most instances, middle-level administrators are not included in either faculty bargaining units or at the bargaining table as part of the employer contingent. Yet, the decisions reached through bargaining affect their salaries and fringe benefits, their professional roles, and their managerial responsibilities. Middle-level administrators consequently fear being squeezed between the opposing forces of collective bargaining and economic retrenchment."

At one level, collective bargaining reduces the power of academic administrators of a college or university; on another level, it reinforces their authority. The managerial and negotiating cultures are interdependent. Gregory Bateson (1972) speaks of this process as complementary "schizomogenesis": as one culture becomes stronger, so does its opposing culture. Because each culture needs the other to survive and to have an identity, they become inextricably linked (Bateson, 1972). Conflict is inevitable and essential to both cultures while also strengthening both.

With regard to ways in which collective bargaining does or can strengthen governing boards, Carr and Van Eyck (1973, pp. 250-252) suggest:

> Collective bargaining will increase the authority and influence of the members of an institution's governing board at a time in higher education when many observers are questioning the continuing usefulness of lay boards and have been noting signs that their role has been declining. The reason for this countertrend is basic. Collective bargaining is a relationship between two adversaries—management and labor. The governing board is management. It possesses and must exercise the responsibility at the institutional level of deciding what is acceptable to management regarding the very wide range of issues that are negotiable at the bargaining table. . . . The governing board must decide how far it will go in meeting the faculty's demands and also whether it will make demands of its own and insist on some degree of tradeoff in the final contract.

Kemerer and Baldridge (1975, pp. 170-171) proposed that college and university administrators will also be in stronger positions as a result of the move toward faculty unionization, for collective bargaining forces a centralization of authority and control in most organizations:

> Until recently, most large four-year institutions were decentralized, with departments, schools, and colleges

traditionally involved in institutional decision making. . . . In both public and private institutions, coordination and centralization of policy making, particularly on economic issues, has moved upward from
departments, to schools, to the central administration
and ultimately to off-campus authorities. . . . In addition to these forces, faculty collective bargaining helps
to push power upward, for boards and administrators
function as "employers" involved in governance. It is
conceivable that some administrations and boards
may reclaim authority once granted to faculty senates
in order to bargain effectively with a faculty union.

The third beneficiary of faculty unionization is mid-level
management—the bureaucratic structure—of the college or university. Though, as we noted above, mid-level managers are often
caught between the two bargaining units, they also can play a key
role as mediators of the conflict and as expeditors of negotiated
policies and procedures. Kemerer and Baldridge (1975) suggest that
bureaucratic red tape increases as procedural rules become more
precise and binding. Though decisions are less likely to be made at
a middle level, instead of being pushed up the line to top management, the actual implementation of the new bureaucracy is in the
hands of the mid-level managers.

We have attended primarily to the impact of collective bargaining on managerial leadership. The issue of faculty leadership,
is obviously also important. A negotiating culture tends to attract
and foster a different type of faculty leadership than does either the
collegial or developmental culture. On the one hand, faculty
members who assume leadership for collective bargaining units
often share with those in the managerial culture a concern for formal structure and procedures. They are interested, and often skillful, in collaborating with many different kinds of people to
accomplish a specific task. On the other hand, collegial faculty
often seem more disposed to work with ideas or with like-minded
faculty members, not so much to achieve some objective as to share
opinions. Developmental faculty also appear more interested in the

process of working with people than with the accomplishment of any specific task.

Faculty members who lead collective bargaining units share with managerial leaders a long-term commitment to their leadership positions. Whereas faculty in the collegial culture are supposed to be reticent about accepting formal leadership responsibilities (being in some sense "called" to these positions for a limited period of time by colleagues), the leaders of collective bargaining units are allowed to indicate their interest. Similarly, faculty in the developmental culture are not supposed to be drawn to leadership or the use of power and persuasion (at least as overtly expressed in formal administrative positions), whereas faculty in unions are accustomed to using power and persuasion in confronting collegiate management. Hence, the latter usually feel comfortable in seeking out and using these resources in attaining leadership within the union.

Unfortunately, most of these faculty leaders have nowhere to go in the union hierarchy. Unlike other unions, there is no extensively staffed national organization to which they can advance after successful performance at the local collegiate union. Many faculty union leaders soon reach the frustrating point of either having to step down as head of the local union (and returning to teaching) or hindering the advancement of others who also wish to move into positions of union leadership. Some leaders of collective bargaining units therefore decide to make the difficult transition from union to management and join the ranks of academic administration.

Assumptions About Institutional Influence and Change

Academic senates and collective bargaining units represent two quite distinct and often incompatible sources of faculty power on a college or university campus. Attempts to make faculty unions out of faculty senates have usually been unsuccessful. Kemerer and Baldridge (1975, p. 142) conclude, "Most senate attempts to usurp traditional union functions will probably be challenged successfully, particularly if the senate has not previously or consistently dealt with economic issues and working conditions." As a rule, the protectionist academics who generally provide leadership in faculty senates hold very little credibility among the deprivation-motivated faculty who start and lead faculty unions.

Kemerer and Baldridge (1975, pp. 29–30) directly address the question of compatibility between collegial and negotiating strategies for influencing collegiate organizations:

> Is collective bargaining compatible with the concepts of collegiality, such as shared governance, professional expertise, and collegial decision-making? . . . In certain institutions, ideas of faculty participation in governance and shared, collegial decision making have always been fictional, for the institutions were actually managed by strong administrators and trustees. Such a pattern of administrative dominance is characteristic of many community colleges, state colleges, and private liberal arts colleges. In institutions where academic collegiality has been a myth, collective bargaining may promote faculty rights and collegial decision making.
>
> Despite the benefits that unionization may bring to some institutions, it is nevertheless true that collective bargaining may threaten some collegial practices. In institutions with long histories of faculty rights, shared governance, and peer judgment, unionization may weaken faculty professionalism, because many collective bargaining practices are in opposition to academic collegiality. In particular, collective bargaining does not accept the presumption of shared governance, which is central to academic collegiality. Instead collective bargaining divides the world into a we-they dichotomy, recognizing that people's perceptions and interests depend largely on their positions within organizations. The best way to guarantee shared decision making, according to many union advocates, is to mandate it in a legally binding contract.

Faculty unions, however, do not necessarily mean the demise of faculty governance systems. Rather, as Kemerer and Baldridge

(1975) observe, collective bargaining typically flourishes in a setting in which faculty participation in governance has been inconsistent and ineffectual. Faculty senates tend to be strong in colleges and universities that have no need for collective bargaining. These are settings in which the collegial culture reigns supreme.

Accountability

At a very basic level, faculty unionization and faculty performance evaluation are in conflict. According to Kemerer and Baldridge (1975, pp. 132–133):

> Unions have many goals, but during a financial crisis, the prime goals are job security and gaining economic benefits. These goals pose a dilemma for academic professionalism because they are complicated by the faculty's traditional responsibility to evaluate professional competence and performance. . . . The major negative consequence of faculty unionism may be a protectionist, job-security orientation that could thwart personnel policies so that incompetency is protected and seniority, not merit, becomes the main decision-making criterion. . . . In discussing this controversial issue we must emphasize both sides of the issue, for in the past evaluation procedures have been unclear, arbitrary, and in many cases indefensible. In short, the older unprofessional procedure of "nonrenewals by default" and by administrative arbitrariness was all too common. Unions have every right, even an obligation, to fight against such processes. Nevertheless, the opposite extreme of "promotion and tenure by default" is equally unprofessional. Somewhere between the two extremes must be a compromise that protects the individual against unreasonable and arbitrary procedures while simultaneously protecting the institution and its students against personnel decisions that occur by default.

In essence, members of the negotiating culture could be said to have no models of performance evaluation. Instead, they have confronted the inappropriate or inequitable use of performance evaluations by members of the managerial culture. Most thoughtful members of the negotiating culture hope, in line with Kemerer and Baldridge's statement above, that their monitoring of managerial practices will yield an effective evaluation system that serves the interests of both the faculty member and institution. In this regard, members of the negotiating culture hold the same optimistic assumption as those in the developmental culture about the ultimate compatibility between personal and organizational well-being.

The negotiating culture also shares an optimism with the other three cultures regarding its ultimate ability to solve the pressing problems of contemporary colleges and universities. As we shall see in the following case study, individual faculty members (and administrators) often move from one culture to another to see if any of them can really deliver on this promise.

Case Study: Bernie Kefelmann

Bernie Kefelmann's life has been shaped by the German Holocaust. His actions and values in the 1990s reflect the haunting impact of being driven out of Germany as a young Jewish boy of two. He arrived in the United States with his mother in 1936; his father was not able to leave Germany and has not been heard from since 1937. Kefelmann received his doctorate from a midwestern university in 1956 and taught philosophy at several large universities between 1957 and 1967.

Since 1967, Bernie Kefelmann has taught at a moderately large state college located in an eastern city in the United States. He is no longer active as a philosopher, though he still teaches excellent introductory courses in philosophy and logic for nonmajors. His primary focus is more political in nature. In a quiet but impressive manner, Kefelmann has become a major leader in the faculty union at his institution (Ferron State College). He is currently leading the faculty at Ferron in its fight against large budgetary cutbacks that would produce both salary freezes and layoffs.

Kefelmann is very frustrated in his current work. He experiences major conflicts between his desire for a contemplative life and his abiding concern for social justice. The current budgetary cutbacks will not directly affect him, but Kefelmann is unwilling to sit back and watch his young colleagues lose their jobs or receive inadequate wages. He wonders if he should retire early (he is expected to retire in six years), so that room might be made for one of his young colleagues who deserves a tenure track position at Ferron.

Unfortunately, Kefelmann may not have sufficient funds to retire at an early age. His salary has never been particularly substantial, and he has done no moonlighting over the years, unlike many of his colleagues in business and the physical and biological sciences. He is also worried about a possible lack of sustained stimulation if he should depart from the college. Would he atrophy intellectually if deprived of daily contact with his colleagues? Is there a way that Kefelmann can remain at Ferron College without taking up the tenure track slot that should be made available to a younger, deserving colleague?

The Negotiating Culture in Interaction with the Other Cultures

Bernie Kefelmann, like many other faculty members who are attracted to the negotiating culture, views collective bargaining as a matter of social justice and principle, rather than simply a means of obtaining better salaries and working conditions. These faculty members are the preservation-oriented representatives of collective bargaining that Kemerer and Baldridge have identified (see Chapter Eight). By contrast, Jim Herbert (See Chapter Three) was willing to join the faculty union at Western State only because of its potential to improve his compensation. Herbert exemplifies Kemerer and Baldridge's deprivation group. Kefelmann is willing not only to join but also to lead his faculty union at Ferron. He firmly believes that formal authority must always be monitored and held in check. Economic repression will inevitably rear its ugly head under conditions of differential power unless those with less authority take collective action and look after one another's welfare.

For many academics in the negotiating culture, the rise of

faculty unionization is linked to the social unrest and student protests of the late 1960s. In many ways, faculty collective bargaining
is part of an old tradition of social awareness and action in academic
settings. In this instance, however, social action is being taken
against a constituency inside the academy—the administration—
rather than an outside adversary, as has traditionally been the case
with academics (as far back as the open-air debates at Oxford University and many German universities more than a century ago). For
Bernie Kefelmann and others at Ferron who feel as he does, faculty
unions are an expression of their social concerns and their criticism
of contemporary Western institutions.

For other faculty members (especially those in vocational
education programs) the union movement represents a quite different set of concerns (the deprivation perspective). They firmly believe
that salaries for trade instructors should be comparable to those that
their years of seniority would entitle them to in the "real world."
These faculty members generally look with dismay or at least suspicion on their more socially active, academic colleagues who wish
to use the union to make political statements about external matters. Bernie Kefelmann does not have to bridge these two worlds in
his college; however, many leaders of faculty collective bargaining
units in community colleges must constantly attempt to reconcile
Kemerer and Baldridge's preservation and deprivation perspectives.

As an older faculty member who has been influenced by both
the collegial and negotiating cultures, Bernie Kefelmann wants to
help young faculty members. Both cultures urge support and concern for the welfare of other faculty members (though both in their
more virulent forms establish old-boy networks and block the advancement of younger faculty). Kefelmann finds himself an imped-
iment to the career advancement of younger faculty members at
Ferron State College. Under stable or even declining enrollment
conditions, many colleges and universities cannot expand the
number of faculty positions; thus, they are unable to hire new faculty members until the old ones retire, are transferred to other positions, or are asked to resign.

The case study of Bernie Kefelmann illustrates the shifting
interests and styles of faculty members over a lifetime of work in the
academic enterprise. What has kept Bernie an interesting, dynamic

teacher all of these years? How does he remain a successful instructor in introductory courses, even though he has taught them many times, over many years? Other faculty members, like Jim Herbert and Kevin Reynolds, lost interest in undergraduate instruction. Bernie Kefelmann did not. Somehow he has managed to find new challenges and variety in his teaching. Perhaps his interest in collective bargaining has enabled him to maintain his vitality as a teacher, as negotiation requires a different set of skills and involves contact with different people. Do faculty members in the collegial culture who devote considerable attention to faculty senate responsibilities also find a way to remain committed teachers and counselors of students? Or are they escaping to the senate meetings because their teaching and counseling have become boring?

Leaders of American colleges and universities must find ways to help faculty remain interesting and motivated teachers over a lifetime. Alternatively, they must devise ways so that faculty members can more easily enter and exit higher education. If a faculty member remains inside the academy, he or she must span the collegial, managerial, developmental, and negotiating cultures—in the process making use of the valuable perspectives and resources to be found in each. In this bridging of cultures, faculty members who remain loyal to the academy can find sufficient challenge and variety to remain vital and informed.

Part Two

❖❖❖❖❖❖❖❖❖❖❖❖❖❖

Leadership Strategies for Academic Organizations

10

❖❖❖❖❖❖❖

Engaging the Four Cultures in Organizational Improvement

How does one improve the quality of life and educational service at an institution such as Plainsville Community College that incorporates all four diverse and often antagonistic academic cultures? What are methods that one can use to work more successfully with the faculty and administrators of Mountain State University—or to help Peter Armantrout or Ellen Vargas find their current academic work more meaningful or at least less burdensome? How does one avoid the pitfalls of an institution like Canon College that finds itself with funds that it does not know how to use? Like the colleges and universities that we have featured in this book, many noneducational organizations increasingly find themselves faced with changing environments (shifting consumer interests, fluctuating economic conditions, and so forth). They also must cope more effectively with their own internal transitions. Organizational development is a concept and process valued in many environments as a tool that leaders can use to deal with these internal changes and with the personal and interpersonal stress they cause. It has gained substantial and growing credibility in meeting these needs in American corporations, human service agencies, and school systems (see, for example, Likert, 1967; French and Bell, 1978; Burke, 1982, 1987).

Furthermore, many corporations, human service agencies, and schools are peopled (like our case-study colleges and universities) by workers with evolving values. Many employees now hold an implicit "psychological contract" (Schein, 1980) with their employers that requires their greater involvement in the decision-making processes of the organization and more meaningful work. Organizational development tools and procedures can be beneficial to employers in addressing these new expectations and needs, as well as assisting employees to articulate their expectations more clearly and constructively.

Finally, and perhaps most importantly, we live in a culture that seems to be particularly directed toward individualism (Bellah and others, 1985). We seem to value individual rights much more than interpersonal responsibility (Gilligan, 1982). As a result, our organizations often lack the "glue" that is found in cultures oriented toward collective welfare and interpersonal responsibility (such as is the case in most countries outside of northern Europe and the United States). American companies risk falling apart, due to the lack of sufficient attention to the ways in which employees can contribute to the overall well-being of their fellow workers. It is not just conditions at Plainsville Community College or at Fairfield College that drive students and faculty away. We find the same alienating forces in many other contemporary organizations.

In many ways, organizational development can be the new glue that binds people together or at least reminds them of the important role played by interpersonal relationships, group decision making, and effective communication. Organizational development certainly cannot compensate for the deeply felt sense of alienation in highly individualistic organizations; however, it does help and is often valued precisely because it seems to counterbalance the pull toward isolation in modern American organizations.

Organizational Development in Higher Education

In view of organizational development's apparent advantages, it is surprising that with minor exceptions (Boyer and Crockett, 1973; Sikes, Schlesinger, and Seashore, 1974; Lindquist, 1978a, 1978b; Bergquist and Armstrong, 1986), few colleges or universities now make use of this valuable behavioral science tool. Why do American colleges and universities avoid organizational development? They certainly are experiencing the stresses associated with change, as we have shown in our discussion of the four cultures and as illustrated in the case studies we have presented. American colleges and universities are also filled with men and women who advocate the values of participation and meaningful work and are experiencing the alienation associated with rampant individualism. When one examines the resistance in the academy to the principles and practices of organizational development, three main hindrances become apparent. All three of these are related to the four cultures we have previously identified.

First, as we noted in our discussion of the collegial culture, higher education is the bastion of rationality in American society (Parsons and Platt, 1973). The collegial culture holds sway over the norms and values of most American colleges and universities. Our students learn about the importance of rational thought and discourse; they are repeatedly taught that irrational, intuitive decision making has disastrous consequences in the laboratory, as well as in the halls of Congress and the White House. This focus on rationality seems to contradict an emphasis on feelings and relationships that is found in the field of organizational development (and more generally in the developmental culture). Many academicians firmly believe that carefully researched and formulated policies and procedures will win over rational, dedicated colleagues. Jack Lindquist (1978b, p. 2) clearly articulates the assumptions underlying this strategy: "Since we change on the basis of reason and evidence, the best way to obtain alterations in attitudes and behavior is to invest in systematic research and development of new knowledge, new practices, new products. Apply a rational process to attain a rational end. If the research is correct and the development sound, the proposed change will sell itself."

Any attempt to formulate a strategy (Havelock and Lindquist's social interaction and human problem-solving models—see Chapter Ten) for presenting a new idea that takes into account the personal interests and expectations of other parties, or that involves group review and negotiation, is considered a retreat into the undesirable realm of "campus politics" or, worse yet, "group think."

Second, the concept of autonomy (another ingredient of the collegial culture) is widely accepted in American colleges and universities. Allegiance to this concept accounts for and increases the alienation many academicians feel; it also prevents the collaboration and problem solving that might best reduce this alienation. Many faculty and administrators enter American colleges and universities precisely because they wish to be left alone to pursue their own teaching, research, writing, or ideas. Though they may regret this choice as they grow older, they are creatures of habit who do not easily change the way they relate to other people or wish to learn the skills needed in a more collaborative environment.

Finally, the colleges and universities of the United States often do not have sufficient financial resources to mount a major organizational development effort. Other human service agencies that are also strapped for funds somehow find the funds to support organizational development; but colleges and universities, under the guidance of the managerial culture, often encounter so many other demands for limited and often declining funds that they have little interest in taking the major risk associated with establishing an organizational development program. Thus, we find that the colleges and universities that provide many organizational development consultants for American corporations, hospitals, churches, and schools do not themselves make use of these services. The prophet remains unheard and misunderstood in his or her own institution.

Given that organizational development is often blocked by financial realities, by the false images that academicians hold about this behavioral science technique, and by the collegial and managerial cultures, how are we to create conditions for the use of these tools? We have three choices. First, we can ignore the four cultures of the academy and push ahead with organizational development strategies. The resistance exerted by at least three of the cultures (the developmental culture being quite supportive of this approach) can perhaps be overcome by particularly skillful organizational consultants (usually from outside the institution). Second, we can attempt to alter one or more of these four cultures, through the use of organizational development techniques. We have little experience to date that would lead us to expect that either of these approaches might be successful. The academic cultures are much too powerful to be either ignored or readily modified.

A third approach holds more promise: making use of the unique perspectives and strengths of each, we can actively engage all four cultures in the processes of organizational development. To take this approach, however, requires an alteration in the ways that organizational development is usually conducted. We must use new tools and concepts regarding organizational change, stabilization, innovation, and analysis that are compatible with the four cultures if we are to engage them in the processes of institutional improvement. The remainder of this chapter and the final two chapters of this book concern the task of identifying these new methods and ideas. We begin with a brief review of the central concepts that govern our thoughts about organizational development. We then introduce two principles regarding organizational change and stabilization that begin to move us beyond our current notions.

Organizational Development: Three Schools of Thought

If we are to expand and modify the tools of organizational development for use in collegiate settings, what is the nature of these tools, and how are they now being used? First, it is important to note that the term *organizational development* tends to be a bit elusive, having been claimed by several different schools of thought with varying perspectives on organizational functioning. One school, endorsing the human relations or American perspective, begins with the assumption that the individual is central to all group and organizational life. For the American school (often identified with the NTL Institute near Washington, D.C.), one improves the functioning of groups and organizations primarily through increasing the skills and knowledge of individual members. Building on the American behaviorist tradition, practitioners in this school emphasize the observable (and therefore changeable) behavior of individuals in groups and organizations. Principles of social psychology (such as situationally based leadership, group norms, stages of group development, and communication patterns) inform these pragmatic and generally optimistic practitioners.

The group relations or British school of organizational development begins with the premise that the group (rather than the individual) is the basic unit in any analysis of organizational life.

Operating from the perspective of this school (often identified with the Tavistock Institute near London), a practitioner will focus on how the unconscious life of the group influences the behavior of its individual members. One will not be successful in improving the effectiveness of a group or organization merely by providing members with new skills and knowledge, for other group members will soon collude unconsciously to rob this member of his or her new skills. Principles of systems theory (such as homeostasis, boundary maintenance, differentiation and integration, and transformation) are combined with psychoanalytic principles (primarily from the Kleinian school of object relations). This school provides a sometimes sobering influence on those who seek to bring about change in organizations. The school's adherents are often pessimistic about the ability or even the desirability of major organizational change and point to the need for a full understanding of the culture and system dynamics of an organization before attempting any development efforts.

The third school does not have a convenient label, for it seems to be newly emerging as a coherent perspective on organizational life. Perhaps best defined as the social-cultural or continental school, it places chief emphasis on such value-related issues as what the purpose of change should be and who should control the organizational development process. Advocates of this school often point to the use of organizational development as a means of placating (Goffman, 1952) disgruntled employees or diverting the legitimate claims of workers with regard to collective action and bargaining. Building on the blended Marxist-Freudian perspectives of the Frankfurt school (Habermas, Fromm, Adorno, and Sanford) and the fields of anthropology and sociology, practitioners often find themselves applying many different concepts and helping to articulate the fundamental issues associated with the complex cultures of contemporary organizations.

Although there are a diversity of perspectives associated with the term *organizational development*, two principles seem to be integral to (though they are often ignored by) all of the schools; these principles provide a basis for dialogue between the schools and for the creation of new methods useful in improving American colleges and universities.

Principle One: First- and Second-Order Change

On the one hand, organizational development consultants are often in the business of promoting first-order change. They help members of an organization do more or less of what they are already doing, or do what they are now doing better: more supervisor-subordinate communication, less disruptive interpersonal conflict, more collaboration in group decision making. This type of change is often appropriate and sometimes effective.

In second-order change, on the other hand, the organizational development practitioner assists members of the organization to do something different. For example, rather than improving supervisor-subordinate communication, a second-order change would entail an alteration in the substance of that communication or in the very nature of the supervisory-subordinate relationship itself. There might be a change in the areas of conflict, rather than just in the strategies being used for management of the conflict. Collaborative group decision making would cease to be a goal; instead, the nature and composition of the group would be modified, or the type and/or number of decisions being made by the group would be altered.

Each of the second-order strategies for the management of change requires a reframing of the context in which they are formulated. Thus, focus is directed less on the content (for example, a new curriculum or administrative policy) than on the process of change. The attention we have given to the cultures in which change must occur places further emphasis on process rather than content. Though most higher education consultants are in the business of promoting or planning for change in a specific content area, there is greater need for these consultants to reflect on the processes involved.

Chris Argyris and Donald Schön (Argyris, Putnam, and Smith, 1985; Schön, 1984) offer us some valuable insights regarding second-order change. They observe that experienced practitioners (in management, teaching, and other fields requiring extensive human relations experience) tend to replicate the specific behavior that they most criticize in other people. If they are most critical of the harsh, judgmental manner in which a supervisor addresses subor-

dinates, then the practitioners may be very severe in their criticism
of the supervisor. If they believe that a teacher is being indirect in
assessing a student's performance, they will often be indirect in their
feedback about the teacher's performance. There are many possible
explanations for our tendency to duplicate those behaviors that we
dislike most. One of the reasons is the culture that both we and our
colleagues share. We copy the disapproved behavior because we
inhabit the same invisible culture that influences or even elicits this
behavior.

Only when we move to a second order—one that requires us
to assess the discrepancy between our own espoused theories of human behavior and the ways in which we actually relate to other
people (theories in use)—will we gain an understanding of our own
behavior and that of other people—the first step toward effective
practice. The insights gained by Argyris and Schön (representing
the American school) may directly relate to the concept of subsystem
mirroring that is central to the British school (subsystems tend to
replicate or mirror the dynamics of the total system). Gregory Bateson (1979), best identified with the social-critical school, also points
to the importance of second-order change (and stabilization) when
he suggests that learning how to learn (deutero-learning) may often
be of greater survival value than first-order (proto-) learning.

In a variety of different ways, each of these theorists and
practitioners is pointing to the importance of culture and the implicitly held theories, assumptions, values, and norms that are associated with each. We identify several second-order strategies in
Chapters Eleven and Twelve that take these cultural factors into
account. Contemporary colleges and universities must have access
to the range of ideas and skills that accompany both first- and
second-order organizational development if they are to remain responsive and viable. In view of the value of these institutions in our
complicated and troubled society, they deserve the best we have to
offer.

Principle Two: Change and Stabilization

Academic institutions often confront problems associated with both
change and stabilization, particularly if all four academic cultures

are present. An organizational development consultant who works in colleges and universities is often asked to assist not in bringing about change, but in bringing about stability in a chaotic and unpredictable academic environment. Change (or, more precisely, the rate of change) is itself the major problem that an organization sometimes faces. This principle can be readily illustrated by a change curve (see Figure 10.1).

When an organization introduces any change, it generally does so because it anticipates improvement in some aspect of the organization (higher worker morale, increased productivity, larger profits). Yet most often when changes are actually introduced, the immediate effect is a decline in the primary index of success (morale is lower, productivity decreases, profits fall). This situation occurs for several reasons: the rest of the system must adjust to the change (typically, other parts of the system are not altered to accommodate

Figure 10.1. The Change Curve.

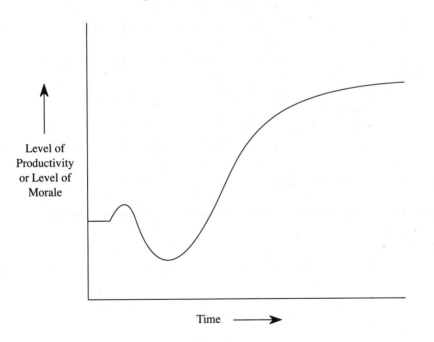

Level of
Productivity
or Level of
Morale

Time ⟶

Source: Adapted from Sprunger and Bergquist, 1978, p. 336.

the new policy, procedure, or structure); new skills, knowledge, and attitudes must be acquired by those critically involved in the change; the initial expectations regarding improvement were unrealistic; and/or those in the organization who resent, or at least resist, the change consciously or unconsciously sabotage it.

With a drop in performance level, disillusionment often sets in. Many organizations will therefore change once again (reverting to the old way or, more often, trying another new way), and a new change curve is initiated. But performance levels decline even further. Then still another change is made. At this point, the organization is experiencing a downward spiral and is most in need of stabilization. Thoughtful reflection on the lessons learned from the previous disasters and patience in allowing the new change to take hold may be needed.

The cycle described above is becoming more prevalent today, as the rate of change accelerates. Organizational development consultants must formulate not only plans for change, but also strategies for stabilization. Chris Argyris and Donald Schön from the American school (1974 and 1978) seem to be articulating some of these strategies, as are many of the systems-oriented members of the British school (see, for example, Colman and Bexton, 1975). With specific regard to higher education, instability is likely to be even more pronounced if the desired change is incompatible with the college's dominant culture(s).

Based in the developmental culture, the new curriculum development program at Canon College, for instance, is basically incompatible with the powerful collegial culture of the college. Even with all of the funds that were made available to Canon College, the inherent resistance of the faculty (as well as administrators and students) to the developmental culture was too strong. Perhaps in part because of the large sum of money that was involved, the resistance became focused and coherent. Typically, the resistance to a new idea is mobilized only after it is shown to be viable and able to be translated into action.

If we return to our original case study (Chapter One) of Peter Armantrout, we see repeated evidence of the change curve in operation. Armantrout chaired a general education committee that attempted to introduce a new curriculum into Fairfield College.

Being directed at overall campus requirements, such a change would inevitably affect many elements of the college and would contribute to a large dip in the curve, as would the requirement for new knowledge, skills, and attitudes.

Many American colleges and universities are strewn with the skeletons of general education programs introduced without adequate provision for the diminished faculty performance, student morale, and administrative efficiency that are inevitable in any major innovation. Armantrout attributes the resistance to his general education program to territorialism. He might instead have recognized the desire of his colleagues for general education programming that did not require significant change (in other words, one built on the existing disciplinary expertise of the faculty). Like faculty at many other American colleges and universities, those at Fairfield College are inclined to select distribution requirements as a means of avoiding the change curve.

The central question thus becomes how one can deal successfully with the change curve when introducing new ideas in a college or university. We offer several suggestions and indicate ways that the faculty members and collegiate institutions featured in our case studies might benefit from the use of these strategies.

First, one must acknowledge the existence of the change curve and recognize that a deterioration in performance and morale is likely when a new idea is introduced. If a college or university cannot withstand this period, the change effort may have to be delayed until the institution is more fully prepared. Thus, in the case of Canon College, the new grant might have been accepted at a point in the history of the college when it was more stable and had developed a clear mandate for curricular change. Quite understandably, some of leaders of Canon College saw the curriculum development grant as a timely antedote to the collective woes of the college; however, until some of these woes (faculty salaries, for example) have been attended to, any similar grant will only cause mischief and potential disruption.

Second, the curve will be less drastic if one or more of the forces that bring about the decline are eliminated or at least considered. Substantial training and education, for instance, can help if introduced prior to the initiation of the change. At Fairfield, faculty might have been encouraged to read about (or, better yet, visit) various other colleges and universities that have recently enacted general education programs. Informal faculty colloquia might have been convened for discussion and review of possible general education models. (These forums should take place at least a year prior to the formal review of any new general education program.) Some senior members of the faculty might also have been given leave time in order to gain an in-depth understanding of alternative general education models.

The integration of the desired change with other new projects at a college or university can also help to buffer the problem. The leaders of curriculum development at Canon College might have met with the leaders of other new programs to coordinate activities. This process is particularly valuable if the other program initiatives are more fully aligned with the dominant culture(s) of the institution. At Canon, a new faculty governance program was being introduced at the same time as the curriculum development plan. The leaders of these two programs might have coordinated efforts and determined their mutual impact, so that they could build on one another rather than competing with, or at the very least disrupting, each other.

Typically, the first-order changes we make in any collegiate institution (or any social institution, for that matter) are evolutionary in nature. This type of change is illustrated in Figure 10.2. Each evolutionary change will be minimal and may represent no qualitative difference from the immediately preceding one. It can be considered transitional rather than transformational. In Thomas Kuhn's terms (1962), the change becomes a part of "normal science" rather than a "paradigm shift." Thus, it is likely to be more acceptable and less stressful for a greater number of people than if the change is large and abrupt. This first-order incremental strategy holds one major disadvantage: in the slow, progressive movement toward a specific goal, the sense of direction and motivation found at the beginning of the initiative may disappear. As a result, the effort may simply fade away before the goal is attained, or it may lose its way and end at a quite different point from that originally intended.

Figure 10.2. Evolutionary Change.

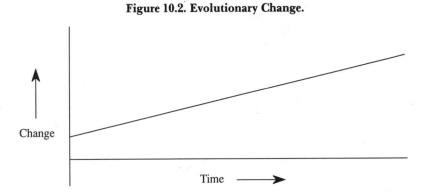

The first-order, incremental model of mediation and compromise is particularly prevalent in the collegial and negotiating cultures. It is not uncommon for faculty committees and faculty union negotiations to produce policies, programs, and objectives that relate only vaguely and often in a very distorted manner to the original goals or visions of those who were engaged in the deliberations. A politicized collegial culture—such as we find at Mountain State University—promotes small changes that are expedient but unrelated in any genuine sense to the basic mission of the institution. For example, the distribution requirements that are advocated by many faculty at Fairfield College (and are found at many colleges and universities) are often forged in a political/collegial crucible. These requirements probably bear very little resemblance to any particular vision of what a college should be.

A graphic depiction of second-order, revolutionary change looks quite different from first-order, evolutionary change (see Figure 10.3). The change that occurs represents a profound transformation in the institution: a paradigm shift. The motivation to begin the change and the sense of the direction that it should take are usually not lost during the course of the change. Levels of stress, however, and resistance to this transformation will be great in most educational institutions. Typically, power and manipulation are required to bring about this type of change—power being most often used by representatives of the managerial culture and manipulation being usually employed by representatives of the developmental culture.

Proponents of the managerial culture look wistfully at

Figure 10.3. Revolutionary Change.

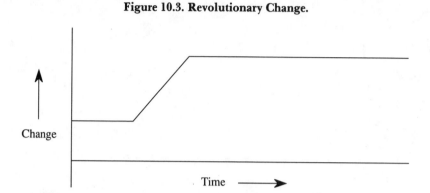

highly driven and rapidly changing corporate environments (such as those found in high technology firms) and long for a similar ability to effect major change in a short period of time. Proponents of the developmental culture also often long for the substantially funded and required training and development programs that are found in these corporations. By contrast, neither the collegial nor the negotiating culture allows for this kind of change. Neither permits administrators (or individual faculty members) to hold the unilateral authority that is needed to bring about revolutionary shifts.

This does not mean that second-order revolutionary strategies are not attractive to representatives of the collegial or negotiating culture. In fact, they are advocated by some of them, but rarely successfully. Someone like Jim Herbert, our dissatisfied physicist at Western State University, is tempted to align with the negotiating culture in part because of its revolutionary potential. If evolutionary change efforts have met with little success (specifically with regard to faculty grievances at Western), Herbert and his faculty colleagues at Western look to revolutionary strategies (such as faculty strikes) as the last hope for genuine change. Similarly, Bernie Kefelmann looks to the negotiating culture as a source of revolution. He lives with the ghost of past social inequities and atrocities and is understandably skeptical about evolutionary, developmentally oriented methods that require patience and trust.

Often, neither evolutionary nor revolutionary strategies are very effective. Kefelmann and Herbert are just as likely to be unhappy with the effects of radical efforts as Armantrout or the faculty at Mountain State University are with their gradual ones. A strategy is required that allows for evolutionary change (in keeping with the collegial and negotiating cultures) but that also enables the people attempting the change (often from the managerial or developmental cultures) to retain their motivation and sense of direction. Temporary educational systems offer a model for educational institutions that combines the best of both the evolutionary and revolutionary strategies. This temporary system of change is graphically portrayed in Figure 10.4.

The desired change is initiated through the first-order, incremental steps of a planning or design process. However, at a certain point, a temporary system is established in which a short-term, second-order revolution can occur. Part or all of the program or idea that has been designed to produce the desired change can be tested in this way. Faculty and administrators can discover what the results of implementing the plan will be, whether it is feasible, and whether or not it is truly desirable. A provisional system provides people involved in change with renewed motivation to continue the effort, provided the results of the trial enactment are found to be desirable. If the trial is successful, such a system also provides a greater sense of direction.

Temporary educational systems can take several different forms, ranging from briefly exposing a new method or content in an existing, ongoing course to establishing an entirely new (though temporary) college with multiple course offerings. Basically, there

Figure 10.4. Temporary Systems.

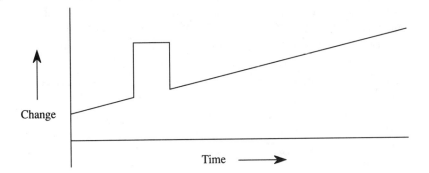

are five different types of temporary educational systems (TESs): (1) program embedded, (2) miniprogram, (3) extended program, (4) minicollege, and (5) experimental college. Each of the five types blend strengths of both evolutionary and revolutionary change.

The program embedded TES is typically conducted by a faculty member or administrator who wishes to test a new idea for the program he or she is now conducting. The virtue of this type of TES is that it does not require that the content of the current program be changed. This TES might be used when a new evaluation procedure (an oral exam or assessment of a critical-thinking competence) is being attempted, an instructional method (a case study or studio work) is being tried in a discipline not usually associated with its use, or a new instructional support service (orientation to library research or use of computer-based editing service) is being tested for the first time.

For instance, Ellen Vargas, the business professor at Midlands Community College, might make effective use of the program embedded TES as she continues to develop her accounting courses and her own instructional competence. With her managerial culture orientation, Ellen might be encouraged to develop specific instructional objectives for each component of her course and to test out alternative instructional designs systematically to determine the extent to which each design moves the students toward her objectives.

Miniprograms are the second type of TES. They generally involve the pilot testing of an entire program unit, though not necessarily an entire program. The miniprogram is often offered during an interim term, during a preterm or postterm session, or as a short course during a regular academic term for which students can receive extra credit or can attend as a regular assignment. If offered at a time when other programs are not being conducted (during freshman orientation week, for example), the miniprogram can readily be observed by nonparticipating faculty or administrators. Because miniprograms are short (as compared to the more lengthy third, fourth, and fifth types of TES) and highly flexible (as compared to the first type of TES), they can be structured in a variety of ways and can easily be repeated in a number of different forms.

Our interdisciplinary scholar, Kevin Reynolds, could use a miniprogram TES in his exploration of the nonacademic world. Reynolds might, for instance, prepare a miniprogram that introduces executives in a corporation to some of the major interdisciplinary themes of our age. His TES could be used by him (and the corporation) to see if executives are truly interested in intellectual matters. He could also use the TES to try out several different interdisciplinary themes to determine which are most appropriate to that particular corporation.

An extended program TES involves the testing of an entire component (course, program service) during a condensed period of time—usually about one month. Often an interterm period is used for this kind of TES. Typically, it requires substantial attention on the part of participants (usually students) and those running the program (faculty or administrators). An extended program holds several advantages over other types of TESs. First, it enables a full component of the academic program to be assessed. Yet because it is confined to a specific period of time, it can readily be observed and subjected to various alterations. This type of TES is not as easily repeated as the first two types; however, it normally requires less planning and coordination than the fourth or fifth type.

An extended program TES might be particularly helpful to Peter Armantrout, who longs for the days when he was teaching mostly mature men and women. Peter could start a interterm program at Fairfield College that is specifically designed for adults or even retired people—possibly in conjunction with the Elderhouse programs that are now being offered in colleges and universities throughout the United States (O'Donnell and Berkeley, 1980). Armantrout and his colleagues could use this temporary setting not only to try out new instructional ideas, but also to evaluate their own feelings about the teaching of mature students. Do they really prefer these students, or had nostalgia misled them?

The minicollege, a fourth type of TES, is used to test several components of an academic program or the interaction of several different programs. This type of TES is of briefer duration than the extended program; often a minicollege will last for only one or two weeks. A series of courses, workshops, or services are provided during this period of time. A university in the Pacific Northwest, for instance, ran a minicollege for several years during the 1970s as a means of developing and assessing the components of their new general education program. The faculty at Canon College might have made similar use of a minicollege in conjunction with their curriculum development project.

A minicollege is particularly helpful if the proposed program change is likely to threaten the dominant culture of the institution. Fairfield's powerful collegial culture, for instance, makes an interdisciplinary, nonpolitical exploration of general education very difficult. A minicollege can provide a safe setting for such an exploration. Given that the program ideas being tested are not permanent, but rather are open to further revision and even rejection, collegially oriented faculty are less likely to be suspicious. The managerial administrators and faculty at Fairfield are also likely to be attracted to the systematic assessment that typically accompanies a minicollege. Even the faculty who represent the negotiating culture are likely to find the minicollege acceptable, if it is held during the regular, contracted academic year. For example, many of the community colleges in western Canada have negotiated a contract with their faculty union that includes a paid month of professional development for all their instructors. A yearly minicollege could be established during this month that is specifically designed for developing and testing new modes of instruction and student service.

The final and most elaborate type of TES is the experimental college. The Paracollege of St. Olaf College exemplifies this model. Faculty participate part-time in the experimental college for several years and then move back to their full-time positions in the regular college. This form of TES can be used in a very successful manner if it is created intentionally as a temporary structure. The act of creating a new institution is itself enriching for students and faculty alike. Furthermore, the experimental college does not exist long enough to become burdened with its own restrictive traditions or precedents. The experimental college is often employed as a means of gradually introducing the developmental culture into a setting that is ruled by the collegial culture. It also can be used as a vehicle for the systematic testing of specific managerially oriented instructional or student service objectives.

What might an experimental college look like if it were introduced at one of our case-study institutions, say, Canon College? First, it would be established around a specific theme that is of central relevance to the college. Canon College might wish to build its experimental college around some aspect of its religious tradition. A liberal arts college in New York City might create an experimental college that focuses on "the city," whereas a community college like Plainsville might concentrate on a need of the local community (historical preservation or environmental pollution).

Second, the experimental college should be designed in a manner that enables all or most Canon faculty members to participate at least once during its existence. In this way, the gradual introduction of a new culture (in this case, developmental) can take place through intensive, short-term involvement of each campus constituency in an experimental college that provides a "taste" of this culture.

Third, the experimental college at Canon should include some mechanisms for accountability. Because the college is experiencing difficulties with regard to finances and student enrollment, it clearly needs an injection of the managerial culture. This might best take the form of marketing and student learning outcome studies conducted in conjunction with the various program units being tested in the experimental college. Faculty and administrators not only learn about the instructional components being tested in the Canon College experimental college but also about the tools used for assessment purposes.

Finally, the Canon College experimental college should provide the faculty and administrators with a new setting in which to explore mutual areas of concern. Quality-of-work-life programs have been developed in corporate and public-service settings as places where union and management representatives can temporarily put aside their differences and solve their shared problems. An experimental college can similarly provide a setting in which estranged faculty and administrators explore new ways to plan, conduct, and evaluate academic programs. An experimental college can never address all the issues that give rise to the need for a negotiating culture, but it can become a setting in which the negotiating culture can interact productively and creatively with the three other cultures of the academy.

Though the TES is not a panacea and is certainly not the only strategy suggested in this book for engaging the four academic cultures, some detailed attention has been given to it because it is frequently overlooked in higher education (Bergquist and Armstrong, 1986) and because it has proven valuable in other organizational settings that are confronting similarly turbulent environments and complex mixtures of perspectives and cultures.

11

Fostering
Organizational Change
and Innovation

We moved in Chapter Ten from some of the more traditional notions about organizational development to the exploration of the very nature of organizational change itself and to the need to balance change and stabilization, particularly in the context of diverse cultural perspectives in higher education. In this chapter, we continue to explore the nature of change in a cultural context by focusing on three domains of change and on four models that are concerned with the processes whereby new ideas and products (in other words, innovations) are diffused in an academic institution. Each of these concepts, which expand the currently available options in the field of organizational development, allows us to be more effective in addressing the diverse needs and styles of representatives of all four academic cultures. Like our exploration of possibilities in Chapter Ten, the expansion of options in this chapter moves our institutional change strategies from a first-order to a second-order perspective; we can do something more to respond to the problems of our colleges and universities than just learn how to improve the status quo.

The first set of concepts that we will consider is Watson and Johnson's (1972) three domains of organizational change; the second set is Ronald Havelock's (1971) and Jack Lindquist's (1978b) models for the diffusion of innovation. We relate our analysis of the four academic cultures to each of these concepts and make recommendations regarding their use. In Chapter Twelve, we study two other concepts that can help us to expand even more substantially our ideas about institutional improvement within the context of the four academic cultures.

Watson and Johnson's Structure, Process, and Attitude Model

According to Watson and Johnson, the strategies that various theorists advocate regarding effective ways to influence organizations usually require change in one of three domains: structure, process, or attitude (1972). Structure is changed when the organizational chart, the reward system, or institutional policies and procedures are modified. Efforts at Canon College to alter the general education curriculum of the college would be considered a structural change, as would Peter Armantrout's attempts to reform the curriculum and governance procedures at Fairfield College.

Changes in process, by contrast, involve alterations in the way that people operate within and relate to others within the existing structures of the organization. Process changes entail shifts in communication patterns, modes of decision making or conflict management, or styles of management. The efforts exerted by Kevin Reynolds (see Chapter Seven) to improve the quality of interdisciplinary dialogue among colleagues at other academic institutions would exemplify the process-oriented approach.

The third domain, attitudes, has to do with how people feel about working with the existing structures and processes of the organization. Changes in attitudes usually involve modifications in organizational culture, as well as personal growth and development among members of the organization. We witnessed an unplanned change in the dominant collegial attitude at Canon College (see Chapter Two) and saw evidence of an unsuccessful attempt to introduce the developmental attitude at Plainsville Community College (Chapter Eight). At a somewhat less ambitious level, Peter Armantrout's attendance at a men's group might influence some of his attitudes (Chapter One), as might Ellen Vargas's participation in one or more instructional improvement programs (Chapter Five).

Concerns about change in all three of these areas are evident in many American colleges and universities. Our case-study institutions and faculty are not exceptions. Structural change, for instance, can be seen in widespread debate about faculty contracts, merit pay programs, and new governance models. Process-oriented change is evident in discussions about consensus building, collaborative management, and conflict resolution. Change directed toward shifts in attitude is to be found in the considerable interest in organizational culture and images of leadership and faculty renewal. Unfortunately, concern for alterations in these three areas does not necessarily translate into useful action. Organizational development is rarely successful, and sensitivity to the dominant academic culture(s) of the organization is rarely evident.

To bring about successful modifications in any of these domains, it is essential, first of all, to recognize that several major strengths and weaknesses are associated with each, especially as it relates to and confronts the four academic cultures. Having acknowledged these strengths and weaknesses, we can prepare strategies that initially incorporate those domains that are particularly compatible with the dominant culture(s) of the institution and then introduce the other domains in a systematic manner to complete a comprehensive project.

Change in Structure

Two major strengths and three weaknesses can be identified with regard to structural change. Its major strengths are low cost and ease of implementation. Structural changes are usually much less expensive than those in either process or attitude. It is not hard to reorganize an organizational chart or modify the compensation program of a college or university. Alterations in structure can be done rapidly, usually with immediate effect. Although the outcomes of the structural change may ultimately be very costly (in higher salaries, new staff appointments, or employee adjustments to new reporting relationships or policies), the change itself is usually quite easily and inexpensively enacted. Furthermore, structural modification is particularly compatible with the managerial and even the negotiating cultures. Collective bargaining and related ingredients of the negotiating culture were established in large part as a means of resisting the ease with which structural changes can be made by an insensitive administration.

The weaknesses of structural changes relate directly to their ease of implementation. First, structural change is organizationally seductive. Many organizational leaders are likely to perceive any problem as amenable to structural amelioration. Second, structural change is easily initiated, often because it can be put into place coercively. Employees are often the victims of thoughtless structural changes that yield demoralizing and negatively accelerating change curves (see Chapter Ten).

Third, employees are not always the victims of structural change. They are also sometimes successful saboteurs. Changes in the formal organizational chart of a college or university often have little effect on the informal, operating network of the institution, for they rarely affect its dominant culture(s), particularly if it is collegial in nature. In the case of Canon College, for instance, even the introduction of a new director of professional development and a new assistant dean for curricular matters did little to increase the capacity of the faculty to implement lasting curricular changes. Five years later, there is no sign of either structural or curricular changes at Canon—despite its substantial funding.

Most collegiate organizations resemble Canon College in this regard. New policies and procedures are ignored, distorted, or made ineffective. Men and women assigned to new positions in an organization are submerged by the dominant, preexisting culture of the units that they join. A new faculty governance system, for example, may be subverted by the negotiating culture (as was the case at Plainsville Community College), in part because this system is viewed by those in the negotiating culture as a mode of faculty collusion with the administration.

Each of these three weaknesses speak to the need for process-oriented and attitudinal change in association with structural alterations. Without the involvement of the other two domains, structural change is usually ineffective and/or destructive. With the development of new skills (process change), people filling new positions can operate skillfully from the outset. With work on attitudes, they can continue to be efficient and supported by other members of the organization. This work requires an understanding of the four cultures described in this book and a recognition of the value (and potential problems) associated with each of them. It does very little good to attempt any diminution in the impact of any of the four cultures; rather, one must work within the context of each to enhance its strengths, avoid its weaknesses, and encourage a tolerance for and understanding of the other three cultures by its advocates.

We can illustrate a successful use of structurally oriented organizational change by turning to the case of a liberal arts college that has become increasingly reliant on part-time faculty to teach a diverse student population. The planning and governance of this college were being performed by the administration and a few full-time faculty members (serving as heads of departments that were filled with part-time faculty). The administrators and part-time faculty tended to represent the managerial culture of the college, whereas the full-time faculty were part of the collegial culture. An organizational change consultant was called in to help these administrators and faculty find a way to involve part-time faculty more fully in the school's operations, while also being respectful of the numerous other demands on the lives of these professionals.

The consultant worked with the administrators, part-time faculty, and full-time academics in devising a new planning model that called for semiannual retreats during which all faculty would meet to solve problems and make plans for the next six months of the college. In addition, a new governance model was devised that included the participation of part-time faculty members, not only through their department heads, but also through the appointment of at-large part-time faculty representatives who were concerned with the unique problems of part-time instructors, regardless of discipline. Part-time faculty are often drawn toward (or they are attractive to) proponents of the managerial culture. This college was able to gradually introduce part-time faculty to the collegial culture by means of this new governance model.

Change in Process

The major strengths of the process domain relate to the empowerment that accompanies skill building and (with specific reference to higher education institutions) the compatibility of process-oriented change with the educational missions of our colleges and universities. An effort that emphasizes alterations in process begins with the assumption that people can change (individually or as a group) and that through training and education people can become more accomplished in their relationships with other people.

Building on the educational philosophy of John Dewey ([1916] 1944, [1929] 1960), the early practitioners of this strategy emphasized the need for men and women in organizations to take responsibility for their individual actions by reflecting on their own behavior, learning new skills, and acquiring new, practical knowledge. This model of education based on experience empowers men and women. It suggests to them that they need not become victims of oppressive structures or attitudes. Such a vision is certainly compatible with the traditional optimism and pragmatism of American higher education and is in keeping with the developmental culture, as well as with the egalitarian goals of the negotiating culture. These goals and values tend to be viewed with greater skepticism in the collegial and managerial cultures.

The major weakness in this approach to organizational change is its emphasis on individualistic solutions to complex, group-centered problems and the ephemeral nature of this seemingly pragmatic approach to training and education. Individual, process-oriented change is usually sabotaged by the group. This lesson has been learned many times over in the painful reentry of men and women into the "real" world who have just experienced an enriching and transforming training program. They return to a unsupportive, unforgiving, and misinformed group of colleagues. Because process-oriented change comes about slowly and at considerable cost (in training, education, and time away from work), it is also difficult to sustain, especially when money is tight and dreams of personal transformation seem at best optimistic.

Process-oriented organizational change must be coupled with shifts in structure and attitude if they are to be effective and sustained. Individuals who are returning to a work group after a training program must find compatible structures and a supportive environment. Better yet, the entire work group should be involved in the training and in the restructuring of the workplace. It may be more difficult to train a whole group, but the skills and knowledge gained in this way generally endure.

Recent examples of process-oriented change are somewhat more abundant than those from the other two areas, in large part because of the upsurge of interest in professional development for faculty and administrators. Over a period of five years, five workshops were recently offered at a large state university for mid-level managers. These workshops focused on collaborative decision making, conflict management, and leadership. The workshops were evaluated in a very positive manner, and workshop participants left each session with a renewed dedication to improved management practices at their own work sites. Little change, however, was evident at this university, for there was no follow-up to this program. In fact, there was significant resistance to these workshops on the part of those who stood astride the collegial and managerial cultures (namely, the department chairs).

Furthermore, no structural changes were made at this university that might help sustain these efforts. Changes in the area of personnel policies and procedures, for instance, would have been of considerable value. The existing policies and procedures at the university often seemed to contradict the principles taught in the workshops. Similarly, lack of support and incompatible management styles at the top of the organization meant that the mixed collegial and managerial culture of the university would not sustain the attitude changes needed to ensure the acceptance of these newly acquired managerial skills. Though the workshops might have been of some benefit, they certainly did not contribute to long-term organizational effectiveness.

A second example of process-oriented change also yielded few lasting results. The president of a private urban university requested that team-building sessions be conducted with his large (ten-person), often unwieldy, management team. Resistance to any examination of the structures (size and function) of this team meant that even successful efforts at improving the functioning of the current group yielded only short-term improvements. Ultimately, the attitudes of the university's president, based firmly in the managerial culture, ensured that no real change would take place— much as the managerially oriented attitudes of the Mountain State

University president seemed to inhibit any real change in process at his institution. At both institutions, the president resisted any redistribution of power in the organization. This resistance was reinforced by the management team's perception that it lacked power.

A powerful, charismatic university presidency is often acceptable to the collegial and managerial cultures and compatible with the fears (and the defensive strategies) of the negotiating and developmental cultures. This state of affairs illustrates the typical ineffectiveness of some first-order change efforts. Training in or sensitivity to new managerial styles and strategies will rarely effect real change, unless they relate in some manner to parallel shifts (second-order changes) that are occurring in the dominant culture(s) of the institution.

The third example indicates the potential for successful process change—provided that structural and attitudinal issues are also considered. The faculty and administrative leaders from a group of Canadian community colleges mentioned earlier formulated an instructional improvement program (process domain and developmental culture) in conjunction with collective bargaining agreements between the faculty and administration (structural domain and negotiating culture). This agreement was reached within the context of a shared faculty-administrative commitment to specific instructional goals (attitudinal domain and managerial-collegial cultures). All parties to the agreement were concerned about the changing learning styles and needs of community college students. The instructional improvement program that was created and sustained in response to these shared concerns made extensive use of both volunteer faculty assistance (attitudinal domain) and faculty release time (structural domain). This program, which began in the late 1970s, has continued for more than a dozen years and has involved more than three thousand faculty members in Canada and the United States.

The success of this instructional improvement project can be attributed in part to the convening of its leaders each year in a personally enriching, community-oriented retreat in the Canadian Rockies (attitude domain). A temporary system is created at this yearly retreat that encourages experimentation in a variety of areas (curriculum, community building, instructional strategies, and so forth). The combining of structure, process, and attitude in this organizational change effort has made a real difference for the participating colleges and has yielded tangible, lasting benefits for those who take part.

Change in Attitude

Many people who attempt to bring about widespread societal change believe that it can only occur if there are modifications in the attitudes of people. In higher education, what is often required is a shift in the relative strength of one or more of the four cultures. As noted in the tenets of many world religions, a change in "spirit" leads not only to better relationships with other people, but also to greater personal fulfillment and enrichment. In the domain of attitude change, the improvement of institutions and people go hand in hand, provided that the attitude change results from mature recommitment or conversion, not from either coercion or immature and uncritical imitation of another person's values or beliefs.

The weaknesses associated with change directed toward shifts in attitude relate primarily to the difficulty of implementing a successful project. Many people have tried, but few have succeeded, except through drastic and usually inhumane methods (often labeled "brainwashing"). Furthermore, even when seemingly successful, attitude change is easily "faked" or disappears, unless it is supported by appropriate structural and process-oriented changes. A classic example of this mistaken use of attitude change is evident in a bitterly humorous movie from the 1960s, *Bob, Carol, Ted and Alice*. Like many who participated in "encounter" workshops during this period, this film's protagonists found their newly discovered openness to be inappropriate in their home and work settings. Their new interpersonal skills were rather fragile and quickly abandoned when confronted with the realities of domestic and work-related conflict.

Examples of organizational change in higher education directed primarily at attitude change include several national and institutionally based programs; these create temporary systems in which participants experience and explore the implications of alternative cultures and value systems. Several national higher education associations have made extensive use of week- or even month-long retreats during which faculty and/or administrators from colleges or universities throughout the country are exposed to new ideas (such as outcomes-based education) or values (such as the importance of student development in higher education). The attitudes of participants in these retreats are often influenced less by what experts in the field say about the issue at hand than by colleagues from other campuses who have tried a new idea or reflected on the growing importance of a particular value.

In his research on change in higher education, Jack Lindquist (1978b) noted that one of the most important ingredients in any collegiate change effort is the increased cosmopolitan perspective of participating faculty members. If faculty members have made connections with colleagues from comparable institutions, then they tend to be more open to new ideas (attitude change), as well as to be more knowledgeable about how to implement these new ideas (process change). A retreat that involves faculty from two or more colleges or universities (through the auspices of a consortium or national association) provides an exceptional opportunity for faculty to break free from the parochial constraints of the dominant culture on their own campus and see that other perspectives (and attitudes) are viable.

We can illustrate this approach to attitude change by focusing on the experiences of faculty in one retreat program (Bergquist, Lounibos, and Langfitt, 1980). A new experimental college was created from scratch for a one-month period each year by ten faculty and thirty students from small liberal arts colleges throughout the United States. Faculty and students found that this experience significantly influenced their own attitudes about the ways in which faculty and students should cooperate and the ways in which people from differing religious, ethnic, and regional backgrounds can and should interact. Students and faculty who participated in the college returned to their home campuses with renewed commitment to or a new appreciation for the developmental culture and for education based on experience. They also came away with a new understanding of the managerial (and also the negotiating) culture, because they had to administer this experimental college themselves.

Another example of attitude-oriented change in higher education builds on the British school's notions of group and organizational life (see Chapter Ten). Leaders of a dysfunctional college in the Midwest identified key ingredients in their organization that seemed not only to resist attempts at improvement but even to benefit from the current dysfunction. These distressed men and women were encouraged by a consultant to consider how their current problems were sustained and protected by the "secondary gains" that came from support for a specific culture and from the disorder and miscommunication that pervaded their use of this culture.

What is it that an organization does very well (such as produce crises, contradictory messages, and/or incompetent leadership), and what is to be gained from this kind of success? This midwestern college was ruled informally by the collegial culture. It was always in chaos. As a result, no one had to feel accountable for his or her own individual performance. In another academic institution (dominated by the negotiating culture, in this case), one leader after another was found to be incompetent. Members of this organization were always able to find evidence for their own continuing mistrust of authority. Administrative inefficiency also helped faculty union leaders to forge an alliance among colleagues that was based on this mistrust and the need for continuing unity and diligence with regard to faculty-administration matters.

If members of an organization recognize these unconscious motivations and the ways in which they help to produce chaos or miscommunication, they often dramatically shift their own attitudes about their organization. Rather than being obsessed about the need for change (while simultaneously sabotaging any idea that is advanced by others), they become more appreciative of the unique and often quite subtle dynamics and strengths of the organization and come to understand the origins and source of continuing support for their own dominant culture(s).

Faculty members at Plainsville Community College (Chapter Eight), for instance, may be quite skillful at undermining competent administrators, just as the administrators may impede the Plainsville faculty. Both the faculty and administrators at Plainsville could explore why questioning and confrontation may have been useful to the organization at one point in its history, as well as why they may now be inappropriate and counterproductive. With this acceptance and a growing mutual appreciation of the organization's managerial and negotiating cultures, Plainsville faculty and administrators could more readily move on to fresh ways of thinking. They might then identify new motivations and approaches that require a more mature organization. The insights gained from this type of organizational change are often "quiet." They produce reflection rather than immediate action and lead first to attitude change, then to alterations in structure and process. This type of change effort requires patience and persistence, for dramatic and early results are rarely apparent. Real change, however, often seems to require this gradual shift in perspective and accompanying modification of attitudes.

Havelock's and Lindquist's Strategies for the Diffusion of Innovation

Like Watson, Ronald Havelock (1971) conducted research during the 1970s on the processes of change and innovation in various human service settings. Working out of the Institute for Social Research in Ann Arbor, Michigan, Havelock focused on strategies for the dissemination and utilization of knowledge in educational institutions. He proposed three different strategies for the dissemination and use of innovative ideas: rational planning, social interaction, and human problem solving. Building on Havelock's work, Jack Lindquist (1978b) added a fourth strategy to the list, which he called the political approach. Lindquist applied Havelock's three models and his fourth one to his analysis of change and innovation in American colleges and universities. The following is a brief description of each of these four strategies and their relationship to the four cultures described in this book, as well as to Watson and Johnson's three change strategies.

Rational Planning

For many contemporary colleges and universities—or at least for their leaders—rational planning reigns supreme. The common rhetoric of our times relies heavily on such terms as *systematic, information-based, research-based,* and *logical.* As noted in our discussion of the collegial culture (Chapter Two), colleges and universities in particular are inclined to be perceived by those within and outside as strongholds of reason and rational deliberation. The rational planning strategy is heartily embraced by three of the four cultures. Only advocates of the negotiating culture seem to be skeptical about its values and effectiveness; representatives of the other three cultures complain that the level of rational discourse in contemporary colleges and universities is insufficient.

What is at the heart of this first strategy? Havelock (1971, p. 5) identified several basic assumptions underlying this model of change:

> First of all, the [rational planning] model suggests that dissemination and utilization should be a rational sequence of activities which moves from research to development to packaging before dissemination takes place. Secondly, this model assumes that there has to be planning, and planning really on a massive scale. It is not enough that we simply have all these activities of research and development; they have to be coordinated; there has to be a relationship between them; and they have to make sense in a logical sequence that may go back years in the evolution of one particular message to be disseminated.

Thus, when this strategy is dominant, we are likely to find detailed descriptions of steps to be taken in designing a five-year plan for the school or a close working relationship between the institutional research office and the faculty curriculum committee. The collegiate leader who believes in rational planning will devote a significant amount of time, money, and energy to the collection of quantifiable information about such aspects of the institution as student enrollment and attrition, unit costs, projections of changing student or community needs, and student-learning outcomes. This approach is exemplified in the work of the National Center for Higher Education Management Systems (Boulder, Colorado),

Educational Testing Service (Princeton, New Jersey), and American College Testing (Ames, Iowa).

Three other assumptions about this strategy are identified by Havelock (1971, p. 5):

> There has to be a division of labor and a separation of roles and functions, an obvious prerequisite in all complex activities of modern society, but one that we sometimes slur over. [This model also] assumes a more or less clearly defined target audience, a specified passive consumer, who will accept the innovation if it is delivered on the right channel, in the right way, and at the right time. The particular process which is supposed to assure this happening is scientific evaluation, evaluation at every stage of development and dissemination. . . . Finally, this perspective accepts the fact of high initial development cost prior to any dissemination activity, because it forsees an even higher gain in the long run, in terms of efficiency, quality, and capacity to reach a mass audience.

If these assumptions are correct, it is clear why Havelock and Lindquist believe that this strategy is in some trouble, given the state of contemporary colleges and universities. First, the traditional hierarchy and passive consumer that this strategy supposes simply do not exist in most contemporary institutions. Some of the more prestigious universities that are permeated with the collegial culture may still live under the myth of control and hierarchy and primarily serve a relatively traditional student body, but even these schools are now subject to major external and internal forces that are neither controllable nor predictable. The boundaries of these institutions have been penetrated, and they must come to terms with the presence of and need for Havelock's and Lindquist's other three strategies. Advocates of the negotiating culture have known of the inherent weaknesses in the rational planning strategy for many years; proponents of the other three cultures have much to learn in this regard.

Social Interaction

Both Havelock and Lindquist specifically identify the social interaction strategy for planned change with Everett Rogers's (1982) description of the ways in which new ideas and technologies are
diffused in communities and organizations. Rogers, in turn, bases
his work on previous research and consultation about how major
social innovations (such as water purification systems) are introduced into non-Western communities and large corporations. In regard to this strategy, Lindquist (1978b, p. 4) observes, "We live in
social networks. One connects us to professional colleagues; another
unites us with family and friends. Through these connections we get
news and views about what's happening in the world around us. We
can gain security, status and esteem from these informal systems, just
as we can from formal organizations. Some researchers maintain that
these contacts are essential to change, for new ideas get communi-
cated and validated through social networks."

According to Rogers, there are predictable stages through
which innovations move as they spread throughout the community
or organization. Initially, they are held closely by those who helped
to develop them. We find that innovators usually work alone or in
small groups and that they generally communicate among themselves or (if they view other innovators as competitors) with no one
at all. When they do begin to share their ideas or products, they
usually communicate with a group that Rogers calls the "early
adopters." These are people open to virtually any innovation. They
are risk takers, who have a high tolerance for ambiguity and short-
term failure. In the 1980s and 1990s, these are the faculty members
from the developmental culture who will inevitably attend a critical-
thinking workshop that is being offered for the first time, or the
faculty members and administrators from the managerial culture
who will be the first to try out a new software program or interactive
video system. The early adopters are excellent first-time users of a
new product, given their willingness to take risks and learn from
their failures. Even if a specific program idea does not work out, the
early adopters are likely to come back to the innovator for a second
try. Rogers estimates that in most communities the early adopters
and innovators make up about 5 to 10 percent of the population. In

most collegiate institutions, these people come from the nondominant cultures (particularly, the developmental culture).

Once an idea or product has been received (and often modified by or in conjunction with) the early adopters, it is examined by a large group that Rogers calls the "early majority." This group, often represented in colleges and universities by the managerial culture, typically requires evidence—a central part of a rational planning strategy. Thus, facts and figures indicating the value of a new administrative policy or a new instructional technology will be persuasive to the early majority. Whereas the early adopters are likely to be receptive to most new ideas, the early majority is quite selective. The case must be made before it will even pay attention to the idea or product, let alone embrace it. In most communities and organizations, this group represents roughly 30 to 50 percent of the population (though the percentages will change depending on the innovation being considered). Taken as a group, the innovators, the early adopters, and the early majority (as the name implies) barely constitute a majority of the population. In most collegiate institutions, the result is that a new idea or product must be acceptable to at least some members of the collegial culture if it is ever to be successful.

At the point that a majority has accepted a specific innovation, Rogers suggests that a new group, the "late majority," forms. Members of this group are completely uninterested in facts and figures. They are concerned only with political realities (as emphasized in Lindquist's political strategy). If it looks as though the new program will be adopted by at least half of the organizational population, then we can expect many of the men and women who first ignored or resisted the idea to support it, if reluctantly. They are also likely to be quite ignorant of the new product or idea and will often misuse it. This period is frequently the most vulnerable for any innovation. While the inventers are celebrating their victory, the innovation is being altered or translated by the late majority into a form that will no longer be recognizable. In many instances, the late majority is composed of the "rank and file" of the collegial culture and by some members of the negotiating culture (unless the innovation involves new personnel policies and procedures, in which case representatives of the negotiating culture may be among the innovators and early adopters, whereas members of the developmental culture will join the late majority).

The final group to be identified by Rogers consists of the "laggards" or recalcitrants, who will resist a new idea until their own deaths or the death of the innovation. Typically, the causes of the laggards' resistance to a specific innovation are irrational and based on reasons that have little to do with the idea itself. They do not like the innovator or are in competition with this person. Perhaps they were themselves innovators at one point in their careers and now find that the success of someone else's project acts like salt in the wound. Thus, when an innovative idea is ignored or rejected by a community or organization, we not only have lost a potentially valuable innovation, but also may have helped to create a laggard who will be resistant to new ideas for many years to come. Laggards are typically stagnant or insecure members of the collegial culture, disillusioned members of the developmental culture (who have seen their own innovative ideas ignored in the past), or betrayed members of the negotiating culture.

Taken together, Rogers's five-stage chronology represents a quite different portrait of planned change than that found in the literature and experiences of many who support the rational planning process. Often, those who advocate rational planning draw very few distinctions between the various audiences that must be considered in presenting a new idea or product. They may overestimate the amount of information that the early adopters need to try out an innovation or offer the wrong kind of information, at a premature point in the dissemination process, to those in the late majority. Furthermore, those from the rational planning perspective (like those from the human relations and political perspectives) often devote too much attention to the laggard group, in part because it seems to challenge any statement made by the innovators and their advocates, regardless of the content and validity of what they say. The laggards are often considered wise about the realities of organizational life at the institution and the keepers of the institution's venerable (though sometimes neglected) values and traditions (to which we turn in Chapter Twelve, where we consider the symbolic functions in organizational life).

Resolution of Human Problems

The third strategy is one often identified with the organizational development movement in American corporations and schools (see Chapter Ten). First introduced by Kurt Lewin and his colleagues associated with the National Training Laboratories, this strategy relies on the improvement of interpersonal relationships and on the critical role played by human emotions and group dynamics. Havelock (1971, p. 13) identifies five basic tenets associated with this strategy:

1. That the user's world ([that of] the person who is to adopt a new idea or practice) is the only sensible place from which to begin to consider utilization;
2. That knowledge utilization must include a diagnostic phase where user need is considered and translated into a problem statement;
3. That the role of the outsider is primarily to serve as catalyst, collaborator, or consultant on how to plan change and bring about his solution;
4. That internal knowledge retrieval and the marshalling of internal resources should be given at least equal emphasis with external retrieval; and
5. That self-initiation by the user or client system creates the best motivational climate for lasting change.

Lindquist remarks that the human problem resolution model assumes that collaboration and openness are better than competition and rigidity and that consensus should always be obtained (as opposed to the use of majority rule or authoritative decree). Advocates of this strategy in American higher education (see Chapter Ten) tend to discount the rational planning approach as ignoring the role of human emotions in decision-making processes and the valuable lessons to be learned about the differing needs of various constituencies exposed to the new idea or product.

The Political Approach

Lindquist's strategy looks neither to the quality of the idea being offered nor to the nature of the interactions among those who are developing or implementing the idea. It focuses instead on the distribution and use of power within the collegiate institution. Lindquist identifies one of the basic tenets that underlies this approach as the need to be sensitive to the wants expressed by various constituencies and the necessity of bringing these to the attention of influential members of the community or organization. Lindquist states that a range of concerns or wants first arises. Change will then begin to take place if these wants are clearly articulated and are relevant to those who have influence in the community (1978b, p. 7): "Unless these various wants are felt strongly by influential people, and the people who hold them bring together various subgroups, no change is likely. People are usually upset about something or other but not sufficiently so to press authorities into a decision. But if the income/expenditure gap widens alarmingly . . . a 'demand' may well be in the offing."

Then, according to Lindquist, it is critical for those who are concerned to make authorities take notice. They must make their stand as people who are confident that a more desirable state of affairs is possible, even with existing resources and expertise. Lindquist (1978b, p. 8) goes on to state:

> Once a demand is made, it must gain access to the formal decision-making system if it is to become a change in policy or program. Key here is a sympathetic "gatekeeper," a person or group who can put the demand on the authorities' agenda. . . . Once on the agenda, the demand gets deliberated. . . . If it survives this buffeting, it emerges as a formulated proposal for change which then gets reviewed, modified, revised, reduced and in general worked over by all the persons or groups concerned about its potential impact on their vested interests. . . . Important to the survival of change proposals in this river of nibbling piranhas are the persistent efforts of highly influential

"issues sponsors" who are determined to carry the change through.

Though this political strategy may, on the surface, look just as systematic as the rational planning strategy, it involves a considerable amount of intuition (like human problem resolution) and a thorough knowledge of the diverse needs of the various constituencies that make up the community or organization (like the social interaction approach). The close connection between political approaches to the diffusion of innovation and the negotiating culture are readily apparent. The connection between this approach and the collegial culture is less apparent, but no less important. Whereas the political processes associated with the negotiating culture are normally public and legalistic (allowing for the informal negotiations that take place behind closed doors), those associated with the collegial culture are likely to be more informal and legislative in nature. For both cultures, however, a political approach is critical, though it becomes particularly effective if connected to the other three dissemination strategies.

Though the political approach is a realistic one, it specifically emphasizes the importance of believing that change is possible and that needs can be met with sufficient commitment on the part of those in power. All four approaches, in fact, require that we begin with the belief that they will work, provided they are given sufficient time, money, or expertise. We would thus expect that each strategy has specific blinders that prevent its advocates from clearly seeing its shortcomings. Certain strategies are compatible with particular cultures in part because they encourage the same world view and provide the same blinders against unfavorable evidence.

The variety of strategies that have been described in this chapter illustrate the diversity of approaches that must be taken when addressing the complicated organizational cultures and problems now facing our colleges and universities. In their three-volume series of handbooks on faculty development in higher education, Bergquist and Phillips (1975, 1977, and 1981) built their own multidimensional strategies for instructional improvement, using Watson's model of structure, process, and attitude, as well as Havelock's and Lindquist's models for the diffusion of innovation. Bergquist and Phillips speak of the importance of bolstering any instructional or professional improvement program (process) with both organizational (structural) and personal (attitudinal) components. They suggest that successful instructional development will inevitably produce new problems at both the organizational and personal levels. They also believe that anyone working in the field of professional development must view the settings in which they work as communities, rather than just organizations; in other words, rational planning and human problem solving must be supplemented with Havelock's social interaction and Lindquist's political strategies.

The same lesson can be learned with regard to general ideas for institutional change and improvement within the context of our four academic cultures. If campus leaders are preoccupied with the managerial or negotiating culture, they are likely to be preoccupied with structural solutions and with rational planning as the chief means of disseminating innovative ideas. As a result, they will often ignore important information about, or be oblivious to needs associated with, changes in process or attitude; they may also fail to take into account the political and communal nature of the institution in which they are trying to effect change. Similarly, campus leaders from the collegial or developmental cultures are frequently ineffective when they look at an organization's problems only through the lenses of either process or attitude or through the use of problem solving, social interaction, or political processes. They will tend to ignore the substance of the change, while plotting complex public relations campaigns.

For many years, there have been proponents of change in each of Watson's three domains. Those favoring modifications of attitudes believe that real change only occurs when the heart has been transformed. By contrast, process-oriented change strategists propose that change will endure only if it involves relationships between people. Structural change advocates suggest that what counts is the financial outcome. For advocates of rational planning, the quality of the evidence and of the message should be sufficient for any academic audience. Those who believe in human problem solving and social interaction are likely to stress the personal factor, whereas political advocates focus on the distribution of power.

None of these positions is adequate by itself. All of these strategies are required if the change effort is to have a deep, enduring impact. We can begin in any of the three domains of change or with any of the four diffusion strategies. The important thing is to start and to recognize that eventually we must draw on all of these strategies if we are to meet the distinctive challenges (and exploit the potential) of each of the four cultures.

12

❖❖❖❖❖❖❖

Acknowledging
Cultural Realities
in Academic Leadership

We provided two models of organizational change and diffusion of innovation in Chapter Eleven. In this chapter, we will examine two additional models. The first is offered by Robert Birnbaum (1988), who described four different kinds of collegiate institutions, each holding a set of distinctive assumptions about the nature of organizational life and change. A second model is presented by Bolman and Deal (1991), who provides us with four frames through which we can view organizational problems and potential solutions. Each of these models (like those in Chapter Eleven) relates directly to our analysis of the four academic cultures and provides us with valuable understanding of ways that we can better comprehend and improve our colleges and universities.

Birnbaum's Four Institutional Types

Whereas Watson, Havelock, and Lindquist offer us general descriptions or principles regarding institutional change, Birnbaum suggests four hypothetical collegiate organizations that illustrate each of four institutional types: collegial, bureaucratic, political, and anarchical. As the reader will note in the similarity of names, Birnbaum and Havelock offer typologies that overlap to some extent and that are akin to the four cultures described in this book. Birnbaum even shares ground with Watson (as we shall discuss later). Never-

209

theless, the analysis that Birnbaum offers is distinctive in many regards. His hypothetical institutions offer rich insights, and the concepts that he introduces help us better understand life within complex, contemporary collegiate organizations.

The Collegial Institution

Birnbaum's collegial institution, like the collegial culture described in this book, is distinctive in its reliance on tradition, precedent, and informal power. According to Birnbaum (1988, p. 88): "The hierarchical structure and rational administrative procedures are absent [in the collegial institution]. Instead, because all members have equal standing, there is an emphasis on thoroughness and deliberation. It often takes a long time to reach major decisions. . . . Decisions are ultimately to be made by consensus, and not by fiat, so everyone must have an opportunity to speak and to consider carefully the views of colleagues."

The president in Birnbaum's collegial institution serves as the first among equals, rather than as the "boss" or even primary leader. The collegial president tends to rely on expertise and informal relationships to exert influence and rarely uses coercion or rewards to bring about institutional change. To be effective, this president must live up to the norms of the group. He or she is not above these very powerful, collegial norms. The president must conform to group expectations regarding leadership, use established channels of communication, and give orders that are fair and appropriate (and, as a result, that will be obeyed). The collegial president must also have excellent listening skills, the ability to learn from errors, and the willingness to minimize differences in status with other members of the organization. A collegial institution must usually remain small if the president is to play this more informal, interactive role.

Birnbaum suggests that there is "loose coupling" of the collegial institution with the external environment, but "tight coupling" within the organization. Put in somewhat different terms, the collegial institution tends to be a closed system; there are strict and impenetrable boundaries established between the institution and the outside world and highly informal boundaries among the subsystems within the organization. It is hard to get into the collegial institution; however, once inside, there is relatively easy access to all constituencies within the institution. According to Birnbaum (1988, p. 98): "Values that guide the administrative and instructional subsystems . . . are tightly coupled and therefore consistent because of the significant overlap in their personnel. But these same values, such as autonomy and academic freedom, lead to loose coupling within the administrative systems, because giving directives challenges the assumption of equality."

Thus, we find informality within the collegial institution and a homogeneity of both processes and attitudes (to use Watson's terms). The norms of rationality are prevalent, though rational planning is often superseded by a quasi-political mode of decision making and problem solving. Birnbaum's collegial institution is a representative of the collegial culture that was dominant prior to the 1960s. As Birnbaum notes, no collegiate institution now exists in this pure form; rather, each is a hybrid of several different institutional types and cultures.

The Bureaucratic Institution

According to Birnbaum, the bureaucratic institution is one with an organizational chart that is clear and that is taken seriously. Although we would expect large universities to rely on careful organization, they are often the least likely to sustain an effective bureaucracy, in large part because of their size and complexity. The author is reminded of an experience that occurred during a consulting assignment with the medical school at a large midwestern university. Leaders in the medical school had determined that one of the reasons members of the department tended to bypass the normal reporting structure of the institution was that they simply did not understand the university's organizational chart.

A representative from the president's office was asked to come to a meeting of the medical school faculty to explain the chart. When she put the graphic display of the university's organizational structure up on the overhead projector, the faculty members broke out in unbridled laughter; the chart closely resembled what one faculty member later called "the wiring diagram for the telephone system in New York City." Straight and dotted lines went out in every direction. One gained a distinct impression of confusion from this chart. It was no wonder that faculty members chose a more informal route when trying to get something done. The unfortunate representative from the president's office was never able to complete her presentation, for she, too, soon acknowledged that the bureaucracy of the university was unfathomable and perhaps unmanageable.

Thus, as we look at Birnbaum's bureaucratic organization, we are more likely to be examining the middle-sized institution (often a community college or mid-level state university) in which, as Birnbaum (1988, p. 111) notes: "The functions of each office are codified in rules and regulations, and officers are expected to respond to each other in terms of their roles, not their personalities. . . . The emphasis on written job descriptions and on rules and regulations that guide behavior increases organizational certainty and efficiency."

Birnbaum goes on to suggest that bureaucratic institutions tend to be rational organizations. There is a conscious attempt to relate explicitly means to ends, plans and the allocation of resources to institutional objectives, goals to mission statements (1988, p. 114): "Administrators and faculty who function within their roles must apply the same criteria to everyone, ensuring fairness and equity rather than personal favoritism, and subordinates are less subject to administrative caprice. The emphasis on rationality, performance, and expertise also limits the extent to which incompetent people can move into higher positions and reduces reliance on extraneous factors such as social status, sex, or religion in personnel decisions."

On the one hand, Birnbaum's bureaucratic institution would seem to embody the rational planning approach described by Havelock and Lindquist. Ideally, in a well-run bureaucratic institution, there would be no need for the negotiating culture. The managerial culture (or some combination of the managerial and developmental cultures) would rule. Everything would be equitable, and rational decision making would prevail. However, as in the case of most collegiate institutions, rational planning is a goal rather than a reality. The rational processes of the institution are diluted or overwhelmed by more irrational processes that are better described and managed through use of the social interaction, human problem solving, and political approaches to planned change. Components of the negotiating culture will mingle with managerial, developmental, and even collegial components to yield a dynamic, hybrid institution that incorporates all of Birnbaum's four institutional types.

With regard to tight and loose coupling, Birnbaum notes that bureaucracies are, in many instances, loose in that their subsystems are autonomous (though interconnected). Furthermore, in order to preserve the continuity and stability of a bureaucratic institution's policies and procedures, the institution must become a relatively closed system that changes only slowly in response to shifting demands from the environment or even from forces operating within the organization. Therefore, the negotiating culture will inevitably emerge, as bureaucratic structures fail to accommodate emerging or increasingly vocal minority or low-status groups.

Leadership in the bureaucratic institution, according to Birnbaum (1988, p. 126), requires skillful use of basic management principles—delegation of authority in particular: "As long as the person receiving an order from a superior believes in the legitimacy of the rule of law that provided for the delegation, that person is likely to expect to receive such orders and to be predisposed to accept them. But we know through our experiences that not all orders are obeyed. To understand why, it is necessary to examine the idea of authority from an organizational, rather than a legal, perspective."

At this point, Birnbaum notes, "Authority is no longer defined by the power of the person giving an order but instead by the willingness of the person receiving it to accept it" (Birnbaum, 1988, p. 126). The result is that "The greater the professional level of institutional staff members, the less effective bureaucratic controls will be in coordinating their behavior. It suggests why bureaucratic controls are usually less influential in dealing with faculty than in dealing with administrators. It also suggests why bureaucratic controls may be more effective [at a college in which fewer faculty] have the doctorate . . . are less professional . . . [and are] more likely to have had experience in secondary school systems and therefore to have been socialized to expect less involvement in decision making" (Birnbaum, p. 127).

Birnbaum's description of the bureaucracy and its functioning is clearly in line with the origins and founding characteristics of the managerial culture that is described in this book.

The Political Institution

Birnbaum observes that the political orientation of most collegiate institutions is nothing new. After all, Oxford University was the site many years ago of debates between constituencies that represented diverse perspectives on the higher educational enterprise. The role of political forces in collegiate institutions has become increasingly important, however, as they have become larger and more complicated:

> In a more complex institution, member groups tend to be more specialized and heterogeneous, with divergent interests and preferences. Subgroups may have their own perceptions of community, but the institution as a whole seldom does. Sometimes these subgroups are work groups, such as academic departments or administrative offices, and sometimes they are based on social factors such as sex, age, ethnicity, or ideology. Those who identify strongly with any of these groups thinks of each other as "we," and "they" can come to refer not just to groups outside the institution but to other groups inside as well [Birnbaum, p. 131].

In general, political institutions tend to evolve from collegial or bureaucratic institutions that have become large and often unwieldy. The organization becomes "too complex to control activities through bureaucratic systems" (Birnbaum, p. 131)—as we noted in our example of the midwestern medical school. Its members are unable to reach consensus regarding basic governing goals and objectives, and its culture and governance structure have become fragmented by special-interest groups that operate autonomously of each other and yet are dependent on each other for power and influence. The information of coalitions becomes critical to the operation of the political institution, as does the role of negotiator and mediator.

As Jack Lindquist also remarked in his description of the political strategy, the key to success in a political institution is to arouse interest in a specific issue: "A central characteristic of most political communities is indifference. Most people . . . are not concerned about most issues most of the time. Most of the time what happens . . . is routine and guided by existing procedures and informal understandings. But at irregular intervals, and for reasons that are not at all clear, a specific issue emerges and become contentious on campus" (Birnbaum, p. 137). Political processes (like bureaucratic ones) can get a bad name in many sectors of society (especially in higher education), but they serve invaluable functions, particularly in colleges and universities that are unable to formulate clear and consistent goals, that have become unstable, and that have immature cultures and values. Birnbaum's political institution, like the negotiating culture we have described, enables decisions to be made in the absence of shared goals and aspirations and helps to provide stability during periods of rapid change and turbulence.

The leader of a political institution or an institution dominated by the negotiating culture must, like Birnbaum's hypothetical President Robinson, strive for "flexible rigidity": a stance that allows for compromise on means but stubbornness with regard to ends. This type of leader tends to be a realist and someone who often works behind the scenes. Moreover, the leader of a political or negotiating-oriented institution must be able to occupy a variety of roles. Birnbaum cites Clark Kerr's description of a university president: "leader, educator, creator, initiator, wielder of power, pump; he is also officeholder, caretaker, inheritor, consensus-seeker, persuader, bottleneck. But he is mostly a mediator" (quoted in Birnbaum, p. 147). Above all, the presidents of most politicized collegiate institutions cease to be controlling forces in their institutions.

The Anarchical Institution

Birnbaum's "anarchical institution" (as we shall see with Bolman and Deal's "symbolic frame") represents the most radical and in many ways the most intriguing model of institutional life. One suspects that Birnbaum is describing an institutional type that is now becoming more prevalent or is already quite common. First of all, the anarchical institution is usually complex and large. It is generally composed of program units of differing sizes and structures, just as its student body (and faculty, administration, and staff) is a diverse mix of ages, ethnicities, and even degree of involvement in the school (full-time versus part-time enrollment). This type of institution often looks chaotic—hence the label anarchical. Yet, as we now know with regard to physical systems (see, for example, Gleick, 1987), this seemingly chaotic system serves specific functions and is in many ways quite effective and appropriate for certain educational purposes. It has its own structure and roles that often contradict the usual textbook notions of organizational behavior (Birnbaum, 1988, p. 154): "The concepts of the organized anarchy are counterintuitive. They defy the common expectations that are part of the more familiar ideas of organizations as communities, as bureaucracies, or as political systems. To understand them requires suspension of some common sense ideas about organizations that we 'know' are correct."

Birnbaum (1988, p. 154) suggests that we begin our analysis of anarchical institutions by abandoning some cherished ideas:

> Among these ideas are that organizational leaders play critical roles in institutional processes, that institutions have goals, that individuals can specify their preferences, that chains of cause and effect lead individuals and organizations to take certain actions in order to effectuate outcomes they consider desirable, that problems are solved by decisions, and that decision making is a primary occupation of organizational participants. In other words, they question common understandings of organizational rationality that presupposes that thinking precedes action, action

serves a purpose, purposes are related to consistent sets
of goals, and choice is based on logical relationships
between actions and consequences.

Other recent books regarding contemporary organizational
life speak in a similar manner of the basic changes that are now
taking place in the way institutions are structured (Peters, 1987) and
also in the parts that human service agencies can realistically play
in the amelioration of deeply embedded social problems (Drucker,
1989). We seem to be entering a postmodern era (Bergquist, forthcoming) in which many institutions—not just colleges and universities—will come to resemble Birnbaum's anarchical institution.

Birnbaum states that an organized anarchy can be defined by
three characteristics: problematic goals, an unclear technology, and
fluid participation. With easily crossed boundaries, the anarchical
institution is constantly being inundated with new participants,
ideas, technologies, and, as a result, needs: "There are probably few,
if any, occasions on which decisions on two related issues are made
by the same people. People tend to move in and out of various parts
of the organization, and their involvement in any issue depends to
a great extent on what other opportunities for their attention
happen to be available at the same time" (Birnbaum, p. 156).

In reading Birnbaum's description of the anarchical institution, one is reminded of the fragmented organizational climates at
both Fairfield College (Chapter Four) and Plainsville Community
College (Chapter Eight). These colleges, like many contemporary
collegiate institutions, discourage participation and commitment.
Their members (whether students, faculty, or administrators) try to
spend as little time as possible on campus. Very little institutional
loyalty accrues, and everyone becomes, in essence, a "commuter"
who goes to school each day (or every second or third day), primarily to obtain a degree or paycheck.

Virtually all elements of the anarchical institution are
loosely coupled. It is never clear what causes what and how one
might best change or improve specific functions within the organization. As Bergquist and Phillips (1977) note, academic institutions often more closely resemble communities than they do
organizations. Their leaders act more like mayors of cities or small

towns than they do leaders of corporations or even other types of educational institutions. Some of the best strategies for leading and managing such institutions are certainly novel and deserve considerable attention and discussion. Bergquist and Phillips (1977) also suggest that community development strategies might be more appropriate in these institutions than organizational development. The techniques first developed by Saul Alinsky (1969) may ultimately prove to be of greater value to academic settings than are the strategies of the gurus of corporate change.

Much as Lindquist speaks of the need for politically based approaches to change, so must the academic leader who confronts structured anarchy employ nonrational techniques. Birnbaum, for example, points to the important role played by "garbage cans" in the management of any decision-making process in an anarchical organization. In essence, the garbage-can strategy is based on the idea that there are programs, groups, or individuals in anarchical institutions that attract (or absorb) problems and concerns—much as the "strange attractors" in chaotic systems create order out of chaos (see Bergquist, forthcoming; Gleick, 1987). A long-term planning committee, for instance, might attract a diverse set of concerns about parking, affirmative action, salaries for nonexempt employees, and new water fountains for the student union. According to Birnbaum (1988, p. 165): "Garbage cans in an organization act like buffers or "energy sinks" that absorb problems, solutions, and participants like a sponge and prevent them from sloshing around and disturbing arenas in which people wish to act. Ad hoc long-range institutional planning committees may be the quintessential garbage cans, temporarily providing "homes" for any conceivable institutional problem, solution, or participant. But there may also be permanent structural garbage cans, such as the academic senate, that function at least in part to draw unwanted participants, problems, or solutions away from decision arenas." Institutional garbage cans, as well as various symbolically rich units within an anarchical organization, permit participants in the institution to "substitute belief for action" (Birnbaum, p. 165).

The primary functions served by the leader of an anarchical organization are spending time on a small number of projects that have symbolic importance to the institution, persisting in the initiation and maintenance of high-priority actions, providing members of the organization with status in exchange for their support of a specific substantive issue, and facilitating the participation of one's opposition in the deliberations of the institution. To ensure that the system does not get overloaded with ideas and competing factions, the anarchical leader must also provide garbage cans "that attract other people's garbage and keep them away from one's own proposal" (Birnbaum, p. 171). The leader must manage in an unobtrusive manner by introducing small, incremental changes rather than highly visible ones and must interpret the history of the institution in a way that supports and provides meaning for the directions in which it is now moving or must begin to move.

Such a leader will gain little specific guidance from any one of the four academic cultures in isolation, though much could be learned from observing the interaction between them in the daily life of the leader's institution. We can hope that the developmental culture will ultimately be responsive to the unique training and development needs associated with the demanding new roles of the anarchical leader. Programs of this kind would both be of value to the leader and also enhance the credibility of the developmental culture in the increasingly anarchical world of American higher education.

Bolman and Deal's Four Frames

The models of institutional functioning that have been offered by Birnbaum describe four different types of institutions. Like the institutional types in Birnbaum's cybernetic institution, the four cultures being proposed in this book are also assumed to be present, to varying degrees, in all contemporary collegiate institutions. Two of the four cultures (collegial and managerial) had their origins in different institutional types; however, both of these and the two newer cultures (negotiating and development) are now evident throughout American higher education.

Similarly, the four frames that are proposed by Bolman and Deal (1991) will be found in all organizations; they represent differing ways of looking at any organization, regardless of its origins or form. One might argue, in fact, that the frames being proposed by

Bolman and Deal are aspects of the four cultures described in this book: in both sets of organizational models, the primary ingredient is the perspective provided on certain institutional phenomena (for example, leadership or decision-making processes).

The Structural Frame

As Watson noted, many organizational analyses of change strategies begin with an examination of the formal roles, responsibilities, and relationships that exist in the organization. Certainly, organizations that are (in Birnbaum's terms) bureaucratic in nature or that are ruled by the managerial culture will encourage a structural approach. According to Bolman and Deal, there are six basic assumptions that underlie the structural perspective:

1. Organizations exist primarily to accomplish established goals.
2. For any organization, a structural form can be designed and implemented to fit its particular set of circumstances (such as goals, strategies, environment, technology, and people).
3. Organizations work most effectively when environmental turbulence and personal preferences are constrained by norms of rationality. (Structure ensures that people focus on getting the job done rather than on doing whatever they please.)
4. Specialization permits higher levels of individual expertise and performance.
5. Coordination and control are essential to effectiveness. (Depending on the task and environment, coordination may be achieved through authority, rules, policies, standard operating procedures, information systems, meetings, lateral relationships, or a variety of more informal techniques.)
6. Organizational problems typically originate from inappropriate structures or inadequate systems

and can be resolved through restructuring or developing new systems [Bolman and Deal, p. 48].

These assumptions are based directly on the dominance of the structural perspective among collegiate leaders who embrace the managerial culture and could be considered their guiding principles. This culture certainly encourages the formulation, clarification, and maintenance of clear goals at all levels of the organization (including instruction). Furthermore, the managerial culture places great emphasis on rationality (as do the collegial and developmental cultures). Innovations in structure are produced and disseminated primarily through what Havelock would call a rational (research and development) diffusion process. As Bolman and Deal also observe (1991), attention is devoted, from a structural perspective, to two major issues: (1) the division of work into specialized roles, functions, and units, and (2) the creation of organizational units and functions that help to coordinate and integrate these specialized elements vertically and horizontally into the organization. As academic organizations become larger and increasingly responsive to diverse and often contradictory community and societal needs, the role of both specialization and integration becomes critical to an organization's survival. Certainly, some of the most important benefits derived from the managerial culture and the structural perspective in higher education are the creation of both traditional and nontraditional organizational structures (see, for example, Bergquist, Gould, and Greenberg, 1981) to meet these complex demands.

The structural perspective, however, has also been a source of considerable disruption and disappointment. First, the formal structures of an organization may or may not be linked to the informal political processes that are required to move ideas and programs through a collegiate institution. Furthermore, formal structures cannot protect individuals in the organization from the abuse of power or from the seeming irrationality associated with these political processes. Structural strategies for bringing about reform and improvement in American higher education will be inadequate and ultimately unsuccessful if they do not take into account Bolman and Deal's political frame, the lessons to be learned from Birnbaum's political institution, or Lindquist's political strategies for the diffusion of innovation. Moreover, those who live within the managerial culture (as well as the developmental culture) must take into account the political aspects of both the collegial and negotiating cultures if they are to survive in contemporary collegiate institutions that are hybrids of all four cultures.

A second problem concerns the need for an appropriate set of attitudes (to use Watson's term) to accompany any structural change. For instance, attitudes regarding structural change found in the collegial, developmental, and negotiating cultures will often distort or at least create resistance to efforts aimed at ameliorating organizational problems with alterations of structure. For those who are deeply embedded in the collegial culture, structural changes are often viewed as ephemeral—as administrative window-dressing that has little impact on the daily life of the institution. Representatives of the negotiating culture, by contrast, tend to view structural changes with considerable alarm and often assume that they are being introduced to undermine or bypass faculty or staff authority. Finally, proponents of the developmental culture are inclined to perceive structural change as misguided and often dehumanizing. They share with those from the negotiating culture a fear of injustice and with those from the collegial culture an ultimate disbelief that such changes will ever have a lasting effect.

A third problem associated with the structural frame concerns the interpersonal skills that are needed for members of an organization to live and work within a specific structure. Watson speaks of the necessity of process-oriented strategies to accompany structural changes, just as proponents of the developmental culture describe the need for personal training as an adjunct to any changes in curriculum, instructional technology, or organizational structure. Similarly, Bolman and Deal's human resource frame, to which we now turn, must accompany any structural plan if it is to be successful.

The Human Resource Frame

The developmental culture is the latest of the four cultures to receive widespread attention in the higher education literature. In the same way, the human resource frame has more contemporary origins than either the structural or political frame offered by Bolman and Deal. Both the developmental culture and the human resource frame grew out of the identification of differing personal needs among members of organizations and the recognition that an organization serves its own best interests by meeting these needs. Bolman and Deal (1991, p. 121) make four specific suggestions with regard to the human resource frame:

1. Organizations exist to serve human needs (rather than the reverse).
2. Organizations and people need each other. (Organizations need ideas, energy, and talent; people need careers, salaries, and work opportunities.)
3. When the fit between the individual and the organization is poor, one or both will suffer: individuals will be exploited, or will seek to exploit the organizations, or both.
4. A good fit between individual and organization benefits both: human beings find meaningful and satisfying work, and organizations get the human talent and energy that they need.

Like the match between the structural frame and the managerial culture, we find a close correspondence between the values and perspectives of the human resource frame and those associated with the developmental culture (as well as with Watson's process-oriented strategy for change and Havelock's human problem solving strategy for the diffusion of innovation). In all of these models, attention is focused on the psychological aspects of organizational life, often at the expense of political, functional, and even financial aspects of life in the organization. Although they will carefully look after the higher-order needs of men and women in an organization (such as recognition and the meaning of the work being performed), human resource practitioners often overlook lower-order requirements (such as adequate pay, decent working conditions, and job security) that are better addressed through the negotiating (and even sometimes the managerial) culture.

All too often, developmentalists become unknowing conspirators in an effort to diffuse or distract legitimate faculty and staff complaints through the provision of cathartic (but not helpful) developmental workshops and team-building sessions. Bolman and Deal (1991, p. 177) state, "Human resource theories have been criticized primarily on two grounds: that they are naive and that they are easily co-opted by power elites." They go on to note (p. 179) that human resource theorists and practitioners "have rarely asked if there are fundamental differences in the interests of workers and management that are rooted in the larger institutional environment." In other words, those from the developmental culture of higher education must learn from those who see the institution through the lenses of the negotiating culture, just as advocates of the negotiating culture must come to see (with the help of a developmentalist) that a collegiate institution is something more than a place of competing interests. There must be shared concern for the teaching and learning enterprise.

The key to successful human resource development resides in the reflections of Watson, who insisted that changes in processes (such as new modes of instruction or new decision-making styles) must be accompanied by shifts in structure and attitude if these changes are to be sustained and are to have a positive, humanizing effect on the life of the organization. The political frame, to which we now turn, is particularly important as a corrective to the naive optimism of the developmental culture and the human resource frame; it is also critical to the initiation and maintenance of any change in either structure or attitude.

The Political Frame

As noted above, those who reside primarily in the negotiating culture of an academic institution are inclined to see it as nothing more than a political arena—and are likely to adopt a political frame when viewing the dynamics of the organization. When organizations are perceived as political arenas, according to Bolman and Deal (1991, p. 186), there are several consequences:

1. Organizations are coalitions composed of varied individuals and interest groups (for example,

hierarchical levels, departments, professional groups, gender and ethnic subgroups).

2. There are enduring differences among individuals and groups in their values, preferences, beliefs, information, and perceptions of reality. Such differences change slowly, if at all.

3. Most of the important decisions in organizations involve the allocation of scarce resources: they are decisions about who gets what.

4. Because of scarce resources and enduring differences, conflict is central to organizational dynamics, and power is the most important resource.

5. Organizational goals and decisions emerge from bargaining, negotiation, and jockeying for position among members of different coalitions.

Most members of the negotiating culture in American higher education would probably agree with some, if not all, of the propositions just outlined. Effective change—as the union leaders at Plainsville Community College or Fairfield State University will acknowledge and as Bernie Kefelmann has reluctantly come to realize—requires the building of coalitions among factions that share concerns and problems. Of course, these coalitions may be short lived and are often based on mutual interest rather than on any ideological agreement.

The acknowledgment of political realities is probably the hardest task for most proponents of the other three collegiate cultures. Those who come from the collegial and managerial cultures often express their dismay at the irrationality of the political process; all three of the other cultures are alarmed at the seeming indifference of the political culture to the educational values, aspirations, or ideals of the institution. Members of the negotiating culture seem to be indifferent to teaching and learning and spend more time in political meetings than in preparation for class.

Yet as we examine the life of a man like Bernie Kefelmann, we find not so much lack of interest in the educational mission of the institution as a new and more realistic appraisal of how long-lasting educational improvement can really take place, given major

decreases in public support for higher education and the exertion
of increasing control in many postsecondary education systems by
lay or politically appointed boards of governors. Kefelmann is
fighting less for his own personal welfare (wages, benefits, working
conditions) than for the right of faculty to determine or at least
influence the nature of their daily work as teachers and counselors.

Though they are healthy additions to the changing world of
politicized higher education, the political frame and the negotiating
culture will benefit significantly from the other frames and cultures.
The collegial and managerial cultures force the academic politician
to reflect on the reasons for doing battle. It is easy to forget what
the battle is really about when one is surrounded by political enemies and is fighting for one's political life. The structural frame and
Watson's structural strategies for change are also critical, for they
help to establish a fair battlefield. Structures provide stability of role
and responsibility and sometimes even become the formal entities
that are negotiated by both parties (for example, a union that bar-
gains for a representative on the board of trustees).

Similarly, the political frame clearly needs the skill-building
components of the human resource frame (and the process-oriented
change strategist); extraordinary talents are required to construct
coalitions, negotiate between competing factions, allocate scarce resources, resolve conflict, and mediate power differentials. Donald
Schön (1973) suggests that these brokering roles are becoming increasingly prevalent and that they will increasingly combine with
the types of roles defined by the symbolic frame, to which we now
turn.

The Symbolic Frame

In their identification and articulation of the symbolic frame, Bolman and Deal have probably made their most valuable contribu-
tion, for it is in this frame that they draw from disciplines other
than psychology and management to advance our understanding of
organizational dynamics. Specifically, Bolman and Deal make use
of anthropology, linguistics, and even literature in their construction of this frame: "Managers who turn to Peter Drucker's *The
Effective Executive* for guidance might do better to study Lewis

Carroll's *Through the Looking Glass*" (Bolman and Deal, 1991, p. 245). Bolman and Deal themselves recognize that the assumptions underlying the symbolic frame are unconventional:

1. What is most important about any event is not what happened, but what it means.
2. Events and meanings are loosely coupled; the same events can have very different meanings for different people because of differences in the schema that they use to interpret their experience.
3. Many of the most significant events and processes in organizations are ambiguous or uncertain—it is often difficult or impossible to know what happened, why it happened, or what will happen next.
4. The greater the ambiguity and uncertainty, the harder it is to use rational approaches to analysis, problem solving, and decision making.
5. Faced with uncertainty and ambiguity, human beings create symbols to resolve confusion, increase predictability, and provide direction. (Events themselves may remain illogical, random, fluid, and meaningless, but human symbols make them seem otherwise.)
6. Many organizational events and processes are important more for what they express than for what they produce: they are secular myths, rituals, ceremonies, and sagas that help people find meaning and order in their experience [1991, p. 245].

In their emphasis on culture and on rituals, symbols, stories, and the role of organizations as theater, Bolman and Deal focus on many of the notions about attitude change that Watson and Johnson (1972) had less clearly articulated at an earlier time. Watson spoke of the assumption that attitudes had to change before real alterations in behavior, structure, or processes could take place. Bolman and Deal suggest that much of this attitude change may occur in the context of a search for personal meaning within an organizational context and of an organization's construction of symbols, rituals, and stories that support this search. Similarly, in building on the work of Everett Rogers, Ronald Havelock and Jack Lindquist have directed our attention, by means of the social interaction model, away from the overt content of a message that is being disseminated in an organization to its inherent meaning. To understand the resistance experienced in any collegiate organization to a new idea or innovative program, one must first determine the way in which this idea or program will be interpreted by those now there—in light of their past history in the organization and, as we have emphasized, the organization's dominant culture(s).

In each of the case studies offered in this book, we have tried to show how events and issues are understood differently by various constituencies. At Canon College, for example, a generous monetary gift that is to be used for curriculum development is perceived in a variety of ways by those in the developmental culture (who see these funds as a blessing), those in the negotiating culture (who see the money as directed toward low-priority problems), those in the collegial culture (who view the grant as a potential source of faculty division and competition), and those in the managerial culture (who believe that the funds are basically an administrative headache). At Plainsville Community College, we see even more dramatically the various constituencies' differing interpretations of events. Newcomers find that they will only be accepted into the Plainsville community if they are willing to reduce their potential level of threat by making a publicly acknowledged blunder, whereas the old-timers think they are demonstrating their willingness to let less experienced faculty try their hand at running the faculty governance system in the college. As we noted in the Plainsville case study, the reoccurring rites of initiation and betrayal in the college confine faculty and administrators to specific roles and scripts. The theatrical metaphor that Bolman and Deal employ in their own analysis of the symbolic frame is quite applicable and illuminating in the Plainsville case.

Bolman and Deal's symbolic frame is clearly connected to Birnbaum's anarchical institution, given its emphasis on style rather than substance, on the reconciliation of diverse perspectives and value systems, and on the role of seemingly chaotic and irrational forces in the implementation of managerial and governance processes. Ironically, although both the anarchical organization and the symbolic frame are geared to the emerging dynamics of postmodern organizations (Bergquist, forthcoming), they are also relevant to our understanding of the oldest of the four academic cultures: the collegial culture. This culture relies heavily on both the complexity of the anarchical institution and the fluidity of the symbolic frame.

Just as the three characteristics attributed by Birnbaum to the anarchical institution (problematic goals, unclear technology, and fluid participation) are all descriptive of the collegial culture, so are the symbolic frame's reliance on precedent, informal roles, and symbolic functions. Perhaps one of the reasons why the collegial culture has remained dominant over many years of change in American higher education is its blend of flexibility and ambiguity, on the one hand, and stability and predictability, on the other.

Our case study of Jim Herbert (the chemist from Western State University) illustrates the clear priority given in the collegial culture to scholarly publications and participation in faculty governance. It also demonstrates the subtle and often elusive ways in which these priorities are shaped, articulated, and sustained. Western State University is committed in all of its official documents (and in the master plan of the state higher education board) to excellence in teaching and student advising, but Jim Herbert is made constantly aware (through the stories, rituals, and symbolic rewards of the university) that this formal commitment to teaching is much less important than either scholarship or involvement in governance.

The analyses of culture offered in this book are potentially of greatest value when applied specifically to the anarchical type of institution that has been identified by Robert Birnbaum and when used in conjunction with Bolman and Deal's highly instructive symbolic frame. These types of institutions and frames will surely not diminish in number and importance as American colleges and universities prepare for a new century. We are also unlikely to see the immediate demise of any of the four academic cultures that were described in this book. Rather, we can look forward to working and finding meaning in colleges and universities that embrace all four cultures. One of the best ways that we can begin to prepare for this task and to cope with challenges posed by these new organizational types and frames is to examine our own institutions in order to appreciate and engage the diverse and often conflicting cultures that reside in them.

References

Adams, H. *The Academic Tribes.* New York: Liveright, 1976.

Alinsky, S. *Reveille for Radicals.* New York: Random House, 1969.

Anderson, S., and others. *Encyclopedia of Educational Evaluation.* San Francisco: Jossey-Bass, 1976.

Argyris, C. *Intervention Theory and Method.* Reading, Mass.: Addison-Wesley, 1970.

Argyris, C. *Reasoning, Learning, and Action: Individual and Organizational.* San Francisco: Jossey-Bass, 1982.

Argyris, C., Putnam, R., and Smith, D. M. *Action Science: Concepts, Methods, and Skills for Research and Intervention.* San Francisco: Jossey-Bass, 1985.

Argyris, C., and Schön, D. *Theory in Practice: Increasing Professional Effectiveness.* San Francisco: Jossey-Bass, 1974.

Argyris, C., and Schön, D. *Organizational Learning.* Reading, Mass.: Addison-Wesley, 1978.

Astin, A., and others. *Faculty Development in a Time of Retrenchment.* New York: Change Magazine, 1974.

Axelrod, J. *The University Teacher as Artist.* San Francisco: Jossey-Bass, 1973.

Axelrod, J. "From Counterculture to Counterrevolution: A Teaching Career." In K. E. Eble (ed.), *Improving Teaching Styles.* New Directions for Teaching and Learning, no. 1. San Francisco: Jossey-Bass, 1980.

231

Bandler, R., and Grinder, J. *Reframing*. Moab, Utah: Real People Press, 1982.

Barber, N. "The Organization as Curriculum: An Exploration of the Learning Implications of Organizational Culture and Administrative Practice in Colleges." Unpublished doctoral dissertation, Wright Institute, Berkeley, Calif., 1984.

Bateson, G. *Steps to an Ecology of Mind*. New York: Ballantine, 1972.

Bateson, G. *Mind and Nature*. New York: Dutton, 1979.

Beckhard, R. *Organization Development: Strategies and Models*. Reading, Mass.: Addison-Wesley, 1969.

Belenky, M. F., Clinchy, B. M., Goldberger, N. R., and Tarule, J. *Women's Ways of Knowing*. New York: Basic Books, 1986.

Bellah, R., and others. *Habits of the Heart*. Berkeley: University of California Press, 1985.

Ben-David, J. *American Higher Education*. New York: McGraw-Hill, 1972.

Bergquist, W. H. *Managing on the Edge: Life in the Postmodern Organization*. Forthcoming.

Bergquist, W. H., and Armstrong, J. L. *Planning Effectively for Educational Quality: An Outcomes-Based Approach for Colleges Committed to Excellence*. San Francisco: Jossey-Bass, 1986.

Bergquist, W. H., Gould, R. A., and Greenberg, E. M. *Designing Undergraduate Education: A Systematic Guide*. San Francisco: Jossey-Bass, 1981.

Bergquist, W. H., Lounibos, J., and Langfitt, J. *The College I Experience*. Washington, D.C.: Council of Independent Colleges, 1980.

Bergquist, W. H., and Phillips, S. *A Handbook for Faculty Development: Volume I*. Washington, D.C.: Council of Independent Colleges, 1975.

Bergquist, W. H., and Phillips, S. *A Handbook for Faculty Development: Volume II*. Washington, D.C.: Council of Independent Colleges, 1977.

Bergquist, W. H., and Phillips, S. *A Handbook for Faculty Development: Volume III*. Washington, D.C.: Council of Independent Colleges, 1981.

Bergquist, W. H., and Shoemaker, W. A. (eds.). *A Comprehensive*

Approach to Institutional Development. New Directions for Higher Education, no. 15. San Francisco: Jossey-Bass, 1976.

Bion, W. *Experience in Groups.* New York: Ballantine, 1974.

Birnbaum, R. *How Colleges Work: The Cybernetics of Academic Organization and Leadership.* San Francisco: Jossey-Bass, 1988.

Blake, R., Mouton, J. S., and Williams, M. S. *The Academic Administrator Grid.* San Francisco: Jossey-Bass, 1981.

Bolman, L. G., and Deal, T. E. *Reframing Organizations: Artistry, Choice, and Leadership.* San Francisco: Jossey-Bass, 1991.

Bowen, H. R., and Douglass, G. K. *Efficiency in Liberal Education.* New York: McGraw-Hill, 1971.

Boyer, R., and Crockett, C. Introduction. *Journal of Higher Education,* Special Issue on Organization Development in Higher Education, 1973, *44,* 339–351.

Briggs-Myers, I. *The Myers-Briggs Type Indicator.* Palo Alto, Calif.: Consulting Psychologist Press, 1976.

Briggs-Myers, I. *Gifts Differing.* Palo Alto, Calif.: Consulting Psychologist Press, 1980.

Brubacher, J. S., and Rudy, W. *Higher Education in Transition.* New York: HarperCollins, 1958.

Burke, W. *Organization Development: Principles and Practices.* Boston: Little, Brown, 1982.

Burke, W. *Organization Development: A Normative Approach.* Reading, Mass.: Addison-Wesley, 1987.

Carlber, R. J., and others. *Faculty Development Manual.* Wenham, Mass.: Gordon College, 1978.

Carnegie Commission on Higher Education. *The Fourth Revolution: Instructional Technology in Higher Education.* New York: McGraw-Hill, 1972.

Carr, R. K., and Van Eyck, D. K. *Collective Bargaining Comes to the Campus.* Washington, D.C.: American Council on Education, 1973.

Chickering, A. W. *Education and Identity.* San Francisco: Jossey-Bass, 1969.

Clark, B. R. *The Open Door College: A Case Study.* New York: McGraw-Hill, 1960.

Clark, B. R. *The Distinctive College: Antioch, Reed, and Swarthmore.* Hawthorne, N.Y.: Aldine, 1970.

Colman, R., and Bexton, W. *Group Relations Reader*. San Francisco: GREX, 1975.

Czesak, K. *Paradigms of Scholarship*. Unpublished doctoral dissertation, Wright Institute, Berkeley, Calif., 1984.

Deal, T. E., and Kennedy, A. A. *Corporate Cultures: The Rites and Rituals of Corporate Life*. Reading, Mass.: Addison-Wesley, 1982.

Deegan, W. L. "Entrepreneurial Management: A Fourth Concept of College Management for the Decade Ahead." In T. O'Banion (ed.), *Innovation in the Community College*. New York: Macmillan, 1989.

Dewey, J. *Democracy and Education*. New York: Free Press, 1944. (Originally published 1916.)

Dewey, J. *The Quest for Certainty*. New York: Capricorn Books, 1960. (Originally published 1929.)

Diamond, R. M. "Syracuse University: A Systematic Approach to Curriculum and Faculty Development." In W. H. Bergquist and W. A. Shoemaker (eds.), *A Comprehensive Approach to Institutional Development*. New Directions for Higher Education, no. 15. San Francisco: Jossey-Bass, 1976.

Diamond, R. M., and others. *Instructional Development for Individualized Learning in Higher Education*. Englewood Cliffs, N.J.: Educational Technology Publications, 1975.

Douglas, J. M. "Unionization among College Faculty." In G. T. Kurian (ed.), *Yearbook of American Universities and Colleges*. New York: Garland, 1988.

Drucker, P. *The New Realities*. New York: HarperCollins, 1989.

Etzioni, A. *Complex Organizations*. Troy, Mo.: Holt, Rinehart & Winston, 1961.

Freedman, M., and others. *Academic Culture and Faculty Development*. Berkeley, Calif.: Montaigne Press, 1979.

French, J.R.P., and Raven, B. "The Bases of Social Power." In D. Cartwright and A. Zander (eds.), *Group Dynamics*. New York: HarperCollins, 1968.

French, W., and Bell, C., Jr. *Organization Development*. (2nd ed.) Englewood Cliffs, N.J.: Prentice-Hall, 1978.

Gaff, J. G. *Institutional Renewal Through the Improvement of Teaching*. San Francisco: Jossey-Bass, 1978.

Genova, W. J., and others. *Mutual Benefit Evaluation of Faculty and Administrators in Higher Education.* New York: Ballinger, 1976.

Gilligan, C. *In a Different Voice.* Cambridge, Mass.: Harvard University Press, 1982.

Gleason, P. "American Catholic Higher Education: A Historical Perspective." In R. Hessenger (ed.), *The Shape of Catholic Higher Education.* Chicago: University of Chicago Press, 1967.

Gleick, J. *Chaos: Making a New Science.* New York: Penguin, 1987.

Goffman, E. "On Cooling the Mark Out." *Psychiatry,* 1952, *15,* 451–463.

Greenleaf, R. K. *The Servant as Leader.* Peterborough, N.H.: Center for Applied Studies, 1970.

Greenleaf, R. K. *The Institution as Servant.* Peterborough, N.H.: Center for Applied Studies, 1972.

Greenleaf, R. K. *Trustees as Servants.* Peterborough, N.H.: Center for Applied Studies, 1974.

Greenleaf, R. K. *Teacher as Servant.* New York: Paulist Press, 1979.

Greenleaf, R. K. *Servant: Retrospect and Prospect.* Peterborough, N.H.: Center for Applied Studies, 1980.

Harper, W. R. "The High School of the Future." *The School Review,* 1909, *11,* 1.

Havelock, R. *Planning for Innovation Through the Dissemination and Utilization of Scientific Knowledge.* Ann Arbor, Mich.: Institute for Social Research, 1971.

Hill, J. *The Educational Sciences.* Oakland, Mich.: Oakland Community College, n.d.

Hillway, T. *The American Two-Year College.* New York: HarperCollins, 1958.

Jencks, C., and Riesman, D. *The Academic Revolution.* Chicago: University of Chicago Press, 1968.

Johnstone, R. L. *The Scope of Faculty Collective Bargaining.* Westport, Conn.: Greenwood Press, 1981.

Kanter, R. M. *The Change Masters.* New York: Simon & Schuster, 1984.

Katz, J., and Associates. *No Time for Youth: Growth and Constraint in College Students.* San Francisco: Jossey-Bass, 1968.

Kemerer, F. R., and Baldridge, J. V. *Unions on Campus.* San Francisco: Jossey-Bass, 1975.

Kerr, C. *The Uses of the University.* Cambridge, Mass.: Harvard University Press, 1963.

Knefelkamp, L., Widick, C., and Parker, C. (eds.) *Applying New Developmental Findings.* New Directions for Student Services, no. 4. San Francisco: Jossey-Bass, 1978.

Kolb, D. *The Learning Style Inventory.* Boston: McBer, 1976.

Kuhn, T. *The Structure of Scientific Revolution.* Chicago: University of Chicago Press, 1962.

Ladd, E. C., Jr., and Lipset, S. M. *Professors, Unions and American Higher Education.* New York: McGraw-Hill, 1973.

Landrith, H. *Introduction to the Community College.* Danville, Ill.: Interstate Printers and Publishers, 1971.

Lawler, E. E., III. *High-Involvement Management: Participative Strategies for Improving Organization Performance.* San Francisco: Jossey-Bass, 1986.

Lawler, E. E., III. *Strategic Pay: Aligning Organizational Strategies and Pay Systems.* San Francisco: Jossey-Bass, 1990.

Lessem, R. *Managing Corporate Culture.* Brookfield, Vt.: Gower, 1990.

Likert, R. *The Human Organization.* New York: McGraw-Hill, 1967.

Lindquist, J. "Approaches to Collegiate Teaching Improvement." In J. Lindquist (ed.), *Designing Teaching Improvement Programs.* Washington, D.C.: Council of Independent Colleges, 1978a.

Lindquist, J. *Strategies for Change.* Washington, D.C.: Council of Independent Colleges, 1978b.

Lippitt, R., Watson, J., and Westley, B. *Dynamics of Planned Change.* Orlando, Fla.: Harcourt Brace Jovanovich, 1958.

London, H. B. *The Culture of a Community College.* New York: Praeger, 1978.

Malinowski, B. *A Scientific Theory of Culture.* Oxford, England: Oxford University Press, 1948.

Martin, W. B. *Conformity: Standards and Change in Higher Education.* San Francisco: Jossey-Bass, 1969.

Medsker, L. L., and Tillery, D. *Breaking the Access Barriers.* New York: McGraw-Hill, 1971.

Millett, J. *The Academic Community: An Essay on Organization.* New York: McGraw-Hill, 1962.

O'Banion, T. "The Renaissance of Innovation." In T. O'Banion (ed.), *Innovation in the Community College.* New York: Macmillan, 1989.

O'Donnell, K. M., and Berkeley, W. D. "Elderhostel: A National Program." In E. Greenberg, K. M. O'Donnell, and W. H. Bergquist (eds.), *Educating Learners of All Ages.* New Directions for Higher Education, no. 29. San Francisco: Jossey-Bass, 1980.

Parlett, M., and Dearden, G. (eds.). *An Introduction to Illuminative Evaluation.* Washington, D.C.: Council of Independent Colleges, 1977.

Parsons, T., and Platt, G. M. *The American University.* Cambridge, Mass.: Harvard University Press, 1973.

Peck, R. D. *Future Focusing: An Alternative to Long-Range Planning.* Washington, D.C.: Council of Independent Colleges, 1983.

Perkins, J. *The University as an Organization.* New York: McGraw-Hill, 1973.

Perry, W. *Forms of Intellectual and Ethical Development in the College Years: A Scheme.* Troy, Mo.: Holt, Rinehart & Winston, 1970.

Peters, T. J. *Thriving on Chaos.* New York: HarperCollins, 1987.

Peters, T. J., and Waterman, R. H. *In Search of Excellence: Lessons from America's Best-Run Companies.* New York: HarperCollins, 1982.

Pettigrew, A. M. "On Studying Organizational Cultures." *Administrative Science Quarterly,* 1979, *24,* 570–581.

Polanyi, M. "Sense-Reading and Sense-Giving." In M. Polanyi (ed.), *Knowing and Being.* Chicago: University of Chicago Press, 1969.

Popham, W. J. *Criterion-Referenced Measurement.* Englewood Cliffs, N.J.: Prentice-Hall, 1978.

Pusey, N. *The Age of the Scholar.* Cambridge, Mass.: Harvard University Press, 1963.

Riechmann, S., and Grasha, A. "A Rational Approach to Developing and Assessing the Construct Validity of a Student Learning

Style Scale Instrument." *The Journal of Psychology*, 1974, *87*, 213-223.

Riesman, D., Gusfield, J., and Gamson, Z. *Academic Values and Mass Education: The Early Years of Oakland Monteith.* New York: Doubleday, 1970.

Rogers, C. *Freedom to Learn.* Columbus, Ohio: Merrill, 1968.

Rogers, E. M. *Diffusion of Innovations.* (3rd ed.) New York: Free Press, 1982.

Rudolph, F. *The American College and University: A History.* New York: Random House, 1962.

Sanford, N. (ed.). *The American College.* New York: Wiley, 1962.

Sanford, N. "Academic Culture and the Teacher's Development." *Sounding*, Winter 1971, pp. 357-371.

Schein, E. *Organizational Psychology.* (3rd ed.) Englewood Cliffs, N.J.: Prentice-Hall, 1980.

Schein, E. *Organizational Culture and Leadership: A Dynamic View.* San Francisco: Jossey-Bass, 1985.

Schein, E., and Bennis, W. G. *Personal and Organizational Change Through Group Methods.* New York: Wiley, 1965.

Schön, D. *Beyond the Stable State.* New York: W. W. Norton, 1973.

Schön, D. *The Reflective Practitioner.* New York: Basic Books, 1984.

Scriven, M. "Pros and Cons about Goal-Free Evaluation." *Evaluation Comment*, 1972, pp. 1-4.

Sennett, R. *Authority.* New York: Random House, 1981.

Sikes, W., Schlesinger, L. E., and Seashore, C. N. *Renewing Higher Education from Within.* San Francisco: Jossey-Bass, 1974.

Sprunger, B., and Bergquist, W. *Handbook for College Administration.* Washington, D.C.: Council of Independent Colleges, 1978.

Tierney, W. G. "Organizational Culture in Higher Education." *Journal of Higher Education*, 1988, *59*, 2-21.

Tierney, W. G. (ed.). *Assessing Academic Climates and Cultures.* New Directions for Institutional Research, no. 68. San Francisco: Jossey-Bass, 1990.

Watson, G., and Johnson, D. *Social Psychology: Issues and Insights.* (2nd ed.) Philadelphia: Lippincott, 1972.

Watson, J. D. *The Double Helix.* New York: W. W. Norton, 1968.

Watzlawick, P., Weakland, J., and Fisch, R. *Change.* New York: W. W. Norton, 1974.

Weber, M. *The Theory of Social and Economic Organization.* New York: Free Press, 1947.

Wilson, R., and others. *College Professors and Their Impact on Students.* New York: Wiley, 1975.

Index